DIGITAL DISCUSSIONS

Big data raise major research possibilities for political communication scholars who are interested in how citizens, elites, and journalists interact. With the availability of social media data, academics can observe, on a large scale, how people talk about politics. The opportunity to study political discussions is also available to media organizations and political elites—examining how they make use of big data represents another fruitful scholarly trajectory. The scholars involved in *Digital Discussions* represent forward thinkers who aim to inform the study of political communication by analyzing the behavior of and messages left by citizens, elites, and journalists in digital spaces. By using a variety of methodological approaches and bringing together diverse theoretical perspectives, this group sheds light on how big data can inform political communication research. It is critical reading for those studying and working in communication studies with a focus on big data.

Natalie Jomini Stroud is an associate professor in the Department of Communication Studies and the School of Journalism, Director of the Center for Media Engagement, and Assistant Director of Research at the Annette Strauss Institute for Civic Life in the Moody College of Communication at the University of Texas at Austin. Her research focuses on selective exposure, media effects, and the role of journalism in a democracy.

Shannon C. McGregor is an assistant professor in the Department of Communication at The University of Utah. Her research interests center on political communication, social media, public opinion, gender, news, and data. Her research has been published in the *Journal of Communication*, *Political Communication*, *New Media & Society*, *Information, Communication & Society*, *Social Media + Society*, and the *Journal of Broadcasting & Electronic Media*.

NEW AGENDAS IN COMMUNICATION

A Series from Routledge and the College of Communication at the University of Texas at Austin

Roderick Hart and Stephen Reese, Series Editors

This series brings together groups of emerging scholars to tackle important inter-disciplinary themes that demand new scholarly attention and broadly reach across the communication field's existing courses. Each volume stakes out a key area, presents original findings, and considers the long-range implications of its "new agenda."

Recent series titles include:

Digital Discussions: How Big Data Informs Political Communication
edited by Natalie Jomini Stroud and Shannon C. McGregor

Work Pressures
edited by Dawna I. Ballard and Matthew S. McGlone

Strategic Communication
edited by Anthony Dudo and LeeAnn Kahlor

Networked China: Global Dynamics of Digital Media and Civic Engagement
edited by Wenhong Chen and Stephen D. Reese

New Technologies and Civic Engagement
edited by Homero Gil de Zúñiga

The full list of series volumes is available at www.routledge.com.

DIGITAL DISCUSSIONS

How Big Data Informs Political Communication

Edited by

Natalie Jomini Stroud and
Shannon C. McGregor

Routledge
Taylor & Francis Group

NEW YORK AND LONDON

First published 2019
by Routledge
711 Third Avenue, New York, NY 10017

and by Routledge
2 Park Square, Milton Park, Abingdon, Oxon OX14 4RN

Routledge is an imprint of the Taylor & Francis Group, an informa business

© 2019 Taylor & Francis

Library of Congress Cataloging in Publication Data
A catalog record has been requested for this book

ISBN: 978-0-8153-8380-2 (hbk)
ISBN: 978-0-8153-8186-0 (pbk)
ISBN: 978-1-351-20943-4 (ebk)

Typeset in Bembo
by Out of House Publishing

CONTENTS

NOTES ON CONTRIBUTORS

Jessica Baldwin-Philippi is an assistant professor in Fordham University's Communication and Media Studies department. Her work is fundamentally concerned with how engagement with new technologies can restructure forms of political participation and ideas about citizenship. Her book, *Using Technology, Building Democracy: Digital Campaigning and the Construction of Citizenship* (Oxford, 2015) investigates the digital strategies and tactics that electoral campaigns have adopted at both the local and national level.

Leticia Bode is an assistant professor in the Communication, Culture, and Technology master's program at Georgetown University. Her work lies at the intersection of communication, technology, and political behavior, emphasizing the role communication and information technologies may play in the acquisition and use of political information.

Frederick Boehm is a Ph.D. candidate in statistics at the University of Wisconsin-Madison. He has research interests in quantitative analyses for online media. His research has appeared in the journal *Political Communication*.

Jake Dailey is a senior data scientist at the Nielsen company. His work focuses on using applications of data science and machine learning to improve audience measurement, particularly for digital audiences. The political communication research featured in this book was conducted at the University of Michigan under the mentorship of Dr Pasek.

Deen Freelon is an associate professor in the School of Media and Journalism at the University of North Carolina at Chapel Hill. His research covers two major areas of scholarship; 1) political expression through digital media; and 2) data science and computational methods for analyzing large digital datasets. He has authored or co-authored more than 30 journal articles, book chapters, and public reports, in addition to co-editing one scholarly book. He has served as principal investigator on grants from the Knight Foundation, the Spencer Foundation, and the U.S. Institute of Peace. He has written research-grade software to calculate intercoder reliability for content analysis (ReCal), to analyze large-scale network data from social media (TSM), and to collect data from Facebook (fb_scrape_public). He formerly taught at the American University in Washington, DC.

Lei Guo is an assistant professor of emerging media studies at Boston University. Her research focuses on the development of media effects theories, computational social science methodologies, and emerging media and democracy in the United States and China. Her research has been published in a number of leading peer-reviewed journals, such as *Journal of Communication, Communication Research*, and *New Media & Society*. Her co-edited book *The Power of Information Networks: New Directions for Agenda Setting* (2015) introduces a new theoretical perspective to understand media effects in this emerging media landscape.

Toby Hopp is an assistant professor at the University of Colorado Boulder. His research interests are broadly related to the uses and effects of digital and interactive media, the social and motivational factors that underlie uncivil online communication, and organizational transparency.

Andreas Jungherr is Assistant Professor for Social Science Data Collection and Analysis at the University of Konstanz, Germany. His research focuses on the impact of digital technology on political communication and the use of digital trace data in the social sciences. His research has been published in the *Journal of Communication, Journal of Computer-Mediated Communication, The International Journal of Press/Politics*, and *Social Science Computer Review*.

Josephine Lukito is a Ph.D. student in the School of Journalism and Mass Communication at the University of Wisconsin-Madison. She specializes in mixed-methods news-linguistics research, with a focus on syntactical analyses of political communication texts.

Shannon C. McGregor is an assistant professor in the Department of Communication at The University of Utah. Her research interests center on political communication, social media, public opinion, gender, news, and data. Her research has been published in the *Journal of Communication, Political Communication, New Media & Society, Information, Communication & Society, Social Media + Society*, and the *Journal of Broadcasting & Electronic Media*.

Ashley Muddiman is an assistant professor in the Department of Communication Studies at the University of Kansas. She is also a Faculty Research Associate with the Center for Media Engagement housed at the Moody College of Communication at the University of Texas at Austin. Her research explores political media effects, specifically those related to political incivility and digital news. Her work has been published in the *Journal of Communication, International Journal of Communication, Communication Research*, and *New Media & Society*.

Josh Pasek is Associate Professor of Communication Studies, Faculty Associate in the Center for Political Studies, and Core Faculty for the Michigan Institute for Data Science at the University of Michigan. His research explores how new media and psychological processes each shape political attitudes, public opinion, and political behaviors. He also examines issues in the measurement of public opinion, including techniques for reducing measurement error and improving population inferences. His work has been published in *Public Opinion Quarterly, Political Communication, Communication Research*, and the *Journal of Communication*, among other outlets.

Ayellet Pelled is a Ph.D. student at the School of Journalism and Mass Communication at the University of Wisconsin-Madison. Her research interests reside at the intersection of media psychology and information processing. Her research has been published in *American Behavioral Scientist* and *Political Communication*.

Dhavan V. Shah is Maier-Bascom Professor at the University of Wisconsin, where he is Director of the Mass Communication Research Center (MCRC) and Scientific Director in the Center for Health Enhancement System Studies (CHESS). His work concerns framing and cueing effects on social judgments, digital media influence on civic and political engagement, and the impact of ICTs on chronic disease management. Across these domains of work, he has increasingly applied computational techniques to tackle social science questions. He is housed in the School of Journalism and Mass Communication, with appointments in Industrial and Systems Engineering, Marketing, and Political Science.

Natalie Jomini Stroud is an associate professor in the Department of Communication Studies and the School of Journalism, Director of the Center for Media Engagement, and Assistant Director of Research at the Annette Strauss Institute for Civic Life in the Moody College of Communication at the University of Texas at Austin. Her research focuses on selective exposure, media effects, and the role of journalism in a democracy.

Chris J. Vargo is an assistant professor specializing in big data and analytics at the University of Colorado Boulder. He specializes in the use of computer science methods to investigate social media, using theories from the communication and political science disciplines.

JungHwan Yang is an assistant professor in the Department of Communication, University of Illinois at Urbana-Champaign. His research focuses on political communication and media effects, using computational methods. He uses digital trace data to examine the diversity of political and risk information that people use and the impact of such information on individuals, groups, and society. His most recent projects have involved the spread of disinformation by state-controlled political trolls and the dynamics of these events, mass media coverages, and social media conversation on mass shootings in the U.S.

1

BIG DATA IN POLITICAL COMMUNICATION

Natalie Jomini Stroud and Shannon C. McGregor

"Big data" has entered the academic lexicon as a new buzzword. Although there are no clear guidelines for what dataset size qualifies as "big," there is widespread recognition that the availability of massive digital datasets provides a novel opportunity for scholars. By using traces of data left behind by people as they navigate their digital environments—the sites they peruse, the social media posts they make, the way they interact with sites—scholars can analyze people's expressed attitudes and behaviors. In this volume, we focus on what political communication scholars can learn by studying digital trace data—the transmission of information and opinions in public, digital spaces. The messages left in comment sections, posted on social media sites, and tweeted by bloggers provide the raw data for new understandings of how citizens, elites, and journalists make sense of the political world. This book aims to examine the theoretical and methodological implications of big data, and to provide new empirical research that makes use of big data.

There are intriguing possibilities from working with these data. Unlike traditional survey and experimental datasets, big data (at least as conceptualized here) are not created under contrived circumstances. And, unlike in-depth interviews or ethnographies, big data are available on a much larger scale. Of course, the datasets have limitations. Big data come from self-selected participants—only those who have a Twitter account and want to tweet about politics, for instance, will be included in a political Twitter dataset. This is only a substantial weakness if one is looking to make inferences about the broader population. Further, the data are constrained by technology. Algorithmic changes, for instance, can affect the data, as can the availability of digital archives.

Nonetheless, big data present major research possibilities for political communication scholars who are interested in how citizens, elites, and journalists interact. Political discussions, for instance, have long been of interest to communication scholars (e.g. Katz & Lazarsfeld, 1955; Mutz, 2006; Price & Cappella, 2002). With the availability of social media data, academics can observe, on a large scale, how people talk about and interact with politics. The opportunity to study political discussions is also available to media organizations and political elites: examining how they make use of big data represents another fruitful scholarly trajectory. The scholars involved in this book represent forward thinkers who aim to inform the study of political communication by analyzing the behavior of and messages left by citizens, elites, and journalists in digital spaces. Using a variety of methodological approaches and bringing diverse theoretical perspectives, this group is poised to shed light on how big data can inform political communication scholarship.

Big Data and Related Terms

Electing to use the term "big data" to describe this book was not an easy choice. It is fraught with complication because there is no definition of what makes data "big." The best definitions offered by contributors to this volume sidestep this issue. Bode, for instance, defines big data as "information that is (1) created digitally and (2) collected in large numbers to facilitate analysis." Guo identifies big data as "any large-scaled numerical, textual, visual, or geographic data, which can be analyzed to reveal patterns and trends of human behavior." She goes further, saying that the size and complexity of big data are beyond traditional tools for gathering and analyzing data.

We tend to agree that there is no bright line distinguishing big data from medium, or small, data. Nonetheless, the term is useful because it conveys the advanced tools required for gathering and analyzing this form of data. Some traditional statistical programs are unable to accommodate datasets of this size. Further, these datasets tax traditional computers' storage and processing capacities. As technology improves, however, this definition of big data seems less relevant (boyd & Crawford, 2012).

We considered other terms that also seem to capture the phenomenon of interest. Most of the authors in this book are interested in a particular type of big data—digital trace data. In this volume, Jungherr, drawing on work from Howison, Wiggins, and Crowston (2011), defines digital trace data as "data documenting the interactions of users with digital devices or services." These data are, quite literally, the traces that people leave behind when they have engaged in digital spaces. This could be browser history, comments, or social media posts, and the list could continue indefinitely. Of course, there are other types of big data beyond digital trace data—you could think about big datasets with relevance to medicine or engineering. For communication scholars, however, digital trace datasets are often of primary interest.

We also considered using the term "computational social science," which captures a method frequently employed by those using big data. As Shah, Cappella, and Neuman (2015) explain, computational social science involves:

(1)   the use of large, complex datasets, often—though not always—measured in terabytes or petabytes; (2) the frequent involvement of 'naturally occurring' social and digital media sources and other electronic databases; (3) the use of computational or algorithmic solutions to generate patterns and inferences from these data; and (4) the applicability to social theory in a variety of domains from the study of mass opinion to public health, from examinations of political events to social movements (p. 7).

This form of analysis is at the intersection of computer and social science, and can require collaborations with computer scientists, as Guo notes in her chapter.

Acknowledging that the work here involves both digital trace data and computational social science, we nonetheless opted for the term "big data." We did so for several reasons. First, "big data" has gained traction in academic communities, and is now widely discussed in popular and scholarly contexts. Second, we wanted to focus on the *data* in this volume, rather than the *method*. The term data, we felt, lent itself to more diverse analyses, such as Baldwin-Philippi's qualitative work on how campaigns are using "big data." So, with an acknowledgment of the complexities of the term, we adopted it as a defining feature of the chapters that follow.

Big Data and Political Communication

Political communication scholars aim to look at how elites, the media, and the public interact around political topics. Big data allow many opportunities to do precisely this work, as all three entities leave volumes of trace data. Research to date has used big data approaches to examine how political elites communicate (McGregor, Lawrence, & Cardona, 2017), how agenda setting occurs across traditional and social media (Neuman, Guggenheim, Jang, & Bae, 2014), and how norms regarding incivility and partisanship are rewarded and punished in news comment sections (Muddiman & Stroud, 2017). Studies like these demonstrate the utility of this approach for answering questions of theoretical interest to political communication researchers.

Methodologically, political communication scholars should be especially well poised to make contributions to the study of big data. Political content is widely distributed on such platforms as Twitter and political news garners extensive comments on news sites (Coe, Kenski, & Rains, 2014). Communication scholars have been pioneers in the analysis of texts and the methods of content analysis (e.g. Krippendorff, 2012): and political communication scholars, in particular, have been developing computerized content-analysis programs that can be used to analyze large corpuses of text (e.g. Hart, 1985; Young & Soroka, 2012). The availability of content and methods relevant to political communication makes this volume particularly apropos.

With that said, the explosion of research related to big data means that this volume will not be comprehensive. Several aspects of big data are not covered in these chapters, but can be found in other places, such as the analysis of networks and the use of algorithms and recommender systems (e.g. Beam, 2014; Colleoni, Rozza, & Arvidsson, 2014; Flaxman, Goel, & Rao, 2016). We also focus on U.S.-based big data analyses, although the methodological issues raised and the theoretical lessons drawn from the chapters will have relevance to political communication scholars regardless of their country of residence. Finally, there has been an overarching use of big data to analyze textual content, and more development is needed to bring this approach to images and video. This gap in our technical abilities is apparent in this volume as well.

Organization of the Book

The book is organized into three sections; the first examines the benefits and drawbacks of political communication researchers' use of big data; the second evaluates the reliability and validity our uses of these datasets; and the third demonstrates the ways in which we can gain new insights by using big data.

The first section of this book offers competing takes on the benefits and drawbacks of the use of big data within the social sciences. While Bode is optimistic, Jungherr is less so. Putting them into these camps is, of course, an oversimplification of their positions, but their chapters do have decidedly different tones which serve to provide an overview of the complexities of using big data. Bode offers a hopeful take on the effects of big data on academic scholarship. She sees big data as being able to answer new communication questions, to push us to consider our methodological choices more deeply, and to offer stronger justifications for our work. She also believes that big data findings are more easily understandable, which represents an opportunity to better engage students and the public.

Jungherr, taking a different tack, is critical of contemporary scholarship that uses digital trace data. He identifies two fallacies that frequently crop up. First, people treat the data as though they have every possible data point (the n=all fallacy). But, often, scholars do not have complete data. Platforms may not store all the data, or may have service agreements that prevent scholars from accessing all available data. Second, people see online data as acting as a mirror of some social phenomenon, but it may not be. Twitter data may simply be statements that people were willing to make on Twitter and nothing more—perhaps they do not capture underlying social maladies. Jungherr urges researchers to think much more carefully about what the data actually capture and to subject digital trace data to rigorous validity testing. In its infancy, studies using digital trace data were accepted merely based on the grounds that they were methodologically innovative. As we enter an era of more normalized use of these datasets, Jungherr makes a compelling case for better conceptualization.

The second section of the book expands upon questions about what big data can tell political communication researchers. The three chapters push researchers to think carefully about the validity of the inferences they can draw from big data.

Freelon discusses the technical and social aspects of social media platforms and how they can constrain our ability to draw valid inferences. Guo looks at analytic strategies for dealing with big data and how they can be more or less valid. Pasek and Dailey tested how well Twitter sentiment can predict candidate preferences. Each of the three chapters models the care researchers should take in thinking through the validity of any inferences drawn from big data.

Freelon takes a close look at the construct validity of social media trace data. He recommends that researchers consider four factors; the technical design and affordances of a social media platform; the terms of service that govern how people act on a social media platform; the context of how people use social media; and the potential for misrepresentation. The chapter, then, takes a critical look at how people can disclose their gender, race/ethnicity, or location based on these four factors. Facebook, for instance, requires users to indicate their gender when they sign up for an account. Other methods of determining gender, such as inferring it from someone's name, have questionable validity on some platforms and among some sub-populations. As Freelon aptly notes, digital trace data were not created for the purpose of research and, because of this, researchers must carefully consider the limitations of any inferences made.

Guo offers several cautionary tales about how we analyze big data. She points out that researchers must make numerous choices when deciding how to analyze the data, and each choice can affect the conclusions reached. By sharing the results of several reliability and validity tests, Guo illustrates the extent to which human decision-making can change the results of big data analyses. Although she shows that changes do occur, the examples she shared do not seem to result in dramatic overturns of the reached conclusions. Productively, Guo offers recommendations to researchers, urging them to work with computer scientists and to ensure that they test the results of any "out-of-the-box" big data analytics packages.

Pasek and Dailey undertake precisely the sort of analysis that Jungherr recommends, seeking to analyze the correspondence between Twitter data and survey data regarding electoral preferences and candidate favorability. They find little evidence that sentiment expressed toward the candidates on Twitter corresponds with survey measures. This is true regardless of whether they look at; (a) candidate favorability or electoral preferences; (b) changes in sentiment or absolute levels of sentiment; and (c) survey data corresponding to demographic attributes of Twitter users. There is some suggestion that the Twitter data more closely conformed to survey data about candidate preferences later in the 2008 presidential campaign, but the authors are rightly cautious about how far they would push this conclusion. Park and Dailey's chapter suggests that Twitter data is what it is—public expressions among a distinct group—as opposed to a proxy for something else.

The third, and final, section of this book provides examples of big data analysis with relevance to political communication scholars. These demonstrations illustrate how big data can be used to answer important questions for political communication scholars and offer both methodological and theoretical insights. The four chapters in this section each examine different sources of big data, whether Yik Yak, comments from The New York Times, campaign uses of big data, or tweets. Each demonstrates the new ways in which scholars must justify the methods that they use to analyze datasets of this size—using the same techniques that communication scholars typically employ when analyzing survey or experimental data is not always possible. This collection of chapters is also particularly important because they analyze the intersections among media, elites, and the public in their communication practices regarding politics.

In their chapter, Vargo and Hopp analyze the use of Yik Yak among college students. Politics, they find, comes up infrequently. Yet, major political events, such as the State of the Union address, yield an uptick in political posts on the platform. Interestingly, political comments on Yik Yak are particularly unlikely at large universities, universities with a higher percentage of large classes, and universities with more fraternities and sororities—perhaps the heterogeneity of these contexts depresses political talk, but more research is needed.

Muddiman looks at comments left on The New York Times website to understand how other people and the architecture of the space affect discourse. Recommendations and being selected as a NYTPick corresponded with greater commenting in the 30 days after receiving these designations, compared to the 30 days before. When journalists commented, there were more comments overall and less incivility. Muddiman, then, analyzes how the presence of politics in the comment section relates to how people behave. Comment sections with at least one political comment tend to be more uncivil, have more comments overall, and have comments receiving more recommendations. These findings demonstrate that the discourse architecture, the topic, and the behavior of others can all contribute to the comments left on news stories.

Baldwin-Philippi takes a qualitative approach to understanding how campaigns use big data. She takes on popular press accounts that claim the dominance of big data in campaigns, and argues that staff working on lower-ballot races tend to use analytics differently than the staff of presidential and competitive senate races. Her much-needed corrective shows that lower-ballot campaign staff members are less likely to use testing and big data approaches. The rationale, however, is not that these staff members are untrained or unable to do so. Rather, for some at least, it is a purposive choice. Dedicating limited staff time and resources to big data analytics is unlikely to yield a return large enough to warrant the action.

Last, but most certainly not least, Pelled, Lukito, Boehm, Yang, and Shah analyze then-candidate Donald Trump's tweets and retweets of his tweets. Using topic modeling, they identify four main targets; Marco Rubio, Ted Cruz, Hillary Clinton, and the news media. For each, they use computerized content-analysis programs, Diction and LIWC, to understand the underlying dimensions of tweets mentioning these targets. The results give a nuanced picture of how Trump, and those retweeting him, constructed these targets during the election.

Conclusion

Across these three sections, this volume aims to provide a contemporary look at how big data is, and could be, used to answer questions of relevance to political communication scholars. The availability of these massive troves of data is of particular note for those studying political communication, as political elites, media organizations, and everyday citizens make frequent use of digital communication channels to voice their political views. The methodological cautions throughout the chapters, however, illustrate the need for further development of the standards for how big data analyses are conducted and reported. What is clear is the tremendous potential to advance our theoretical understanding through the use of these new sources of data.

References

Beam, M. A. (2014). Automating the news: How personalized news recommender system design choices impact news reception. *Communication Research, 41*(8), 1019–1041.

boyd, d., & Crawford, K. (2012). Critical questions for big data: Provocations for a cultural, technological, and scholarly phenomenon. *Information, Communication, & Society, 15*(5), 662–679.

Coe, K., Kenski, K., & Rains, S. A. (2014). Online and uncivil? Patterns and determinants of incivility in newspaper website comments. *Journal of Communication, 64*(4), 659–679.

Colleoni, E., Rozza, A., & Arvidsson, A. (2014). Echo chamber or public sphere? Predicting political orientation and measuring political homophily in Twitter using big data. *Journal of Communication, 64*, 317–332.

Flaxman, S., Goel, S., & Rao, J. M. (2016). Filter bubbles, echo chambers, and online news consumption. *Public Opinion Quarterly, 80*(S1), 298–320.

Hart, R. P. (1985). Systematic analysis of political discourse: The developments of diction. In K. R. Sanders, L. L. Kaid, & D. Nimmo (Eds.), *Political communication yearbook 1984* (pp. 97–134). Carbondale: Southern Illinois University Press.

Howison, J., Wiggins, A., & Crowston, K. (2011). Validity issues in the use of social network analysis with digital trace data. *Journal of the Association for Information Systems 12*, 767–797.

Katz, E., & Lazarsfeld, P. F. (1955/2006). *Personal influence: The part played by people in the flow of mass communications.* New Brunswick, NJ: Transaction Publishers.

Krippendorff, K. (2012). *Content analysis: An introduction to its methodology* (3rd ed.). Thousand Oaks, CA: Sage Publications.

McGregor, S. C., Lawrence, R. G., & Cardona, A. (2017). Personalization, gender, and social media: Gubernatorial candidates' social media strategies. *Information, Communication & Society, 20*(2), 264–283.

Muddiman, A., & Stroud, N. J. (2017). News values, cognitive biases, and partisan incivility in news comment sections. *Journal of Communication, 67*(4), 586–609.

Mutz, D. C. (2006). *Hearing the other side: Deliberative versus participatory democracy.* New York, NY: Cambridge University Press.

Neuman, W. R., Guggenheim, L., Jang, S. M., & Bae, S. Y. (2014). The dynamics of public attention: Agenda-setting theory meets big data. *Journal of Communication, 64*(2), 193–214.

Price, V., & Cappella, J. N. (2002). Online deliberation and its influence: The electronic dialogue project in campaign 2000. *IT & Society, 1*(1), 303–329.

Shah, D., Cappella, J. N., & Neuman, W. R. (2015). Big data, digital media, and computational social science: Possibilities and perils. *The ANNALS of the American Academy of Political and Social Science, 659*(1), 6–13.

Young, L. & Soroka, S. (2012). Lexicoder Sentiment Dictionary. Available at lexicoder.com.

2

NORMALIZING DIGITAL TRACE DATA

Andreas Jungherr

Digital Trace Data in the Social Sciences: A Promise yet to Be Realized

Gradually, over the last ten years, social scientists have found themselves confronting a massive increase in available data sources. The digitalization has, for example, opened up vast textual corpora (Grimmer & Stewart, 2013) and provided researchers with cheap and fast alternatives to telephone or face-to-face surveys (Callegaro, Manfreda, & Vehovar, 2015). Additionally, the growing use of digital services in everyday life provides social scientists with an ever increasing reservoir of digital data traces documenting slices of users' everyday interactions with various digital devices or services (Howison, Wiggins, & Crowston, 2011). This increase in the variety and size of data available to researchers has been heralded by some as a measurement revolution for the social sciences (Golder & Macy, 2014; Lazer, Pentland, Adamic, Aral, Barabási, Brewer, Christakis, Contractor, Fowler, Gutmann, Jebara, King, Macy, Roy, & Van Alstyne, 2009; Schroeder, 2016; Watts, 2011). Especially, the research potential of digital trace data (Howison et al., 2011) has featured prominently in these accounts.

Digital trace data are data documenting the interactions of users with digital devices or services (Howison et al., 2011). They potentially include a full set of these interactions. This has led some prominent commentators to declare an age of big data, in their view, characterized by the ability of researchers to measure everything and everyone of interest to them. This view is exemplified by the catchy term n=all (Mayer-Schönberger & Cukier, 2013). However, in fact, researchers are usually very far from being able to realize this potential, as they depend on data access policies set by service providers. So, n=all becomes "n=sample with unknown properties from unknown populations determined by third parties." In practice, these data access policies vary between services which are open (Wikipedia), largely restricted (e.g. Facebook), and completely closed off to outsiders (e.g. Google or mobile phone providers) (Resnick, Adar, & Lampe, 2015; Schroeder, 2016).

Another characteristic of digital trace data is that they are found data. They are not produced and provided based on research designs. Instead, they document user interactions through the lens of a service's specific data retention and access policies (Howison et al., 2011). On one hand, this makes these data immensely valuable as they provide researchers a view of actual behavior in the field. On the other hand, researchers do not have the ability to fine tune their data collection to specific research questions. Instead, more often than not, they have to adjust their research question to the data available. Through this, the field runs the risk of producing largely data-driven studies instead of carefully testing developed hypotheses based on current theoretical debates. This raises the importance of careful conceptualization of digital trace data in the context of specific research questions, behavior, or populations. This becomes all the more important when we move from an optimistic early reading of digital trace data as true mirrors of human behavior, attitudes, or social phenomena to a more realistic reading. Digital trace data are the result of very specific data-generating processes that are framed by, among other factors, the affordances of the service providing the data, its code, cultural usage practices associated with the service, users' usage motives, and the level of data access granted to researchers. This makes digital trace data the result of highly specific mediation processes that filter social or political phenomena of interest (Jungherr, 2015; Jungherr, Schoen, & Jürgens, 2016a). It is important for researchers to account for the specific mediating steps that produce digital data traces, if they want to present findings which go beyond a digital ethnography of the device or service that produces their data source or an isolated proof of concept that illustrates the workings of their algorithm or model of choice.

Surprisingly, these two challenges, which are at the center of the work with digital trace data, have only received limited attention in the debate on how to use these data sources in the social sciences. This is surprising as the literature has become very sophisticated with regard to other characteristics of these data, such as problems associated with data access, the dissemination of necessary analytical skill sets, or ethics (boyd & Crawford, 2012; Freelon, 2015; King, 2011). Only recently have questions explicitly addressing the need for theory-driven research, research designs, careful conceptual work, or indicator validation been raised (González-Bailón & Paltoglou, 2015; Howison et al., 2011; Jungherr et al., 2016a; Jungherr, Schoen, Posegga, & Jügens, 2016b; Lazer, Kennedy, King, & Vespignani, 2014; Salganik, 2017).

This has led to a use of digital trace data largely based on an implicitly held naive measurement theory. Practitioners seem to implicitly assume signals found in digital trace data directly inform on phenomena of interest. This runs counter to measurement theories in the social sciences and statistics. These fields have developed sophisticated understandings of how phenomena of interest must be translated into theoretical concepts; these concepts, in turn, must be translated into measures; these measures must be tested as to their validity; and, finally, statistical procedures must be developed regarding how to draw inferences on the respective phenomena based on available data. Social sciences and statistics look back on a long and fruitful debate on this process (Donoho, 2015; Efron & Hastie, 2016; Gerring, 2012; Goertz, 2005; Hand, 2004).

So far, this debate has no equivalent in the use of digital trace data. This indifference has given rise to two central fallacies in the use of digital trace data in the pursuit of social or political research questions:

(1) The n=all fallacy
(2) The mirror fallacy

These fallacies permeate much of the most prominent work with digital trace data and often limit its access to the social science mainstream. As I will argue below, these fallacies can be addressed by developing a measurement theory for the use of digital trace data. For this, researchers will have to test the consequences of variations in research designs, account for sample problems arising from digital trace data, and explicitly link signals identified in digital trace data to sophisticated conceptualizations of social phenomena. Continuing to ignore these challenges will limit the reach of work that is based on digital trace data. The development of a sophisticated measurement theory is a precondition for digital trace data being meaningfully integrated in the social sciences. The alternative is the relegation of this work to a subfield of applied computer research. Instead of meaningfully examining social or political phenomena, this research runs the risk of only speaking to the applicability of a specific algorithm or model to a specific data set. The social or political phenomena in the focus of this research would, thus, become nothing more than vehicles to illustrate computational and quantitative prowess.

Below, I will outline the two fallacies in greater detail. Then, I will discuss their consequences with regard to three general areas in the work with digital trace data in the social sciences; digital ethnography, proxies for other data sources, and hybrids. In these sections, I will present selected prominent studies, predominantly from political communication research. Still, the points raised are general and, thus, should hold for work in other fields. I will close with a short assessment of the road ahead and how these fallacies might be constructively addressed by the systematic development of a measurement theory for the work with digital trace data in the social sciences.

Before we start, let me emphasize that this is a work in progress. The studies listed here are meant to be illustrative of approaches typical for the work with digital trace data in the social sciences. Also, some aspects of the studies below are discussed critically. This is not meant to be a critique of the authors who are pioneers in this field and have proven themselves to be highly original and innovative. Still, as we now look back at nearly ten years of working with digital trace data, specific practices have begun to limit the development of the field, even though their first applications were highly original and promising. So, the arguments presented below are meant to move the debate further and do not judge the inspiring work of past pioneers whose work enables us to have this debate in the first place.

Two Fallacies

There are two central fallacies permeating current research with digital trace data – the n=all fallacy and the mirror fallacy. Both form implicit or explicit foundations of much of current research with digital trace data. As I will argue below, they are rooted in misconceptions about the nature of digital data traces and a widespread indifference among researchers toward sophisticated conceptual debates in the social sciences. They, therefore, severely limit the reach of research based on digital trace data in the established social science core discourses. Yet, as I will argue below, once identified, both fallacies can be addressed by the use of well-established scientific practices. If applied, these practices promise a clearer road forward for the work with digital trace data to be integrated into the core of social science discourses.

The n=all Fallacy

In its design, much of current research with digital trace data is largely indifferent toward questions of sampling. To more classically oriented quantitative social scientists, this might seem surprising. In fact, this indifference is deeply rooted in an understanding that all relevant interactions with devices and services by all users leave digital data traces and are, therefore, complete. Sampling would be, thus, somewhat beside the point. Why limit your potential information by actively discarding data when, instead, you can just analyze everything? The apparent possibility of working with datasets that document all interactions with a device or service by a complete population is presented by some as one of the defining characteristics of digital trace data, or, as they call it, "big data":

> Sampling is an outgrowth of an era of information-processing constraints, when people were measuring the world but lacked the tools to analyze what they collected. As a result, it is a vestige of that era too. [...]
>
> The concept of sampling no longer makes as much sense when we can harness large amounts of data. The technical tools for handling data have already changed dramatically, but our methods and mindsets have been slower to adapt.

Yet sampling comes with a cost that has long been acknowledged but shunted aside. It loses detail. In some cases there is no other way but to sample. In many areas, however, a shift is taking place from collecting some data to gathering as much as possible, and if feasible, getting everything: n=all.
Mayer-Schönberger & Cukier, 2013, p. 26

While some of the early enthusiasm of Mayer-Schönberger and Cukier (2013) begins to ring hollow by now, they clearly captured the mood in the field. This fallacy, n=all, is a catchy formula and makes explicit central assumptions that underlie much of the work with digital trace data. We find studies concerned with collecting all relevant content of a topic (Ausserhofer & Maireder, 2013; Bruns & Highfield, 2013) or all content posted by selected populations (Jungherr, 2015; Lin, Keegan, Margolin, & Lazer, 2014). Why limit yourself if you can get it all? Yet, in the case of digital trace data, it turns out the term "all" just means "all that was collected and made available to researchers by commercial third-party entities." A meaning quite distinct from the word's more common usage. So, what are the limits of digital trace data's "all"?

First and foremost, digital trace data come with a series of technical limitations. Here, the question of data access is key. While it is certainly true that, in theory, all interactions by all users of specific devices or services can be collected by said device or service, it does not necessarily mean that this is the case. Even in an age when data storage is cheap, service providers do not save every data trace available to them. Instead, they make a choice about which data seem valuable to their business case or which data could conflict with their company's policies, such as privacy concerns. But, even to this subset of all interactions, researchers still do not have full access. Instead, they can only access these data directly (e.g. through application programming interfaces (API)) or indirectly (e.g. by web scraping) from the service. Both approaches only provide researchers with subsets of all potentially relevant data. The data quality of these subsets and their relationship to all potentially relevant data can only be guessed (Morstatter, Pfeffer, Liu, & Carley, 2013; Ruths & Pfeffer, 2014). Here, it is always important to keep in mind that the interests of service providers, regarding what to make public and what to keep confidential, are not necessarily identical to the interests of researchers. For example, increasingly such services as Facebook or Twitter show users algorithmically ordered feeds and allow the pushing of posts' prominence through ad buys. These algorithmic and commercial interventions, thus, influence the use of these tools considerably but do not necessarily appear in the digital trace data available to researchers. What researchers might take for social processes, which give rise to specific patterns in these data, might in fact be results of algorithmic interventions (Strohmaier & Wagner, 2014). Recently, various scholars have tried to avoid these challenges by partnering directly with the providers of digital tools (Bakshy, Messing, & Adamic, 2015; Bond, Fariss, Jones, Kramer, Marlow, Settle, & Fowler, 2012). While these studies have been highly original and imaginative, this approach raises serious questions with regard to scientific practices. Obvious issues are replicability, potential conflicts of interest between researchers and partners leading to the focus on or avoidance of specific research questions, and, ultimately, a divide between options open to researchers at prestigious institutions with connections to digital service providers and those without these connections.

Varying access policies across digital services leads to another problem for researchers. The use of digital devices and services inherently encompasses the use of many different devices, services, and channels for overlapping or divergent patterns (Rainie & Wellman, 2012). A user might call a family member from her smartphone and start exchanging views on current events while receiving an email from a colleague with a link to an article covering politics. In following, she might post a link to the article on her Facebook page for her contacts to see, exchange acerbic comments on the article's subject with a friend on her favorite chat program, and post an especially funny quip on her Twitter feed. This whole interaction chain comprises political talk online but only slices are available to researchers working with digital trace data. A researcher focusing on only one of the services in this interaction chain will invariably come to different assessments of the nature of political talk online from those made by a researcher focusing on another service. This interaction between various communication channels is a central challenge and yet only few studies using digital trace data try to explicitly account for it (Leskovec, Backstrom, & Kleinberg, 2009).

A final limitation to the "all" provided by digital trace data to be discussed here stems from digital services' limited and skewed user base. While it is certainly true that many people use digital devices and services in their daily lives, this user base is far from including all members of a society. In fact, digital devices and services are predominantly used by a skewed subset of the population, tending to be younger, wealthier, and better educated. This skewness becomes stronger when we focus on the use of specific services and usage practices (Blank, 2016; Hargittai, 2015). Also, the composition of this self-selected unrepresentative population sample seems to drift unpredictably and non-randomly over time, making the adjustment for the underlying skewness with regard to overall populations infeasible (Diaz, Gamon, Hofman, Kiciman, & Rothschild, 2016). So again, n=some seems to be a more accurate description of what we find in the work with digital trace data than n=all.

All of this does not invalidate the work with digital trace data. Instead, this eerily resembles challenges known from other approaches to data collection in the social sciences. Here, we find sophisticated methodological debates addressing the potential benefits and limits of traditional data-collection approaches (Groves, Fowler Jr., Couper, Lepkowski, Singer, & Tourangeau, 2009; Tourangeau, Rips, & Rasinski, 2000). Yet, in the work with digital trace data, the n=all fallacy misleads researchers to ignore systematic limitations of their datasets—limitations that could be addressed head-on by open testing and discussion of different sampling procedures, allowing systematic assessment and maybe even control of potential biases inherent in digital trace data. Only recently, these questions are beginning to be raised in the field (Salganik, 2017). The early exceptionalism, a mood so evocatively captured by Mayer-Schönberger and Cukier (2013), has stood in the way of social scientists working with digital trace data, profiting from the deep and long-ongoing methodological debates at the intersections between social science and statistics. Joining this debate holds very high promise in addressing the limitations of digital trace data listed above (Donoho, 2015; Efron & Hastie, 2016).

The Mirror Fallacy

The second fallacy is a subtler one. Other than the n=all fallacy, the mirror fallacy is seldom stated explicitly but lies implicitly at the core of many works based on digital trace data. The perceived potential of digital trace data is based on the assumption that digital trace data reflect political or social phenomena in users' data traces (Golder & Macy, 2014; Lazer et al., 2009). This position emerged in reaction to the increasing growth and variety of digital services and the subsequent growing availability of data. Some authors have framed it as a shift from using data collected on the internet for the examination of online phenomena or behavior—cyber-ethnography—to using these artifacts and data traces to draw inferences on larger social or political phenomena (Rogers, 2013). This was a decisive shift in the focus of researchers interested in the use of digital trace data and significantly increased the perceived potential of these data, even for researchers who before had not shown interest in the internet or digital services as objects of study. Yet, this originally immensely liberating hypothesis has become a trap for researchers. A lazy reading tempts them to ignore the inherent mediated nature of digital trace data and the skewness that this might introduce to the reflection of social and political phenomena.

Digital data traces are always the product of the design of digital services and devices, cultural usage practices, and users' usage motives. The reflection of social and political phenomena arising from these data traces are, therefore, mediated by these factors (Jungherr, 2015; Jungherr et al., 2016a). If we accept this, we cannot simply take signals contained in digital trace data at face value but, instead, have to interpret them in the context of the likely mediating processes that lead to their emergence. This renders the process of interpreting signals in digital trace data and linking them explicitly to concepts of interest of paramount importance (Howison et al., 2011). And, yet, this step is nearly always neglected. Instead, researchers seem to share a highly simplistic measurement approach. They mainly take for granted that signals extracted from digital trace data, indeed, measure their given phenomenon of interest. For such a quantitatively advanced field, this is a surprisingly unsophisticated approach to the measurement of social reality (Hand, 2004). Most of the time, researchers appear to be satisfied by statistically linking signals identified in digital trace data to arbitrarily chosen metrics that document social or political phenomena. Alternatively, they might simply point to patterns identified in digital trace data and take them as direct expression of underlying social or political processes. This and an often superficial reading of conceptual debates in the social sciences have led to works based on digital trace data to have limited impact on central debates in the social sciences.

In light of this, the tendency to approach signals in digital trace data uncritically as indicators for micro-level attitudes and behavior or macro-level phenomena seems highly troubling. For example, a very influential study showed that Twitter mentions of a selection of German parties seemed to correspond with their vote shares (Tumasjan, Sprenger, Sandner, & Welpe, 2010). Parties' Twitter mentions, thus, seemed to mirror their level of public support. This was surprising. Given the well-known skewness in Twitter's user base and the prevalence of political snark and public critique on the service, one would have expected parties with young and online-savvy supporters and those at the center of public controversy to be overrepresented. As it turns out, this pattern emerges once one changes only a few parameters of the original study. Simply by including mentions of the Pirate Party, a party focused on digitalization's social impact and civil rights, the surprising link between Twitter mentions and vote shares breaks spectacularly (Jungherr, Jürgens, & Schoen, 2012).

Tumasjan et al. (2010) clearly fell victim to the mirror fallacy. In their analysis, the team found a promising pattern. After all, who would not jump at the possibility of predicting elections by simply counting tweets? Instead of critically investigating their data guided by a realistic reading of Twitter's data-generating process, the authors simply took their welcome results at face value and declared aggregates of Twitter messages as valid indicators of public support for parties. Following this practice, digital trace data became a mirror for everything enterprising researchers wanted to see in them. For example, Twitter messages have been taken, among other phenomena, as expression of political support (Tumasjan et al., 2010), the onset of depression (De Choudhury, Counts, & Horvitz, 2013), or signs of imminent stock market movements (Bollen, Mao, & Zheng, 2011). If true, this would make the micro-blogging service the most universally applicable concoction since the discovery of snake oil.

At the heart of the mirror fallacy lies the predominant practice of statistically linking metrics without seriously proposing and testing a mechanism that plausibly leads to the emergence of this association (Jungherr et al., 2016b). A research environment characterized by big datasets necessarily comes with many correlations between variables. Most of these correlations will be spurious, they do not speak to a systematic or causal link between variables but, instead, emerge by chance. Especially in scientific contexts, the goal is to differentiate between spurious correlations and those speaking to a systematic link between variables. Social science methodology is rich in debates on how to correctly identify causal links between phenomena and variables (Gerring, 2012). At the very least, researchers should propose a mechanism linking two concepts or variables of choice, explaining the nature of any reported correlation. This provides a series of explicit steps linking two concepts or variables. Each of these steps can then be tested on its plausibility or correspondence with available evidence. In this process, the identification of statistically linked metrics is only the first step. The true test of a correlation's meaning lies in the proposal and testing of a potential mechanism leading to its emergence (Gerring, 2008, 2010).

In practice, most contemporary work with digital trace data ignores this crucial second step and, instead, follows a purely data-driven logic when reporting statistical links between arbitrarily chosen metrics. Pair this with a publication culture showing a clear bias toward the reporting of positive findings, with economic pressures on labs and researchers to provide outside funders and the media with spectacular and often counter-intuitive results, and you have the perfect storm drowning the field in reports of positive but irrelevant statistical associations between digital trace data and social or political phenomena. To avoid this, careful conceptual work (Goertz, 2005), the proposal and testing of likely causal mechanisms (Gerring, 2008), and measurement validation (Adcock & Collier, 2001) are of paramount importance in the work with digital trace data.

As with the n=all fallacy, the mirror fallacy does not render the work with digital trace data futile. Instead, it simply means researchers have to account for the mediated nature of their data sources in their interpretation of data traces. As with other data sources, data-generating processes determine the meaning we can plausibly assign to identified patterns. Yet, currently questions in the interpretation and conceptualization of digital trace data are predominantly neglected by the field. This might be due to some researchers' hope of having finally found a data source large enough to turn social science into a "true" science, allowing for the identification of a physics of social life. Ignoring the questions raised by the mediated nature of digital trace data is only logical from this point of view. Interpretation and conceptualization "scale up" badly, thereby getting in the way of finding the gravitational laws of social systems. Yet, collectively ignoring a problem usually does not make it disappear. Instead, it is much more likely that work done based on a common consensus in a small community of practice does not travel far beyond the borders of said community. Accounting for the mediated nature of digital trace data in research designs, conceptualization, and interpretation, therefore, is very likely a necessary step for research that uses these data to extend beyond the small group of the converted.

The Fallacies at Work

The two fallacies discussed above permeate the work with digital trace data. Here, I will exemplarily illustrate their presence by discussing selected prominent papers using digital trace data in political communication research. We can group these studies by their research interests. First, studies using digital trace data to analyze politically relevant behavior online—digital ethnography. Second, studies using digital trace data to draw inferences on offline phenomena, traits, or attitudes—proxies. Third, studies focusing on interactions between political behavior online and offline—hybrids. Especially in the first two groups, we find prominent studies explicitly or implicitly falling for the n=all or mirror fallacy.

Digital Ethnography: The Dangers of Conceptual Stretching

Using digital trace data to examine political behavior of users online and on specific services is an intuitive first step. Here, phenomena of interest are closely connected to data-generating processes that give rise to signals identified in digital trace data. Yet, as I will show, most authors are not content with simply speaking of online political phenomena but instead take them as expression of larger political phenomena. Here, the question arises if patterns found in digital trace data truly speak of political phenomena as conceptualized in the mainstream social science discourse. Authors have to consciously engage with contemporary conceptualizations and provide explicit interpretations of how their signals of choice, identified in digital trace data, connect with them. In neglecting this step, researchers run the risk of concept stretching—extending concepts developed in specific contexts to others without appropriately testing their fit to the new environments (Collier & Mahon, 1993; Sartori, 1970, 1984). This risk is especially relevant in regard to online communication, as it is far from obvious which concepts and theories predominantly developed in the context of mass media will travel to the new environment (Neuman, 2016).

Let us take a closer look at two prominent studies ostensibly examining a prominent topic in political science—political polarization—through the lens of digital trace data. One of the early studies that used digital trace data to examine specific usage patterns of political online use is Adamic and Glance (2005). The authors analyzed linking patterns between 1,000 political blogs and the content of 22,884 posts on 40 prominent political blogs. They found:

> a divided blogosphere: liberals and conservatives linking primarily within their separate communities, with far fewer cross-links exchanged between them. This division extended into their discussions, with liberal and conservative blogs focusing on different news, topics, and political figures.
>
> *Adamic & Glance, 2005, p. 43*

In a similar vein, Conover, Ratkiewicz, Francisco, Gonçalves, Flammini, and Menczer (2011) examined 252,300 politically relevant tweets, focusing on retweet interactions between 18,470 users, and @message interactions by 7,175 users. The authors were interested in whether users sharing the same political leaning were more likely to interact with other users sharing their political convictions. They found that:

The retweet network is highly polarized, while the mention network is not. To explain these observations we highlight the role of hashtags in exposing users to content they would not likely choose in advance. Specifically, users who apply hashtags with neutral or mixed valence are more likely to engage in communication with opposing communities.

Conover et al., 2011, p. 95

Both studies are highly instructive with regard to the benefits and limitations of work that is based on digital trace data in political communication research. Both studies use digital services and technology to collect, prepare, and analyze large datasets of political behavior online. They, then, focus on features of the datasets allowing for easy automated analysis. In this, they jettison some of the potential depth of their analysis. Nevertheless, this approach allows them to use advanced quantitative methods—in both cases network analysis—to identify specific structures of interactions between users on the services under analysis (i.e. blogs and Twitter). In this, both research teams are highly creative and original.

Still, the relevance of the analysis of linking behavior between blogs and the network structures of political talk on Twitter might not be apparent to all. To account for this, both teams situate their work within the larger discourse on political polarization in the USA and the internet's perceived impact on this. Here, we find both studies to be representative of many others in this field. The connection to the theoretical debate on political polarization is provided either in the most fleeting of ways (Adamic & Glance, 2005) or in a highly selective and suggestive reading of the literature (Conover et al., 2011). Neither team acknowledges the depth and conflicting empirical evidence in the larger debate on political polarization in the USA (DiMaggio, Evans, & Bryson, 1996; Fiorina & Abrams, 2008) or the rich debate on the perceived role of media technology (Prior, 2013; Scheufele & Nisbet, 2013).

What constitutes a graver shortcoming is that both studies do not discuss or propose convincing mechanisms of why the data traces analyzed—links between political blogs, retweets, or @messages—can be truly interpreted as expressions of political polarization. This depends on the data-generating process that give rise to the signals used in the analysis. If we interpret links and retweets as being predominantly driven by the intent to point to supporting evidence, additional information, or to point out new content to readers, it is far from surprising to find predominantly ideological homogenous linking patterns in politically focused blogs or Twitter feeds. After all, who, while in a political debate, points consistently to conflicting evidence or content provided by the opposing side? But, is this form of public political expression and the performance of allegiance truly a sign of political polarization?

If we take the influential definition provided by DiMaggio et al. (1996), we can either see polarization as a state or a process:

> Polarization as a state refers to the extent to which opinions on an issue are opposed in relation to some theoretical maximum. Polarization as a process refers to the increase in such opposition over time.
>
> *DiMaggio et al., 1996, p. 693*

To truly speak of political polarization online as a state, studies would, thus, have to measure positions on political issues and demonstrate their systematic and extreme divergence between specific populations or political partisans. To detect a process of polarization online, studies would have to identify an increased spread between issue positions amongst specific populations or sources over time. In contrast, the approach chosen by Adamic and Glance (2005) and Conover et al. (2011), interpreting clusters in public communicative interactions as evidence of polarization, seems a far from ideal measurement strategy.

Both studies illustrate the problems arising from falling for the mirror fallacy by simply assuming chosen signals to be unmediated reflections of phenomena of interest. In doing so, the authors take a specific pattern in the data—homogenous linking or retweet patterns among groups of politically likeminded sources—as evidence of a larger phenomenon—political polarization in the USA—without providing any evidence regarding why the signals chosen by them should actually speak to the underlying phenomenon as expressed in contemporary conceptualizations. Instead of speaking to political polarization online, their studies, thus, fall victim to conceptual stretching.

Again, my goal is not to single studies out. In fact, the chosen examples are highly cited and very influential for research that uses digital trace data. This makes identifying their strengths and limitations all the more important. Both studies are highly data-driven. They seem primarily motivated by the analytical potential provided by digital trace data and, only secondarily, by engaging with the theoretical debate about the phenomena used to situate their findings. This leads to the studies being very sophisticated in their use of data but, at the same time, very superficial in meaningfully linking signals identified in digital data traces to concepts used in larger debates in the social sciences.

Here lies a central challenge in the work with digital trace data. As long as researchers interested in the use of digital trace data cannot or will not provide links between their data traces and larger political phenomena, their research remains isolated and potentially only relevant to enthusiasts of internet phenomena. Given the growing social, political, and economic importance of digital communication, for some, this might constitute no issue. Yet, in connecting their findings with more general concepts and phenomena at the center of social science discourse, many researchers neglect the contingency of behavior documented in digital trace data. In this, they fail to provide evidence of whether their data can truly speak to the concept ostensibly at the center of their study or if their operationalization stretches concepts beyond their accepted use. Showing the potential of digital trace data in contributing to social science mainstream requires careful conceptualization of the phenomena giving rise to specific data patterns. These conceptualizations have to consciously account for the mediated nature of the data traces under analysis and of social processes beyond the service providing the data (Jungherr et al., 2016a). Here, it is necessary for researchers working with digital trace data to engage more sophisticatedly with the current state of scientific debate in their chosen fields of interest, as well as to develop a research culture more aware of the need for interpretation in linking signals to concepts of interest.

Proxies: Recognizing What's Too Good To Be True

A second group of studies uses digital trace data as proxies for other measures of political phenomena and individuals' traits and attitudes. Here, digital trace data become substitutes for other traditional data sources, such as surveys (Schoen, Gayo-Avello, Metaxas, Mustafaraj, Strohmaier, & Gloor, 2013). For this approach, the central question is how one can ensure that signals identified in digital trace data truly measure or predict phenomena, whose traditional and tested measurements they hope to replace.

Of these, one of the most prominent approaches—also one of the most controversial—is the attempt to use digital trace data as indicator of political support in election campaigns (DiGrazia, McKelvey, Bollen, & Rojas, 2013; O'Connor, Balasubramanyan, Routledge, & Smith, 2010; Tumasjan et al., 2010). These studies often share a highly sophisticated approach to data collection and analysis. Their authors also share an understanding of digital trace data containing explicit or implicit signals on political attitudes of individuals or public opinion in general. Yet, the quality of digital trace data in replacement of survey results is inconclusive (Murphy, Link, Childs, Tesfaye, Dean, Stern, Pasek, Cohen, Callegaro, & Harwood, 2014; Schober, Pasek, Guggenheim, Lampe, & Conrad, 2016). The problems with this approach become apparent when we examine some of the most prominent studies more closely.

Let us start with a study not directly concerned with political communication, but with public health. Nevertheless, the study is highly influential for expectations in the diagnostic and predictive power of digital trace data for offline phenomena. In 2009, Choi and Varian (2012) demonstrated the apparent possibility of predicting—among other things—the spread of influenza based on Google search terms. Google even built a tool, Google Flu Trends[1], with which users could see real-time predictions of influenza trends worldwide. Quickly, this became one of the most highly cited cases for the perceived diagnostic and predictive potential of digital trace data. Yet, in 2013, the model started to fail spectacularly. This eventually led to the website being shut down. A detailed examination of this failure, by Lazer et al. (2014), offers a very instructive account of the potential and limitations of digital trace data inferring offline phenomena.

Lazer et al. (2014) pointed out that the initial algorithm provided by Google fundamentally focused on identifying signals in a large collection of digital trace data that were successful in statistically predicting a much smaller set of data points identifying flu dynamics:

> Essentially, the methodology was to find the best matches among 50 million search terms to fit 1152 data points. The odds of finding search terms that match the propensity of the flu but are structurally unrelated, and so do not predict the future, were quite high. [...] In short, the initial version of GFT [Google Flu Trends] was part flu detector, part winter detector.
>
> *Lazer et al., 2014, p. 1203*

This points to a central problem for theory-free statistical predictions based on big datasets. The larger the data set: the higher the probability you find correlations. These may point to systematic relationships between two data points, yet they also might be spurious correlations. In specific contexts, this might not be much of an issue. For example, if the online-vendor Amazon uses theory-free algorithms to detect correlations in the consumption patterns between product A and product B, the nature of these correlations does not matter much. Amazon will use this information to post contextually relevant ads or they may even adjust prices to point consumers of product A to product B. Once it detects a weakening of the correlation between the sales of both products, it might simply adjust its recommendations accordingly. In cases like this, correlations may, in fact, be all that is needed to achieve an increase in sales (Mayer-Schönberger & Cukier, 2013). Yet, once we try to use digital trace data for other purposes—be it scientific research or large-scale diagnostics of public health—eliminating spurious correlations becomes of central importance. Instead of falling for the mirror fallacy, by accepting at face value a signal found in digital trace data as indicator of a phenomenon of interest, we have to demand and perform serious tests of indicator validity and reliability (Gerring, 2012).

Also with regard to the n=all fallacy, Google Flu Trends proves to be instructive. As Lazer et al. (2014) show, changes to a platform's code might break a prediction algorithm based on historical data collected on the platform at an earlier development stage:

> Google reported in June 2011 that it had modified its search results to provide suggested additional search terms and reported again in February 2012 that it was now returning potential diagnoses for searches including physical symptoms like "fever" and "cough". The former recommends searching for treatments of the flu in response to general flu inquiries, and the latter may explain the increase in some searches to distinguish the flu from the common cold. [...] Oddly, GFT bakes in an assumption that relative search volume for certain terms is statically related to external events,

but search behavior is not just exogenously determined, it is also endogenously cultivated by the service provider.

Lazer et al., 2014, p. 1204

This discussion shows that researchers need a clear understanding of the data-generating process and its changes over time on the platform providing their data. This data-generating process essentially guides user behavior and as such filters which phenomena of interest leave imprints in digital trace data and which remain invisible. Inherently, the data-generating process determines how thick the slice of social or political phenomena is, that we can expect to find in digital trace data collected on specific services. To simply declare the specific slice available to us as "all" might be at best an attempt to define the problem away but at worst invalidate our studies.

The central issues with Google Flu Trends raised by Lazer et al. (2014) can also be found in other studies using digital trace data to predict or infer attitudes, behavior, or phenomena. Probably the most visible effort of this kind is the attempt to predict election results based on Twitter data. Efforts of this kind range from the use of very simple approaches—for example, based on the counting of political actors' mentions (DiGrazia et al., 2013; Tumasjan et al., 2010)—to the use of very sophisticated advanced computational methods—such as attempts at theory-free identification of statistical properties in Twitter corpora that are statistically linked to positive or negative showings of political actors in opinion polls (Contractor & Faruquie, 2013; Marchetti-Bowick & Chambers, 2012). The literature has been heavily criticized for its methodological inconsistencies (Gayo-Avello, 2012, 2013; Metaxas, Mustafaraj, & Gayo-Avello, 2011) and the arbitrariness of some of its choices (Jungherr et al., 2012). These arguments need no restating here. Instead, I want to focus on what this literature tells us about the persistence of the mirror fallacy.

The claim that Twitter data would allow us to infer present levels of political support or even the prediction of elections rests on a series of papers showing successful statistical associations between some metrics identified in Twitter data and some metrics of political support, such as opinion polls or election results. At first sight, this might seem like a successful collective exercise in indicator validation. But, in fact, these studies turn out to be largely isolated and only seemingly examine the same phenomenon. While studies abound showing positive statistical associations between some signal identified on Twitter and some metric of political support, we find next to no successful replication of the relationship between specific signals and specific metrics of support (Jungherr et al., 2016b). One of the few studies explicitly testing the stability of the link between Twitter-based metrics and election results over time clearly illustrates the instability of once established statistical relationships over time (Huberty, 2015). This points to the likelihood of positive cases being simply cases of over-fitting, such as the one identified by Lazer et al. (2014) in their discussion of Google Flu Trends.

To make matters worse, the practice of exclusively reporting positive statistical associations between Twitter-based metrics and measures of political success, without seriously testing mechanisms potentially giving rise to these links, might lead researchers to mistake the phenomenon indicated by their data. A central element of indicator validation is discriminant validation—a check for an indicator validly measuring a concept of interest and not a related one. In the case of measuring political support through Twitter-based metrics, a likely candidate for a concept sometimes—but far from always—related is public attention. So, instead of showing positive cases of Twitter identifying political support, studies finding positive results might simply identify cases in which Twitter was successful in identifying public attention toward political actors, which, in these cases, was positively linked with their success (Jungherr et al., 2016b).

Either way, be it through over-fitting or by mistaking the phenomena measured by digital trace data, the practice of relying on face validity in the demonstration of statistical associations between signals identified in digital trace data and other measures of phenomena of interest has proven to produce unreliable research of inconclusive meaning. Given the obvious problems illustrated above, the ongoing popularity of using digital trace data as substitutes for other data sources to directly infer political phenomena or individuals' traits and attitudes is somewhat surprising—apparently exaggerated hope renders myopic. Through this collective myopia, the attempt to use digital trace data as proxies for other data sources has risen to considerable prominence among quantitatively oriented social scientists who are not interested in internet-based phenomena as such. Here, a central weakness in overly quantitatively oriented social science research becomes apparent. To a regression model, every data point seems the same no matter the data-generating process. Yet, as the examples above have shown, the research community should be very careful in accepting this. Balanced reviews in the public opinion research community point to the limits of digital trace data as substitutes for other measurement approaches in the social sciences (Murphy et al., 2014; Schober et al., 2016). To ensure we are using digital trace data meaningfully, we have to move from the early enthusiasm-driven stage and its reliance on a proof-of-concept logic. Instead, we should apply and demand the rigorous application of social scientific methodology and indicator validation. If those are applied, the chances for digital trace data providing substitutes for other data-collection approaches to measure individuals' attitudes, traits, or social phenomena seem slim, rendering the endeavor a likely case of misplaced academic industry. Instead, the true potential of digital trace data might lie in their combination with established measurement approaches, not their substitution.

Hybrids: Connecting Different Data Sources

A third group of studies is characterized by the use of a combination of digital trace data and traditional data sources—here lies significant research potential.

On the one hand, hybrid designs allow validity checks of signals identified in digital trace data by comparing them to a ground truth established by traditional methods, which are much better understood with regard to the benefits and problems arising from their measurement approaches. On the other hand, hybrid designs are tailor-made to better understand the growing interconnection between digital technology and society. Here, I want to focus on studies examining this second question with regard to politics.

The analysis of the interconnection of political behavior on- and offline can take many forms. For example, various authors have looked at the content of Twitter messages and linked this to content in media coverage (Jungherr, 2014; Neuman, Guggenheim, Mo Jang, & Bae, 2014; Vargo, Guo, McCombs, & Shaw, 2014; Wells, Shah, Pevehouse, Yang, Pelled, Boehm, Lukito, Gosh, & Schmidt, 2016) to the dynamics of specific media programs and comments on Twitter (Trilling, 2015), or to offline behavior (Bond et al., 2012). These studies follow the lead of various pieces theorizing and qualitatively demonstrating that political communication on online channels appears to be highly interconnected with political phenomena—such as political coverage in traditional mass media or political participation—but, potentially, follows distinct patterns (Anstead & O'Loughlin, 2015; Chadwick, 2013; Kreiss, 2016). By explicitly addressing this link, researchers are able to anchor their analyses of behavioral patterns online in central debates of political communication research by demonstrating that online communication has become an integral part of the contemporary political communication environment. They, thereby, offer a convincing answer to the relevancy question that pure digital ethnography remains vulnerable to. By conceptualizing political behavior online as only one element of political communication in general, albeit one potentially following distinct and channel-specific patterns, these studies avoid overgeneralizing their findings—a problem inherent in the use of digital trace data as substitutes for other measurement approaches.

One promising area for the linking of digital trace data with other data sources is the analysis of political media coverage and public reactions to it. Here, various studies have demonstrated the research potential inherent in Twitter data by comparing the mentions of specific topics or actors on Twitter and their coverage in traditional media, either over extended time periods or over the course of one program (Jungherr, 2014; Neuman et al., 2014; Trilling, 2015; Vargo et al., 2014; Wells et al., 2016). These studies allow the analysis of attention dynamics in a political vocal population on Twitter. Thus, digital trace data hold the potential of providing insights into the interconnection between everyday political talk and political coverage in mass media—a topic largely neglected for methodological reasons but of clear interests to political communication research (Dayan & Katz, 1992; Gamson, 1992). These studies also allow a deeper understanding of the potential effects of political media coverage on online activity and vice versa. Thus, the combination of digital trace data and conventional data sources promise insights in the dynamics of the "hybrid media system" (Chadwick, 2013).

Another possibility is the linking of digital trace data with data collected by surveys. For example Jungherr, Schoen, Posegga, and Jürgens (2015) compared political topics identified in Twitter messages with topics mentioned in survey responses, to the query for an assessment of the most important problem facing Germany. There was only very limited overlap between topics identified from tweets referring to politics and the most-important-problem question. On one hand, this shows that Twitter provides a poor proxy for identifying public agendas—another refutation of the mirror hypothesis. On the other hand, the findings also point to the necessity to explicitly conceptualize the nature of political talk on Twitter. Is the frequency of topic mentions on Twitter an indicator of their central importance to political life? Or, is the frequency of mentions better understood as an indicator of which objects are central to public attention? If so, what drives the differences between these lists? Is it that people only publicly post on topics they want to be seen as being associated with (i.e. a bias arising from social desirability)? Or, is it that not everything we pay attention to in everyday interactions is automatically prominent if we are asked to reflect and provide a ranked list of important political problems? In other words, do the data speak to a divide between salience and relevance of topics? Currently, these are unanswered questions, which potentially provide insights into the nature of political talk and political communication in general. The difference between the measurements of seemingly related concepts in digital trace data and conventional data collection approaches, thus, may point to promising research puzzles to which we would have remained blind if we had only used established data sources. In these cases, errors (deviations between signals identified in different data sources) may carry meaning. This means we would have remained oblivious if we had only focused on trying to make digital trace data fit patterns identified in established data sources.

The prominence of studies combining different types of data sources is only set to increase. Increasingly journalists, campaigners, and politicians take to digital trace data to identify supposed trends in public opinion or test messages (Anstead & O'Loughlin, 2015). This can lead patterns in digital trace data to influence politics or media coverage without truly mirroring the supposed phenomena (Jungherr et al., 2016b). This process can only be understood and evaluated using hybrid designs.

Hybrid designs are, of course, also vulnerable to the n=all and the mirror fallacies. Yet, by connecting digital trace data to other more conventional data sources, they become less exceptional and questions of adequate research designs and conceptual linkages arise naturally. Still, also with studies falling within this category, we have to critically ask ourselves if digital trace data accurately speak to the phenomena of interest or if authors simply follow a data-driven impulse and, after settling on a data set, only link their data superficially to a seemingly vibrant concept in social science discourse. Here, the link between concepts and measurements is as important as it was with the other approaches and the social sciences in general.

The Road Ahead: A Measurement Theory for Working with Digital Trace Data in the Social Sciences

As discussed above, the use of digital trace data in the social sciences is dominated by two fallacies severely limiting the application of these data. These fallacies are deeply rooted in a naive reading of signals extracted from digital data traces as directly representing social or political phenomena of interest and the indifference of leading practitioners to sampling procedures accounting for inherent limits in coverage and availability of digital trace data. Overcoming these fallacies is central for digital trace data to develop into an accepted data source in the social science mainstream. The alternative is that digital trace data end up as a sandbox for applied computer scientists.

To social scientists, the widespread influence of these fallacies is surprising. The social sciences and statistics look back on a long and fruitful debate on capturing phenomena of interest in concepts, linking these concepts to measurements, and statistical procedures allowing researchers to draw valid inferences based on these data (Donoho, 2015; Efron & Hastie, 2016; Gerring, 2012; Goertz, 2005; Goertz & Mahoney, 2012; Hand, 2004). As shown above, digital trace data share much more characteristics with traditional measurement approaches than early enthusiasts claimed, rendering the former subject to much of the same limitations as the latter. Yet, the current debate in the field focuses much more on the perceived exceptionality of digital trace data than the characteristics they share with other data sources.

Measurement theories are a central feature of quantitative approaches in the social sciences and psychology. Measurement theories conceptualize and test the relationship between signals found in data and their relationship toward phenomena of interest (Hand, 1996, 2004). Central is the acknowledgement that phenomena of interest are not directly connected with signals found in data. Instead, they are linked through a chain of mediating steps. Phenomena of interest have to be translated into meaningful and sophisticated concepts (Goertz, 2005). These concepts then have to be linked to signals found in data. It is crucial that this step accounts for the data-generating process underlying specific datasets and their consequences for the applicability of the linked concepts (Gerring, 2012). In a final step, measurement theories have to discuss valid modes of inference based on the underlying datasets and research interests (Efron & Hastie, 2016). Only a sophisticated understanding of this mediating process allows for the robust use of specific datasets and research methods in scientific work.

In the case of digital trace data, this mediating process is generally ignored in favor of a simplistic implicit reading of signals found in digital trace data as direct expressions of social or political phenomena of interest. As shown above, this limits the use of digital trace data in the social sciences severely. For their work to be taken seriously, researchers, who are interested in the use of these data for significant contributions to core discourses of the social sciences, should, therefore, push for the development of a measurement theory. This means focusing on the development or adaptation of concepts for the research environment of digital devices and services and critically linking these concepts to measurements found in digital trace data. Here, we also need to move away from a computer-science-publication logic based on proofs of concepts and prototyping of algorithms or models. This approach, while giving rise to a quick succession of innovative research methods, more often than not, accepts face validity as test for plausible links between signals and phenomena of interest. This leads papers to have only dubious connections with underlying social or political phenomena ostensibly of interest and only to speak to the application of a specific method or algorithm in a specific case with ill-understood contextual conditions and effects. Instead, social scientists working with digital trace data should push actively for a culture of serious and sophisticated concept validation (Jungherr et al., 2016). Similarly, researchers should focus not only on the novelty of new approaches, but, instead, on checking very consciously for the potential biasing effects of specific approaches to data collection and the reliability of specific quantitative methods (González-Bailón & Paltoglou, 2015; Ruths & Pfeffer, 2014).

Of similar importance is the development of explicit research designs for the work with digital trace data in the social sciences (Salganik, 2017). By now, it has become obvious that the early expectations of being able to neglect addressing research designs, since researchers were wandering through an n=all world, were misplaced. Instead, the inherent limits in reach and coverage of digital trace data have become common knowledge. Now, it is time for this common knowledge to find expression in research designs. This includes addressing questions of sampling, the reliability of different approaches to data selection and collection, and the valid combination of digital trace data and other data sources—such as surveys or digital trace data collected on various services following different data access politics. The relevance of this is only likely to increase when data access policies of digital service providers become more restrictive as they increasingly try to monetize this aspect of their services.

These demands might seem overly ambitious for researchers interested in testing the use of digital trace data in service of specific research questions. Yet, it is important to note that the research agenda sketched above does not necessarily have to be realized at once. Instead, it is highly likely that the steps sketched above constitute a collective project over many years. Still, while the establishment of a complete measurement theory of the work with digital trace data in the social sciences might seem prohibitively ambitious, it is necessary for researchers to address the issues raised above. More often than not, this will mean becoming more transparent in linking signals found in digital trace data to concepts of interest and underlying phenomena. This is very much in the reach of single research papers and would be a very big step forward from the state of "unconscious thinking" (Sartori, 1970) that we, as a field, currently seem to be more fond of than appropriate.

This adjustment in the work with digital trace data in the social sciences is necessary for this work to seriously contribute to the core debates in the social sciences. This means taking the "social science" in "computational social science" seriously. The social sciences have a rich tradition of grappling with social and political phenomena. This has led to the emergence of sophisticated pluralistic approaches to conceptualization, measurement, and inference (Brady & Collier, 2010; Gerring, 2012; Goertz & Mahoney, 2012). Currently, these debates are largely ignored in the work with digital trace data. This seems mostly due to an approach to data analysis predominantly driven from a software developer perspective where the inherent divide between signal and concept of interest features less prominently. Therefore, it is no surprise to find that work with digital trace data that seemingly addresses questions on social and political life currently can be best characterized as a subfield in applied computer science. Instead of meaningfully contributing to contemporary debates in the social sciences, these studies run algorithms and models on data without validly linking them to relevant concepts. Thus, these studies speak more to the workings of underlying algorithms and methods than the phenomena ostensibly being examined. Instead of following this lead, social scientists interested in working with digital trace data should push actively for the development of a serious measurement theory of digital trace data in the social sciences.

Normalizing Digital Trace Data

It is time to dispense with the exceptionalist rhetoric of the early days and to integrate digital trace data in the social science workflow and toolset. This means adapting established research practices to the work with digital trace data, instead of proclaiming a new age based on the perceived exceptionalism of this data source. As shown above, obvious tasks for this normalization lie in the conceptualization of digital trace data in ways that reflect their service-specific mediating data-generating processes (Jungherr, 2015; Jungherr et al., 2016a), the development of a measurement theory of the work with digital trace data in the social sciences to identify which phenomena of interest are reflected by the data and which phenomena remain hidden from it (Jungherr et al., 2016b), and approaches that allow the linking of digital trace data with traditional social science data sources, such as surveys or content analyses of political media coverage.

This also means thinking more consciously about research design. Currently, the n=all fallacy tempts researchers to spend very little time thinking about potential biases to their data collection. Digital trace data are found data (i.e. data produced as byproducts of online interactions by users) (Howison et al., 2011). Currently, researchers have predominantly taken these data as found and constructed research based on their features available to them, not necessarily the features providing the best basis for interesting inferences. Various studies have shown that taking a more active approach in their research design (e.g. through experiments) provides interesting avenues for future research (Bond et al., 2012; Salganik & Watts, 2009).

Other studies have shown that taking a more conscious approach to sampling specific populations on Twitter is providing a more robust footing than simply claiming to collect "all" relevant data (Diaz et al., 2016; Lin et al., 2014).

In short, to realize the potential of the "measurement revolution" (Watts, 2011) provided by digital trace data in the social sciences, we have to subject this new data source to the same rigorous tests in conceptualization and methodology as we do other data sources (Gerring, 2012; Hand, 2004). Currently, the novelty of digital trace data has given researchers somewhat of a free pass with regard to these questions. This free pass has to be revoked as the work with this data source slowly moves closer to the center of social science discourse. For researchers working with these data, this means, on one hand, a considerable chance to contribute foundational studies at the center of social science core discourses. On the other hand, this also means they have to become more disciplined in addressing the limits of their data sources. In this, the way forward very likely holds fewer exceptional, counter-intuitive, or spectacular findings than we are made to believe. Instead, we might witness incremental progress based on highly contextually dependent findings. While this might not be the most promising way to make one's way into airport bookstalls or Buzzfeed's list of "10 research results that will absolutely shock you," there is no reason for disappointment. After all, this is the natural progression of scientific fields and method development.

Acknowledgments

The arguments developed here result from a continuous conversation with colleagues from the social sciences and computer science. Especially, I want to thank Daniel Gayo-Avello, Pascal Jürgens, David Lazer, Helen Margetts, Takis Metaxas, Oliver Posegga, Harald Schoen, Ralph Schroeder, Sebastian Stier, Markus Strohmaier, and Yannis Theocharis.

Note

1 www.google.org/flutrends/about/

References

Adamic, L. A., & Glance, N. (2005). The political blogosphere and the 2004 U.S. election. In J. Adibi, M. Grobelnik, D. Mladenic, & P. Pantel (Eds.), *LinkKDD 2005: Proceedings of the 3rd International Workshop on Link Discovery* (pp. 36–43). New York, NY: ACM.

Adcock, R., & Collier, D. (2001). Measurement validity: A shared standard for qualitative and quantitative research. *American Political Science Review, 95*(3), 529–546. doi:10.1017/S0003055401003100

Anstead, N., & O'Loughlin, B. (2015). Social media analysis and public opinion: The 2010 UK general election. *Journal of Computer-Mediated Communication, 20*(2), 204–220. doi:10.1111/jcc4.12102

Ausserhofer, J., & Maireder, A. (2013). National politics on Twitter: Structures and topics of a networked public sphere. *Information, Communication & Society, 16*(3), 291–314. doi:10.1080/1369118x.2012.756050

Bakshy, E., Messing, S., & Adamic, L. A. (2015). Exposure to ideologically diverse news and opinion on Facebook. *Science, 348*(6239), 1130–1132. doi:10.1126/science.aaa1160

Blank, G. (2016). The digital divide among Twitter users and its implication for social research. *Social Science Computer Review.* doi:10.1177/0894439316671698

Bollen, J., Mao, H., & Zheng, X. J. (2011). Twitter mood predicts the stock market. *Journal of Computational Science, 2,* 1–8.

Bond, R. M., Fariss, C. J., Jones, J. J., Kramer, A. D. I., Marlow, C., Settle, J. E., & Fowler, J. H. (2012). A 61-million-person experiment in social influence and political mobilization. *Nature, 489*(7415), 295–298. doi:10.1038/nature11421

boyd, d., & Crawford, K. (2012). Critical questions for big data: provocations for a cultural, technological, and scholarly phenomenon. *Information, Communication & Society, 15*(5), 662–679. doi:10.1080/1369118x.2012.678878

Brady, H. E., & Collier, D. (Eds.). (2010). *Rethinking social inquiry: Diverse tools, shared standards* (2nd ed.). Lanham: Rowman & Littlefield Publishers Inc.

Bruns, A., & Highfield, T. (2013). Political networks on Twitter: Tweeting the Queensland state election. *Information, Communication & Society, 16*(5), 667–691. doi:10.1080/1369118x.2013.782328

Callegaro, M., Manfreda, K. L., & Vehovar, V. (2015). *Web survey methodology.* London, UK: SAGE Publications.

Chadwick, A. (2013). *The hybrid media system: Politics and power.* New York, NY: Oxford University Press.

Choi, H., & Varian, H. R. (2012). Predicting the present with Google trends. *Economic Record, 88,* 2–9. doi:10.1111/j.1475-4932.2012.00809.x

Collier, D., & Mahon, J. E. (1993). Conceptual "stretching" revisited: Adapting categories in comparative analysis. *American Political Science Review, 87*(4), 845–855. doi:10.2307/2938818

Conover, M. D., Ratkiewicz, J., Francisco, M., Gonçalves, B., Flammini, A., & Menczer, F. (2011). Political polarization on Twitter. In N. Nicolov, J. G. Shanahan, L. A. Adamic, R. Baeza-Yates, & S. Counts (Eds.), *ICWSM 2011: Proceedings of the 5th International AAAI Conference on Weblogs and Social Media* (pp. 89–96). Menlo Park, CA: Association for the Advancement of Artificial Intelligence (AAAI).

Contractor, D., & Faruquie, T. A. (2013). Understanding election candidate approval ratings using social media data. In D. Schwabe, V. Almeida, H. Glaser, R. Baeza-Yates, & S. Moon (Eds.), *WWW 2013: Proceedings of the 22nd International Conference on World Wide Web* (pp. 189–190). Geneva, CH: International World Wide Web Conferences Steering Committee.

Dayan, D., & Katz, E. (1992). *Media events: The live broadcasting of history.* Cambridge, MA: Harvard University Press.

De Choudhury, M., Counts, S., & Horvitz, E. (2013). Social media as a measurement tool of depression in populations. In H. Davis, H. Halpin, A. Pentland, M. Bernstein, & L. A. Adamic (Eds.), *WebSci 2013: Proceedings of the 5th Annual ACM Web Science Conference* (pp. 47–56). New York, NY: ACM.

Diaz, F., Gamon, M., Hofman, J. M., Kiciman, E., & Rothschild, D. (2016). Online and social media data as an imperfect continuous panel survey. *PLoS One, 11*(1), e0145406. doi:10.1371/journal.pone.0145406

DiGrazia, J., McKelvey, K., Bollen, J., & Rojas, F. (2013). More tweets, more votes: Social media as a quantitative indicator of political behavior. *PLoS One, 8*(11), e79449. doi:10.1371/journal.pone.0079449

DiMaggio, P., Evans, J., & Bryson, B. (1996). Have Americans' social attitudes become more polarized? *American Journal of Sociology, 102*(3), 690–755. doi:10.1086/230995

Donoho, D. (2015). *50 years of data science.* Paper presented at the John W. Tukey 100th Birthday Celebration at Princeton University, Princeton, NJ. http://courses.csail.mit.edu/18.337/2015/docs/50YearsDataScience.pdf

Efron, B., & Hastie, T. (2016). *Computer age statistical inference: Algorithms, evidence, and data science.* Cambridge, UK: Cambridge University Press.

Fiorina, M. P., & Abrams, S. J. (2008). Political polarization in the American public. *Annual Review of Political Science, 11*(1), 563–588. doi:10.1146/annurev.polisci.11.053106.153836

Freelon, D. (2015). On the cutting edge of big data: Digital politics research in the social computing literature. In S. Coleman & D. Freelon (Eds.), *Handbook of digital politics* (pp. 451–472). Northampton, MA: Edward Elgar Publishing.

Gamson, W. A. (1992). *Talking politics.* Cambridge, UK: Cambridge University Press.

Gayo-Avello, D. (2012). No, you cannot predict elections with Twitter. *IEEE Internet Computing, 16*(6), 91–94. doi:10.1109/mic.2012.137

Gayo-Avello, D. (2013). A meta-analysis of state-of-the-art electoral prediction from Twitter data. *Social Science Computer Review, 31*(6), 649–679. doi:10.1177/0894439313493979

Gerring, J. (2008). The mechanismic worldview: Thinking inside the box. *British Journal of Political Science, 38*(1), 161–179. doi:10.1017/S0007123408000082

Gerring, J. (2010). Causal mechanisms: Yes, but … *Comparative Political Studies, 43*(11), 1499–1526. doi:10.1177/0010414010376911

Gerring, J. (2012). *Social science methodology: A unified framework* (2nd ed.). Cambridge, UK: Cambridge University Press.

Goertz, G. (2005). *Social science concepts: A user's guide.* Princeton, NJ: Princeton University Press.

Goertz, G., & Mahoney, J. (2012). *A tale of two cultures: Qualitative and quantitative research in the social sciences.* Princeton, NJ: Princeton University Press.

Golder, S. A., & Macy, M. W. (2014). Digital footprints: opportunities and challenges for online social research. *Annual Review of Sociology, 40*(1), 129–152. doi:10.1146/annurev-soc-071913-043145

González-Bailón, S., & Paltoglou, G. (2015). Signals of public opinion in online communication: A comparison of methods and data sources. *The ANNALS of the American Academy of Political and Social Science, 659*(1), 95–107. doi:10.1177/0002716215569192

Grimmer, J., & Stewart, B. M. (2013). Text as data: The promise and pitfalls of automatic content analysis methods for political texts. *Political Analysis, 21*(3), 267–297. doi:10.1093/pan/mps028

Groves, R. M., Fowler Jr., F. J., Couper, M. P., Lepkowski, J. M., Singer, E., & Tourangeau, R. (2009). *Survey methodology* (2nd ed.). Hoboken, NJ: Wiley.

Hand, D. J. (1996). Statistics and the theory of measurement. *Journal of the Royal Statistical Society. Series A (Statistics in Society), 159*(3), 445. doi:10.2307/2983326

Hand, D. J. (2004). *Measurement theory and practice: The world through quantification.* London, UK: Wiley.

Hargittai, E. (2015). Is bigger always better? Potential biases of big data derived from social network sites. *The ANNALS of the American Academy of Political and Social Science, 659*(1), 63–76. doi:10.1177/0002716215570866

Howison, J., Wiggins, A., & Crowston, K. (2011). Validity Issues in the use of social network analysis with digital trace data. *Journal of the Association for Information Systems, 12*(12), 767–797.

Huberty, M. (2015). Can we vote with our tweet? On the perennial difficulty of election forecasting with social media. *International Journal of Forecasting, 31*(3), 992–1007. doi:10.1016/j.ijforecast.2014.08.005

Jungherr, A. (2014). The logic of political coverage on Twitter: Temporal dynamics and content. *Journal of Communication, 64*(2), 239–259. doi:10.1111/jcom.12087

Jungherr, A. (2015). *Analyzing political communication with digital trace data: The role of Twitter messages in social science research.* Cham, CH: Springer.

Jungherr, A., Jürgens, P., & Schoen, H. (2012). Why the Pirate Party won the German election of 2009 or the trouble with predictions: A response to Tumasjan, A., Sprenger, T. O., Sander, P. G., & Welpe, I. M. "Predicting elections with Twitter: What 140 characters reveal about political sentiment". *Social Science Computer Review, 30*(2), 229–234. doi:10.1177/0894439311404119

Jungherr, A., Schoen, H., & Jürgens, P. (2016a). The mediation of politics through Twitter: An analysis of messages posted during the campaign for the German federal election 2013. *Journal of Computer-Mediated Communication, 21*(1), 50–68. doi:10.1111/jcc4.12143

Jungherr, A., Schoen, H., Posegga, O., & Jügens, P. (2016b). Digital trace data in the study of public opinion: An indicator of attention toward politics rather than political support. *Social Science Computer Review.* doi:10.1177/0894439316631043

Jungherr, A., Schoen, H., Posegga, O., & Jürgens, P. (2015). *Characterizing political talk on Twitter: A comparison between public agenda, media agendas, and the Twitter agenda with regard to topics and dynamics.* Paper presented at the American Political Science Association (APSA) Annual Meeting 2015, San Francisco.

King, G. (2011). Ensuring the data-rich future of the social sciences. *Science, 331*(6018), 719–721. doi:10.1126/science.1197872

Kreiss, D. (2016). Seizing the moment: The presidential campaigns use of Twitter during the 2012 electoral cycle. *New Media & Society, 18*(8), 1473–1490. doi:10.1177/1461444814562445

Lazer, D., Kennedy, R., King, G., & Vespignani, A. (2014). The parable of Google flu: Traps in big data analysis. *Science, 343*(6176), 1203–1205. doi:10.1126/science.1248506

Lazer, D., Pentland, A., Adamic, L. A., Aral, S., Barabási, A.-L., Brewer, D., Christakis, N., Contractor, N., Fowler, J. H., Gutmann, M., Jebara, T., King, G., Macy, M., Roy, D., & Van Alstyne, M. (2009). Computational social science. *Science, 323*(5915), 721–723. doi:10.1126/science.1167742

Leskovec, J., Backstrom, L., & Kleinberg, J. (2009). Meme-tracking and the dynamics of the news cycle. In J. Elder, F. Soulie-Fogelman, P. Flach, & M. Zaki (Eds.), *KDD 2009: Proceedings of the 15th ACM SIGKDD International Conference on Knowledge Discovery and Data Mining* (pp. 497–506). New York, NY: ACM.

Lin, Y.-R., Keegan, B., Margolin, D., & Lazer, D. (2014). Rising tides or rising stars? Dynamics of shared attention on Twitter during media events. *PLoS One, 9*(5), e94093. doi:10.1371/journal.pone.0094093

Marchetti-Bowick, M., & Chambers, N. (2012). Learning for microblogs with distant super-vision: Political forecasting with Twitter. In W. Daelemans (Ed.), *EACL '12: Proceedings of the 13th Conference of the European Chapter of the Association for Computational Linguistics* (pp. 603–612). Stroudsburg, PA: Association for Computational Linguistics.

Mayer-Schönberger, V., & Cukier, K. (2013). *Big data: A revolution that will transform how we live, work, and think.* New York, NY: Houghton Mifflin Harcourt.

Metaxas, P. T., Mustafaraj, E., & Gayo-Avello, D. (2011). How (not) to predict elections. In A. Vinciarelli, M. Pantic, E. Bertino, & J. Zhan (Eds.), *SocialCom 2011: The 3rd IEEE International Conference on Social Computing* (pp. 165–171). Washington, DC: IEEE.

Morstatter, F., Pfeffer, J., Liu, H., & Carley, K. M. (2013). Is the sample good enough? Comparing data from Twitter's streaming API with Twitter's firehose. In E. Kiciman, N. B. Ellison, B. Hogan, P. Resnick, & I. Soboroff (Eds.), *ICWSM 2013: Proceedings of the 7th International AAAI Conference on Weblogs and Social Media* (pp. 400–408). Menlo Park, CA: Association for the Advancement of Artificial Intelligence (AAAI).

Murphy, J., Link, M. W., Childs, J. H., Tesfaye, C. L., Dean, E., Stern, M., Pasek, J., Cohen, J., Callegaro, M., & Harwood, P. (2014). Social media in public opinion research: Executive summary of the Aapor task force on emerging technologies in public opinion research. *Public Opinion Quarterly, 78*(4), 788–794. doi:10.1093/poq/nfu053

Neuman, W. R. (2016). *The digital difference: Media technology and the theory of communication effects.* Cambridge, MA: Harvard University Press.

Neuman, W. R., Guggenheim, L., Mo Jang, S., & Bae, S. Y. (2014). The dynamics of public attention: Agenda-setting theory meets big data. *Journal of Communication, 64*(2), 193–214. doi:10.1111/jcom.12088

O'Connor, B., Balasubramanyan, R., Routledge, B. R., & Smith, N. A. (2010). From tweets to polls: Linking text sentiment to public opinion time series. In M. Hearst, W. Cohen, & S. Gosling (Eds.), *ICWSM 2010: Proceedings of the 4th International AAAI Conference on Weblogs and Social Media* (pp. 122–129). Menlo Park, CA: Association for the Advancement of Artificial Intelligence (AAAI).

Prior, M. (2013). Media and political polarization. *Annual Review of Political Science, 16*(1), 101–127. doi:10.1146/annurev-polisci-100711–135242

Rainie, L., & Wellman, B. (2012). *Networked: The new social operating system.* Cambridge, MA: The MIT Press.

Resnick, P., Adar, E., & Lampe, C. (2015). What social media data we are missing and how to get it. *The ANNALS of the American Academy of Political and Social Science, 659*(1), 192–206. doi:10.1177/0002716215570006

Rogers, R. (2013). *Digital methods.* Cambridge, MA: The MIT Press.

Ruths, D., & Pfeffer, J. (2014). Social media for large studies of behavior. *Science, 346*(6213), 1063–1064. doi:10.1126/science.346.6213.1063

Salganik, M. J. (2017). *Bit by bit: Social research in the digital age.* Princeton, NJ: Princeton University Press.

Salganik, M. J., & Watts, D. J. (2009). Web-based experiments for the study of collective social dynamics in cultural markets. *Topics in Cognitive Science, 1*(3), 439–468. doi:10.1111/j.1756-8765.2009.01030.x

Sartori, G. (1970). Concept misformation in comparative politics. *American Political Science Review, 64*(4), 1033–1053. doi:10.2307/1958356

Sartori, G. (1984). Guidelines for concept analysis. In G. Sartori (Ed.), *Social science concepts: A systematic analysis* (pp. 15–85). London, UK: Sage.

Scheufele, D. A., & Nisbet, M. C. (2013). Online news and the demise of political disagreement. In C. T. Salmon (Ed.), *Communication yearbook 36* (pp. 44–53). New York, NY: Routledge.

Schober, M. F., Pasek, J., Guggenheim, L., Lampe, C., & Conrad, F. G. (2016). Social media analyses for social measurement. *Public Opinion Quarterly, 80*(1), 180–211. doi:10.1093/poq/nfv048

Schoen, H., Gayo-Avello, D., Metaxas, P. T., Mustafaraj, E., Strohmaier, M., & Gloor, P. (2013). The power of prediction with social media. *Internet Research, 23*(5), 528–543. doi:10.1108/IntR-06-2013-0115

Schroeder, R. (2016). Big data and communication research *Oxford Research Encyclopedia of Communication*. Oxford, UK: Oxford University Press.

Strohmaier, M., & Wagner, C. (2014). Computational social science for the World Wide Web. *IEEE Intelligent Systems, 29*(5), 84–88. doi:10.1109/mis.2014.80

Tourangeau, R., Rips, L. J., & Rasinski, K. (2000). *The psychology of survey response.* Cambridge, UK: Cambridge University Press.

Trilling, D. (2015). Two different debates? Investigating the relationship between a political debate on tv and simultaneous comments on Twitter. *Social Science Computer Review, 33*(3), 259–276. doi:10.1177/0894439314537886

Tumasjan, A., Sprenger, T. O., Sandner, P. G., & Welpe, I. M. (2010). Predicting elections with Twitter: What 140 characters reveal about political sentiment. In M. Hearst, W. Cohen, & S. Gosling (Eds.), *ICWSM 2010: Proceedings of the 4th International AAAI Conference on Weblogs and Social Media* (pp. 178–185). Menlo Park, CA: Association for the Advancement of Artificial Intelligence (AAAI).

Vargo, C. J., Guo, L., McCombs, M., & Shaw, D. L. (2014). Network issue agendas on Twitter during the 2012 U.S. presidential election. *Journal of Communication, 64*(2), 296–316. doi:10.1111/jcom.12089

Watts, D. J. (2011). *Everything is obvious: How common sense fails us*. New York, NY: Random House.

Wells, C., Shah, D.V., Pevehouse, J. C.,Yang, J. H., Pelled, A., Boehm, F., Lukito, J., Gosh, S., & Schmidt, J. L. (2016). How Trump drove coverage of the nomination: Hybrid media. *Political Communication, 33*(4), 669–676. doi:10.1080/10584609.2016.1224416

3

EVERYTHING OLD IS NEW AGAIN

Big Data and Methodological Transparency

Leticia Bode

Over the past ten years, a combination of increased availability of digital trace data (as well as other large datasets generated by technologies like magnetic resonance imaging (MRI), corneal eye tracking, and electroencephalogram (EEG)), and the development of computational power and methods allowing us to examine it, have contributed to the rise of so-called "big data" in the social sciences[1], and, more specifically, in political communication more specifically (boyd & Crawford, 2012; Mayer-Schönberger & Cukier, 2013). Researchers and public commentators alike are concerned about this "paradigm shift" (AAPOR, 2015, pp. 11) and what it might mean for society, fearing a world in which "people may give algorithms the authority to make the most important decisions in their lives" (Harari, 2016). I will refrain from commenting on the changes big data will entail for society, focusing instead on what it might mean for the social sciences. While this is not an essay on ethics, the choices we make as researchers—including what data we choose to employ and how we make use of those data—are necessarily ethical ones, and some subjectivity and normativity cannot be avoided when it comes to this subject.

As recent research has indicated, big data often means "different things to different audiences" (Halavais, 2015, pp. 584). Definitions alternate between short and catchy (volume, velocity, and variety from Laney, 2012) and long and cumbersome, owing to the fact that big data is speaking to different audiences, but also to the idea that big data is still an ever-changing phenomenon, and likely will be for the foreseeable future. Most researchers avoid defining the term at all, relying on an assumption that their audience will share a "know-it-when-I-see-it" understanding of what constitutes big data (*Jacobellis v Ohio*)[2]. The most comprehensive definition of big data I have come across is the following, offered by boyd & Crawford in 2012:

A cultural, technological, and scholarly phenomenon that rests on the interplay of:

(1) Technology: maximizing computation power and algorithmic accuracy to gather, analyze, link, and compare large datasets.
(2) Analysis: drawing on large datasets to identify patterns in order to make economic, social, technical, and legal claims.
(3) Mythology: the widespread belief that large datasets offer a higher form of intelligence and knowledge that can generate insights that were previously impossible, with the aura of truth, objectivity, and accuracy (pp. 663).

However, this definition goes beyond the purposes of this essay. My discussion of big data relies only on the first two prongs of this definition, leaving any mythology aside. To be sure, there is still some mythology about big data as a result of its relative novelty in the social sciences, but, as will become clear later on, I see that novelty as a feature, rather than a bug. Therefore, for the remainder of my discussion, when I refer to big data, I mean data (1) which exist in a large dataset and (2) which rely on computational power for data gathering, data analysis, or both. This is a simplistic and capacious definition, allowing for a flexible understanding of big data as it has changed and will continue to change over time, and also allowing for inclusivity when it comes to the different nuances individuals adopt in their own understandings of big data.

Most commonly, big data in political communication is generated by digital traces. Digital trace data can include any data that are generated as a result of people engaging in behaviors in a digital way. The range of what this includes is, therefore, vast. People go online to find others to partner with, and this generates OkCupid digital traces, allowing us to examine what people really value in a mate or in a one-night stand (Rudder, 2011). Trackers in taxi cabs allow the generation of maps of trips taken, distance traveled, and fare for different areas in Chicago, providing new insight into how people get around (New, 2016). People create vast networks of users interested in similar things, allowing us to see how ideas cluster on blogs (Adamic & Glance, 2005), how Tumblr users and their pages relate to one another (Chang, et al, 2014), how Facebook users create communities (Ellison, Steinfeld, & Lampe, 2007), and how Twitter users relate to one another in terms of political ideas (Bode et al, 2015), clusters of users, such as Lady Gaga's "little monsters" (Click, Lee, & Willson Holladay, 2013), or around parenting topics (Bode et al, 2017).

All of these are valuable contributions to the study of communication, and provide insight not just into the digital behaviors of users, but also their broader behaviors (Bode, et al., 2016), attitudes (Barberá, 2015), and opinions (O'Connor, et al., 2010), and how these relate to world events (Sayre, et al., 2010).

History of Political Communication Research: How Big Data is Different

How revolutionary is big data? To properly contextualize it, a bit of history is required. In general, most research in political communication falls into a relatively small group of methodological approaches. Importantly, these approaches have been consistently used for the duration of the existence of the discipline, with changes consisting of incremental adjustments, as I outline below, rather than major transformations.

The earliest research in political communication dates back to the early 20th century, with work from such luminaries as Walter Lippmann (Lippmann, 1922) and Charles Horton Cooley (Cooley, 1909) revealing the fundamentally important place of communication in society. The earliest work was observational in nature, drawing on philosophy and political thought more than modern research methods. The discipline quickly developed, though, with such institutional infrastructure as professional organizations and university departments in place by the mid-century. Work at that time relied mostly on qualitative work and critical theory, focusing on big questions of media and communication in society. Methods diversified in the following decades, with quantitative and qualitative research producing findings on media effects (Lasswell, 1927; Lazarsfeld, Berelson, & Gaudet, 1944) agenda-setting (McCombs & Shaw, 1972), uses and gratifications (Katz, Blumler, & Gurevitch, 1973), and other foundational communication theories.

Most research in political communication, though—either quantitative or qualitative—relies on a handful of sources of data. This includes media and communication content, which is most frequently analyzed using discourse analysis or qualitative or quantitative content analysis (Neuendorf, 2001). A second source of data comes from interviews, which can take the form of ethnography, focus groups, qualitative interviews, or participant observation on the qualitative side, but, most commonly, take the form of survey research on the quantitative side (Berger, 2014). Finally, communication has borrowed from other social science disciplines (but especially Psychology) in its use of experiments.

Over the decades, improvements in methods in communication (and, more specifically, political communication) have primarily focused on new computational abilities, made possible by the rapid expansion of computing power in the late 20th and early 21st centuries (Westland & Clark, 1999). Computational power allows for better statistical modeling (Beck & Katz, 2007), computer-assisted content analysis of existing content (Bode & Hennings, 2012), and even automated transcription of interview data (Franz, et al., 2003). The *sources* of data, however, have remained relatively constant.

In this way, big data represents a fundamental change in the political communication discipline. There is no one way in which these data are different, due to the wide variety of data that the term encompasses. Therefore, none of the generalizations I am about to make hold true for every case of big data.

But, in general, big data is often some combination of communication and behavior, falling somewhere between the first two categories outlined above. A tweet could be construed as an act of communication, or as a separate behavior. A data point in a dataset of gaze data produced by an eye tracker, likewise, is a sort of behavioral indication of attention or general preference—it is not an interview, it is not quite observational data, and it may be a part of an experiment—but none of the three wholly encompasses it.

One of the major ways in which big data differ from previous sources of data is that they are often obtained without the explicit awareness of the person gen-erating the data. Whereas for interviews, surveys, and experiments the methods of data collection are generally quite salient to participants—much of big data is trace data that is collected without participants really thinking about their data being used for research (Freelon, 2014).

Big data is also, as might be expected, an order of magnitude larger than trad-itional sources of data. Whereas researchers might interview a couple of dozen of people, enroll a few hundred people in an experiment, or survey as many as tens of thousands of people: big datasets regularly reach into the millions of units of analysis, whether that is tweets, gaze data, or hyperlinks.

Digital trace data offer an entirely new source of data and, in doing so, an entirely new way of seeing the world. The analysis may change as well, but many of the approaches to big data are reliant on existing methods of analysis, giving communication a rich set of analytical tools to bring to bear on new sources of data. So, how does this new source of data change the social sciences and, more specifically, political communication?

Acknowledged Benefits of Big Data for Big Data Researchers

In addition to the substantive contributions big data research provides, as briefly outlined above, big data more broadly—as a data source and/or a methodological approach—has numerous contributions which have already been documented by others, so I will outline them only briefly here.

One major benefit is that big data allows us to see people in their natural habitat, so to speak. Many other common methods, including experiments and surveys, require some degree of artificiality—users are asked to do things that they wouldn't otherwise do. For this reason, experiments suffer from external validity, which can skew their findings (Schram, 2005), and surveys suffer from the fact that many questions we ask are questions that respondents have never given much thought to (Zaller, 1992), which renders them vulnerable to question-wording bias and other limitations such as social-desirability bias (Groves et al., 2009). Big data, on the other hand, finds users where they are and does not require any more of them than they are already prepared to give.

A second benefit of big data is that it allows us access to people that would otherwise be very difficult to reach. Some populations are difficult to find almost by definition. Those with minority viewpoints, and particularly unpopular minority viewpoints, don't tend to make themselves available to researchers, or even known to their communities. Those engaged in any sort of "deviant" act, including everything from illicit drug use to unconventional sexual habits, have every motivation to conceal that behavior from others (Groves, et al., 2009). This makes them difficult to identify in traditional research settings, to interview them, survey them, measure the content they produce, or observe their behavior. Big data allows us to identify these populations by virtue of their communications, and then to observe their behaviors and content without presenting any meaningful risk to the research subjects, as well as allowing them to stay anonymous throughout the process (though it is worth noting that researchers must take proactive action to ensure this anonymity).

Finally, perhaps the most obvious benefit of big data is volume. Big data is big. It allows insights into events and behaviors that are relatively rare and, therefore, difficult to capture in a smaller dataset. It, sometimes, allows us to see an entire population, where other methods would only allow a sample. This also facilitates mapping entire networks of interactions, communications, and affiliations (Chatfield & Brajawidagda, 2012; Khonsari, Nayeri, & Fathalian, 2010; Tremayne, 2014; Ullrich, Borau, & Stepanyan, 2010), which was impossible on any sort of scale prior to the advent of big data.

As a result of this volume, big data is often much cheaper than other forms of data acquisition. Traditional means of acquiring data in communication are often very involved and, therefore, very expensive. Content analysis, when done on any significant scale, requires a small army of coders, and the content being analyzed often costs a substantial amount to access in the first place (see for example, Freedman & Goldstein, 1999). Survey research is extremely expensive, regularly costing between $5 and $15 per respondent, even for a straightforward poll over the phone or online (Groves, et al., 2009). For more intensive survey work, such as the General Social Survey (GSS), respondents must be contacted in person for a lengthy interview, running costs per participant as high at an astounding $1300 per completed interview for the 2010 GSS (Dixon, Singleton, & Straits, 2016). Big data acquisition, on the other hand, often involves relatively limited upfront costs—including server space and other appropriate infrastructure—and costs even less on an ongoing basis. However, to be fair, this is not always the case. When big data are proprietary data, costs can skyrocket. But, many forms of big data collection can be done relatively cheaply. This also facilitates data collection over time, at a fraction of the initial cost, whereas other data acquisition methods often scale up costs dramatically when they are extended from cross-sectional to time series data.

Benefits of Big Data for Non-Big Data Researchers

But, these benefits extend only to those researchers who are engaged in so-called big data research. Researchers who are uninterested in big data, who lack access to

appropriate data sources, or who have not learned the skills required for computational methods associated with accessing, cleaning, analyzing, and visualizing big
data (Koltay, 2014), are not benefiting from the aspects of big data outlined above.
In a zero-sum game, it might be assumed that those researchers not engaging in
big data are in fact *disadvantaged* by the benefits of big data which are being con-
ferred to other researchers.

But, I see things differently. I see big data as more than just a shiny new data
source available to some social scientists to the exclusion of others. Big data, instead,
represents a fundamental shift in social science methods, which has not been seen
for decades. This shift is important for the evolving political communication community as a whole—not just for those who choose to use big data in their research.

While there are likely more, I will discuss three overlooked benefits of big data,
particularly those that extend beyond the researchers actually using big data and to
the entirety of the discipline of communication. These include external visibility,
increased accessibility, and, most importantly, method transparency.

The first benefit for communication as a discipline is increased visibility. For
better or worse, big data is exciting and novel—at least for now. This makes it of
greater interest to journalists, which increases the likelihood that communication
research will get covered by the media and be seen by the public as well. Recent
examples of big data research making headlines include a post-campaign network analysis of Trump supporters, Clinton supporters, and journalists on Twitter
(Thompson, 2016), analysis of the prevalence of white supremacist movements and
their followers on social media (Nickalls, 2016), use of Twitter messages to gauge
natural disaster impact (Hotz, 2016), and victim blaming in comment sections on
news articles reporting on sexual assault (Kingkade, 2016).

More broadly, journalistic interest in big data research is shown, in Figure 3.1.
Clearly, this interest is growing substantially over time. Interest of the general
public, as captured in Google search data, has, likewise, skyrocketed over time,
particularly when compared with trendlines for other, more traditional research
methods (see Figure 3.2). Time will tell whether this novelty will persist, but, for
now, big data seems to get more coverage than other types of research.

Related to this benefit, big data is often based on information about people's
daily lives—dating profiles, purchases, tweets—which makes it, and, by extension,
research based on it, more accessible to the average citizen. People tend to be
interested in research that involves the everyman and (somewhat unfortunately)
are intuitively more persuaded by census-based research as compared to research
based on samples. This makes big data research interesting to people, but also
allows them to grasp it in a personalized way, whereas experiments or surveys
require specific training to interpret and, therefore, may not be as intuitive. This
also makes big data more accessible (in terms of understanding and interest) to
students, which may have the added benefit of making them aware of how much
digital trace data they generate and how to control their privacy online to min-
imize any negative impact of such data (Madden & Rainie, 2015).

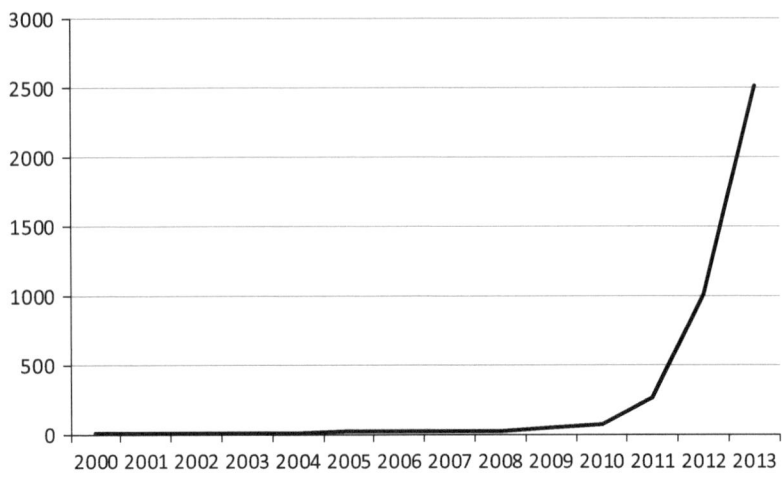

FIGURE 3.1 Mentions of "Big Data" and "Research" in News Articles Over Time

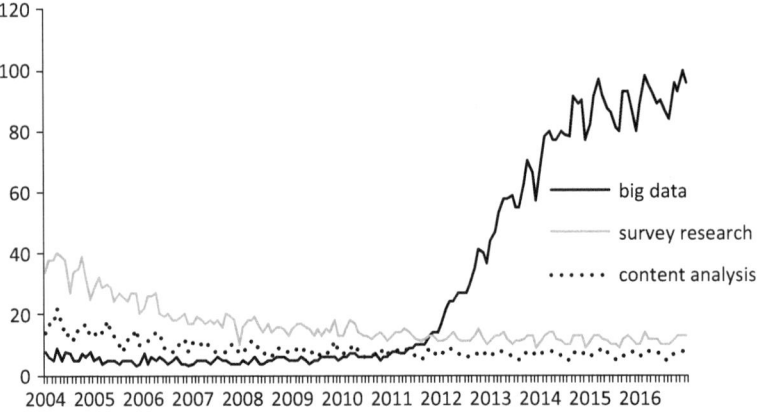

FIGURE 3.2 Google Searches for "Big Data" Over Time

The largest benefit I see of the big data entrance into communication research, however, exists entirely within academia. As described above, most progress in political communication methods has been methodological, rather than data-based. This represents a fundamental change in political communication research, and it is my hope that this change leads to an increased awareness of methods and increased transparency in the choices we make as researchers.

Let me explain. While big data is somewhat intuitive, given its familiarity, the choices that researchers must make around how to collect, clean, sample, analyze, and visualize big data are anything but intuitive. Because these data are so new, we have very few assumptions about how they should be examined, and have yet to develop clear and straightforward best practices (though see the chapters by Deen Freelon and Lei Guo in this volume for some suggestions). As a result, when we review research based on big data, we revert back to fundamental basic questions related to the research design.

First, there are questions about the population or the sample. These include asking who is in the population, what assumptions we are making about who those people are, how they got into the population, and what their motivations are. But, they also include asking who is left out of the population, by virtue of not being willing to engage in that online community or behavior or by not having access to the platform or the online world in general (Anderson & Perrin, 2016).

Questions must also be answered with regard to how the data were obtained, as different processes can return different data, with different issues of completeness which could lead to bias. Sampling the Twitter firehose (all of Twitter), for instance, will return different data than the Twitter garden hose (10% of Twitter), and different API (Application Program Interface) access can also result in different data. Pulling relevant data using keywords demands attention to what the list of keywords was and how it was generated. Retrieving data using hashtags will return different data, but also must address these questions. More specificity means a lower rate of false positives, or data that are unrelated to the topic in question, but a greater likelihood of false negatives, or the possibility that something related is being missed. But, the more general, the more data cleaning that must be done, which involves its own set of choices.

Best practices are beginning to emerge on the choices surrounding cleaning big data, but researchers must still decide how to refine the data to make it more useable for analysis. This may involve removing spam or bots, which first requires identifying them (Wu, Morstatter, & Liu, 2016). For any text-based analysis, it may also involve the choice to get rid of stop words or words that are otherwise relatively uninformative (Wilbur & Sirotkin, 1992). Outliers must also be considered, and choices made about whether they contribute to the overall story or detract from it.

With digital trace data, the question of what the appropriate unit of analysis is also arises, as answers related to users are often very different when compared to answers based on the dataset as a whole. That is, some users are outliers and can significantly skew the data of an entire population. Is it therefore better to examine each single tweet or the corpus of tweets generated by each user? The appropriate analysis to undertake is also an open question, and how to interpret results is equally important, especially given that, in sufficiently large datasets, statistical significance is no longer a meaningful concept.

All of these choices require a significant amount of transparency to convince the reader or the reviewer that appropriate steps were taken at each turn.

So, what does this have to do with all the non-big data researchers in communication? My hope is that this increased transparency demanded by a new source of data will have trickle-down effects to the rest of communication research. Because other sources of data—communication content, survey data, interview data, and ethnographic data—have existed for so long, we have come to accept certain assumptions about them, without properly interrogating research to determine if the choices made at each step were appropriate. Examples of accepted assumptions exist throughout all the ways in which transparency is demanded of big data, as outlined above. I regularly review manuscripts that do not give any defense as to the appropriateness of the method chosen, nor the potential biases or tradeoffs involved in its use. When samples are taken in content analysis, rarely is it discussed how we can be confident that those samples are unbiased representations of the whole corpus of content. Some discussion of sample representativeness is more common in survey data, but non-representative samples are regularly used without any conversation about what bias that likely introduces or to what population we can realistically generalize. More broadly, information about who is recruited into a sample, how they got into the population of interest, and what their motivations are in answering survey questions often goes unreported (even though we have significant evidence that people mislead and, sometimes, outright lie to pollsters (Robinson-Cimpian, 2016); for a recent example of how this matters, see Cramer 2016 on people's claims about intentionally lying to polling organizations during the 2016 election).

This is something I have observed in my own work, both as an author and as a peer-review referee. Because big data is unfamiliar to others, they ask more questions about where it comes from and what it really means—questions we should be asking about all research, but don't always remember to. This has then had a spillover effect into my work (and my reviewing) that does not deal with big data, such that I have a greater drive to think about big questions surrounding my own data and their assumptions, and greater curiosity to know more about data origins and choices when reviewing.

As an example, an article that I wrote with several colleagues, about how Twitter users cluster together in their political hashtagging, had a hard time getting published (Bode et al., 2015). The article uses followers of politicians on Twitter as its sample, and then considers the most frequently used hashtags within that group of users and how they cluster together. We were pushed by reviewers—rightfully—to think more about what we were able to say about these particular users, especially given that we know that Twitter users who follow politicians are an extremely engaged population and are not particularly representative of the broader electorate (Bode & Dalrymple, 2016). We were also pushed about the choices we made in terms of how many hashtags to use and what critical threshold determined an actual cluster of users. These criticisms improved the work, but they also helped us think more seriously about the underling questions and assumptions we were making. This is a common issue I have had when publishing innovative or relatively novel methods.

As a result of these experiences, I am a better scholar in general, even when I am not doing big data research. I am more careful about the claims I make, more explicit about the assumptions inherent in my data, and more thorough when describing the many choices that I make in going from research question to research design, and then to execution and analysis. These are choices that we all make, but with more traditional methods, we are often able to slide through the research process without addressing them head-on.

This taps into a broader trend toward increased transparency in the social sciences. As a recent treatise on the subject put it, "the view that social science is a group activity, requiring inter-subjective knowledge being created using public processes that are warranted to add value, is common to virtually every scholarly tradition" (Lupia & Elman, 2014, pp. 20). That is, our knowledge is more reliable, more understandable, and more accessible to our community and to outside communities when we are as transparent as possible about the choices we make in generating that knowledge.

So, what does it mean to be transparent? Ethics guidelines from the American Political Science Association focus on three elements of transparency; 1) data access (providing access to the data and to thorough replication files); 2) production transparency (outlining the choices made in producing and cleaning the data); and 3) analytic transparency (forthrightness in the many decisions made when analyzing the data) (Lupia & Elman, 2010; 2014).

These guidelines are useful for the methodologically diverse sub-discipline of political communication (Edgerly, et al., 2013), because they apply equally well to a variety of methods. Whether one is conducting quantitative content analysis (Lupia & Alter, 2014), qualitative interviews (Elman & Kapiszewski, 2014; Moravcsik, 2014), detailed experiments (McDermott, 2014), extensive survey research (Dafoe, 2014), or big data analysis, readers still deserve to know about the choices they made about data, production, and analysis, and authors can reasonably be expected to provide each.

To be sure, there are downsides of increased transparency as well. Under the wrong conditions, transparency can itself impose a certain power structure on research, favoring some types or styles of research over others (Ananny & Crawford, 2016). Other potential downsides include putting vulnerable groups at risk by threatening their privacy or their autonomy, and conflating seeing with understanding (Ananny & Crawford, 2016). And, more generally, individual researchers may be put at risk by virtue of their research transparency when it opens them up to greater criticism. Even if more transparent research is objectively better than opaque research, it is also sometimes easier to find fault with, given that there is simply more information about it available. In the peer-review process, this can be frustrating and act as a disincentive for offering more information rather than less.

Nonetheless, we cannot have confidence in our research, and the knowledge it purports to produce, if it is not able to respond to these types of criticism.

> Transparency is therefore not simply a precondition for assessing the quality of existing qualitative work, but also for encouraging and rewarding

empirical, theoretical and methodological excellence in qualitative research. Without transparency, relatively little incentive exists to acquire new skills, collect better evidence, conduct superior data analysis, or render theory more accurate empirically.

Moravcsik, 2014, pp. 50

So, this essay serves as a call to political communication researchers, to use the big data revolution as an opportunity to revisit the assumptions we make in *all* our research and to push one another to talk more thoughtfully about the choices we make. If we do this, the big data revolution will be a boon to the entire political communication research community. If we fail to do so, the risks are real:

when social scientists fail to document their assumptions, decisions, and actions and are unwilling or unable to share this information with others, it limits others' abilities to understand the meaning of the scientists' claims. When such failures are frequent in a research community, the credibility and legitimacy of the community as a whole are imperiled.

Lupia & Elman, 2014, pp. 20

Notes

1 For the purposes of this essay, I will refer to big data as a singular term, even though its meaning is by no means singular, and the words from which it is composed are plural.
2 In his concurrence in *Jacobellis v Ohio*, Justice Potter Stewart famously avoided defining pornography: "I shall not today attempt further to define the kinds of material I understand to be embraced within that shorthand description; and perhaps I could never succeed in intelligibly doing so. But I know it when I see it" (*Jacobellis v Ohio*, 378 U.S. 184, concurrence).

References

AAPOR. (2015). AAPOR report on big data. American Association for Public Opinion Research. 12 February 2015. Retrieved from www.aapor.org/AAPOR_Main/media/MainSiteFiles/images/BigDataTaskForceReport_FINAL_2_12_15_b.pdf

Adamic, L. A., & Glance, N. (2005). The political blogosphere and the 2004 U.S. election: Divided they blog. *Proceedings of the 3rd International Workshop on Link Discovery* (pp. 36–43).

Ananny, M., & Crawford, K. (2016). Seeing without knowing: Limitations of the transparency ideal and its application to algorithmic accountability. *New Media and Society*, online first.

Anderson, M., & Perrin, A. (2016). 13% of Americans don't use the internet. Who are they? *Pew Research Center*. 7 September 2016. Retrieved from www.pewresearch.org/fact-tank/2016/09/07/some-americans-dont-use-the-internet-who-are-they/

Barberá, P. (2015). Birds of the same feather Tweet together. Bayesian ideal point estimation using Twitter data. *Political Analysis, 23*(1), 76–91.

Beck, N., & Katz, J.N. (2007). Random coefficient models for time-series–cross-section data: Monte Carlo experiments. *Political Analysis, 15*(2), 182–195.

Berger, A.A. (2014). *Media and communication research methods: An introduction to qualitative and quantitative approaches.* Thousand Oaks, CA: Sage Publications.

Bode, L., Davis-Kean, P., Ryan, R., & Singh, L. (2017). Vaccinations and autism: A case study in parenting information on Twitter. *Presented at the annual meeting of the Society for Research in Child Development,* Austin, Texas, April 6–8.

Bode, L., Hanna, A., Yang, J.H., & Shah, D.V. (2015). Candidate networks, citizen clusters, and political expression: Strategic hashtag use in the 2010 midterms. *The ANNALS of the American Academy of Political and Social Science, 659*(1), 149–165.

Bode, L., & Hennings, V. (2012). Mixed signals? Gender and the media's coverage of the 2008 vice presidential candidates. *Politics & Policy, 40*(2), 221–257.

Bode, L., Lassen, D.S., Kim, Y.M., Shah, D.V., Fowler, E.F., Ridout, T., & Franz, M. (2016). Coherent campaigns? Campaign broadcast and social messaging. *Online Information Review, 40*(5), 580–594.

Bode, L., & Dalrymple, K. (2016). Politics in 140 characters or less: Campaign communication, network interaction, and political participation on Twitter. *Journal of Political Marketing,* online first.

boyd, d., & Crawford, K. (2012). Critical questions for big data: Provocations for a cultural, technological, and scholarly phenomenon. *Information, Communication & Society, 15*(5), 662–679.

Chang, Y., Tang, L., Inagaki, Y., & Liu, Y. (2014). What is Tumblr? A statistical overview and comparison. *ACM SIGKDD Explorations Newsletter* – Special issue on big data archive, *16*(1), 21–29.

Chatfield, A., & Brajawidagda, U. (2012). Twitter tsunami early warning network: A social network analysis of Twitter information flows. In J.W. Lamp (Eds.), *ACIS 2012: Location, Location, Location: Proceedings of the 23rd Australasian Conference on Information Systems 2012* (pp. 1–10). Australia: Deakin University.

Click, M.A., Lee, H., & Willson Holladay, H. (2013). Making monsters: Lady Gaga, fan identification, and social media. *Popular Music and Society, 36*(3).

Cooley, C.H. (1909). *Social organization: A study of the larger mind.* New York, NY: Charles Scribner's Sons.

Cramer, K. (2016). For years, I've been watching anti-elite fury build in Wisconsin. Then came Trump. *Vox.* 16 November 2016. Retrieved from www.vox.com/the-big-idea/2016/11/16/13645116/rural-resentment-elites-trump

Dafoe, A. (2014). Science deserves better: The imperative to share complete replication files. *Political Science and Politics, 47*(1), 60–66.

Dixon, J.C., Singleton Jr., R.A., & Straits, B.C. (2016). *The process of social research.* New York, NY: Oxford University Press.

Edgerly, S., Bode, L., Kim, Y.M., & Shah, D.V. (2013). Campaigns go social: Are Facebook, YouTube, and Twitter changing elections? In Ridout, T. (Ed.), *New directions in media and politics.* New York, NY: Routledge.

Ellison, N.B., Steinfeld, C., & Lampe, C. (2007). The benefits of Facebook "Friends": Social capital and college students' use of online social network sites. *Journal of Computer-Mediated Communication, 12*(4), 1143–1168.

Elman, C. & Kapiszewski, D. (2014). Data access and research transparency in the qualitative tradition. *Political Science and Politics, 47*(1), 43–47.

Franz, M., Ramabhadran, B., Ward, T., & Picheny, M. (2003). Automated transcription and topic segmentation of large spoken archives. *Eurospeech, 2003, Geneva Switzerland.*

Freedman, P., & Goldstein, K. (1999). Measuring media exposure and the effects of negative campaign ads. *American Journal of Political Science, 43*(4), 1189–1208.

Freelon, D. (2014). On the interpretation of digital trace data in communication and social computing research. *Journal of Broadcasting and Electronic Media, 58*(1), 59–75.

Groves, R.M., Fowler Jr., F.J., Couper, M.P., Lepkowski, J.M., Singer, E., & Tourangeau, R. (2009). *Survey methodology* (2nd ed.). New York, NY: Wiley Publishing.

Halavais, A. (2015) Bigger sociological imaginations: Framing big social data theory and methods, *Information, Communication & Society, 18*(5), 583–594.

Hotz, R.L. (2016). Twitter storms can help gauge damage of real storms and disasters, study says. *Wall Street Journal,* 11 March 2016. Retrieved from www.wsj.com/articles/twitter-storms-can-help-gauge-damage-of-real-storms-and-disasters-study-says-1457722801

Jacobellis v Ohio, 378 U.S. 184, concurrence

Katz, E., Blumler, J.G., & Gurevitch, M. (1973). Uses and gratifications research. *Public Opinion Quarterly, 37*(4), 509–523.

Kingkade, T. (2016). Comment sections are cesspools of rape culture, research finds. *Huffington Post,* 19 August 2016. Retrieved from www.huffingtonpost.com/entry/comment-sections-rape-culture_us_57b606bfe4b00d9c3a1647c0

Khonsari, K.K., Nayeri, Z.A., Fathalian, A., & Fathalian, L. (2010). Social network analysis of Iran's Green Movement opposition groups using Twitter. 2010 International Conference on Advances in Social Networks Analysis and Mining (ASONAM), Odense, Denmark, August 9–11, 2010.

Koltay, T. (2014). Big data, big literacies? Читалиште, *24,* 3–8.

Laney, D. (2012). *The importance of "big data": A definition.* Gartner Inc.

Lasswell, H.D. (1927). *Propaganda technique in the world war.* Cambridge, MA: MIT Press.

Lazarsfeld, P.F., Berelson, B., & Gaudet, H. (1944). *The people's choice: How the voter makes up his mind in a presidential campaign.* New York, NY: Columbia University Press.

Lerman, J. (2013). Big data and its exclusions. *Stanford Law Review Online, 66,* 55–63.

Lippmann, W. (1922). *Public opinion.* New York, NY: Harcourt, Brace, and Company.

Lupia, A., & Alter, G. (2014). Data access and research transparency in the quantitative tradition. *Political Science and Politics, 47*(1), 54–59.

Lupia, A., & Elman, C. (2014). Openness in political science: Data access and research transparency: Introduction. *Political Science and Politics, 47*(1), 19–42.

Lupia, A., & Elman, C. (2010). Memorandum on increasing Data Access and Research Transparency (DA-RT). Submitted to the Council of the American Political Science Association, September, 2010.

Madden, M., & Rainie, L. (2015). Americans' attitudes about privacy, security and surveillance. *Pew Research Center.* Retrieved from www.pewinternet.org/2015/05/20/americans-attitudes-about-privacy-security-and-surveillance/

Mayer-Schönberger, V., & Cukier, K. (2013). *Big data: A revolution that will transform how we live, work, and think.* New York, NY: Houghton Mifflin Harcourt.

McCombs, M.E., & Shaw, D.L. (1972). The agenda-setting function of mass media. *Public Opinion Quarterly, 36*(2), 176–187.

McDermott, R. (2014). Research transparency and data archiving for experiments. *Political Science and Politics, 47*(1), 67–71.

Moravcsik, A. (2014). Transparency: The revolution in qualitative research. *Political Science and Politics, 47*(1), 48–53.

Neuendorf, K.A. (2001). *The content analysis guidebook.* London: Sage Publications.

New, J. (2016). Tracking Chicago's taxis. *Center for Data Innovation.* 8 December 2016. Retrieved from www.datainnovation.org/2016/12/tracking-chicagos-taxis/

Nickalls, S. (2016). Twitter has a huge white supremacist issue, according to new research. *Esquire.* 3 September 2016. Retrieved from www.esquire.com/news-politics/news/a48316/twitter-white-supremacist/

O'Connor, B., Balasubramanyan, R., Routledge, B.R., & Smith, N.A. (2010). From Tweets to polls: Linking text sentiment to public opinion time series. *Proceedings of the Fourth International AAAI Conference on Weblogs and Social Media.* Washington, DC, May 23–26, 2010.

Robinson-Cimpian, J.P. (2016). Inaccurate estimation of disparities due to mischievous responders: Several suggestions to assess conclusions. *Educational Researcher, 43*(4), 171–185.

Rudder, C. (2011). The mathematics of beauty. OkCupid Blog. 10 January 2011. Retrieved from https://blog.okcupid.com/index.php/the-mathematics-of-beauty/

Sayre, B., Bode, L., Shah, D.V., Wilcox, D., & Shah, C. (2010). Agenda setting in a digital age: Tracking attention to California proposition 8 in social media, online news, and conventional news. *Policy & Internet, 2*(2), 7–32.

Schram, A. (2005). Artificiality: The tension between internal and external validity in economic experiments. *Journal of Economic Methodology, 12*(2), 225–237.

Thompson, A. (2016). Parallel narratives: Clinton and Trump supporters really don't listen to each other on Twitter. *Vice News.* 8 December 2016. Retrieved from https://news.vice.com/story/journalists-and-trump-voters-live-in-separate-online-bubbles-mit-analysis-shows

Tremayne, M. (2014). Anatomy of protest in the digital era: A network analysis of Twitter and Occupy Wall Street. *Social Movement Studies, 13*(1), 110–126.

Ullrich, C., Borau, K., & Stepanyan, K. (2010). Who students interact with? A social network analysis perspective on the use of Twitter in language learning. *Sustaining TEL: From innovation to learning and practice: Volume 6383 of the series Lecture Notes in Computer Science* (pp. 432–437). Berlin, Germany: Springer-Verlag Berlin Heidelberg.

Westland, J.C., & Clark, T.H.K. (1999). *Global electronic commerce: Theory and case studies.* Cambridge, MA: MIT Press.

Wilbur, W.J., & Sirotkin, K. (1992). The automatic identification of stop words. *Journal of Information Science, 18*(1), 45–55.

Wu, L., Morstatter, F., & Liu, H. (2016). Misinformation in social media: Diffusion, detection, and intervention. SBP-BRiMS, June 28–July 1, 2016; Washington, DC.

Zaller, J. (1992). *The nature and origins of mass opinion.* Cambridge, MA: Cambridge University Press.

4

IGNORANCE OR UNCERTAINTY

How the "Black Box" Dilemma in Big Data Research May "Misinform" Political Communication

Lei Guo

In the morning of my writing, 328,756,321 tweets were sent, 33,190,759 Instagram photos were uploaded, and 5,845,873,656 YouTube videos were viewed around the world (Internet Live Stats). An analysis of these texts and visuals can quickly tell us what people think and how they think about certain things on that morning. To political communication researchers, the wide availability of these social media data has created unprecedented opportunities for us to gauge the public's mind without intruding on their lives. To understand how voters perceived Hillary Clinton or Donald Trump during the 2016 U.S. presidential campaign, for example, analyzing millions of tweets seems to be a viable alternative to polling or experimenting.

Scholars and practitioners began to celebrate and embrace the revolutionary potential big data has brought to communication research. The past few years has witnessed a rapidly increasing number of big data studies (see Communication & Mass Media Complete database). More and more open-access and commercial software programs emerged, claiming that they can deal with big data analytics. The growing interest in big data research is also reflected by the recent formation of a new interest group on Computational Methods at the International Communication Association in June 2016.

While big data offers big promises to transform communication research, it also comes with myths and misinformation. Big data research is challenging not only because it is too big and too complex for traditional communication research methods to handle, but also because of our unfamiliarity with and uncertainty about new analytical tools. Indeed, an inappropriate use of big data analytics may create more problems than benefits. Scholars have already documented a number of big data challenges and problems (e.g. Grimmer & Steward, 2013; Guo, Vargo, Pan, Ding, & Ishwar, 2016; Kitchin, 2014). This chapter focuses on the black box dilemma in conducting big data research in our field. While an ignorance of the big data algorithm may lead to invalid research results, tuning parameters in the "box" may yield unreliable and ambiguous findings. The discussion is based on my own experience of conducting and reviewing empirical big data research, my use of several big data software programs, and my collaboration with computer science/engineering researchers. Before I set out to discuss the "black box" issue, it is helpful to first clarify what qualifies as a big data study.

What Qualifies a Big Data Study?

One salient problem in the field of communication research is an inconsistent use of the term big data. The definition of big data varies in different studies. It is agreed that big data is a moving target. Still, clarifying some major misunderstandings about the concept is necessary.

While the emergence of social networking sites has significantly contributed to the development of big data research, big data, in essence, is not necessarily associated with social media. It may refer to any large-scaled numerical, textual, visual, or geographic data, which can be analyzed to reveal patterns and trends of human behavior. For example, by collecting tons of past taxi pick-up data points, Uber—the online transportation network company—is able to suggest several pick-up locations where riders could have the chance to limit their wait time (Constine, 2015). In this case, the "big" spatial and temporal data are used to predict human behavior. In the field of communication research, however, big data research usually focuses on the examination of "big *social* data," often text-based big data collected from various social networking sites such as Twitter, Facebook, and Reddit.

Big data not only points to the volume of the data. An analysis of one million tweets about Donald Trump does not automatically qualify as a big data study. The nature of data and the complexity of analysis both matter. To define, the data is "big" because its *size* (e.g. dimensionality, volume, and velocity of generation) and *complexity* (e.g. diversity and variability) exceed the capabilities of traditionally used tools for capturing, processing, curating, and analyzing data within a tolerable time frame (e.g. Beyer & Laney, 2012; Laney, 2001). In addition, the definition of big data is domain-dependent and ever evolving. In communication research, big data typically means data where n is too big or too complex for humans to code a representative sample of the entire dataset (Riffe, Lacy, & Fico, 2014).

"Computational research" does not necessarily involve big data. While the growing size and complexity of data urges the need for advanced computational methods, not all computational studies deal with big data. In fact, a number of computational methods, such as data mining and machine learning, have been long established in the field of computer science and computer engineering. For example, for the task of text categorization, the research community began to use machine-learning paradigms as early as the 1990s to organize and analyze textual documents, such as newspaper articles (Sebastiani, 2002). In other words, computational methods can also be applied to provide an understanding of "small data."

Based on the above clarifications, in communication research, a typical big data study generally involves the use of computational methods to process a large dataset (10,000s for larger documents or 100,000s for smaller documents), the analysis of which is beyond the capabilities of traditional manual methods (Riffe et al., 2014). Big data analytics can help identify human behaviors and interactions with a large amount of information, which can be used to explain communication phenomena and further test communication theories. However, the question remains whether these analytics can, indeed, generate valid and reliable results, or to what degree those results are of sufficient rigor for communication contexts. Unfortunately, a few empirical studies, including some of my own, revealed that machines can be untrustworthy in some circumstances.

The Mysterious "Black Box"

Computational science, especially when it applies to big data, is a completely different discipline than communication research. Rather than developing their own algorithms, communication scholars usually have to rely on the use of *existing* commercial software programs or analytical packages in R, Python, or other programing languages to conduct "big data" research. In particular, "layman" commercial programs make it possible for communication researchers with little or no computational background to automate the analysis of various large datasets. For example, one can easily "click and run" an analytical program and find the proportion of male versus female users in a sample of tweets, which in turn could be used in a study to explain gendered political behaviors. The problem is, however, that the underlying computer algorithms of many of these commercial programs are not publicly available. It is like a "black box," where the process of transforming input information into output is not transparent. Oftentimes, it is not an option for researchers to tune the parameters of the algorithms behind the commercial programs. In the above example, it is likely the algorithm that determines whether a Twitter user is male or female is unknown and cannot be changed. Is it through reading the user's self-reported information, reviewing the public profile, or by analyzing the language the user used in the previous tweets? Suppose it is through analyzing the user's profile, what approach has been employed? With these questions unanswered, the extent to which the programs can produce valid and reliable results is suspicious.

Rohde and Wu (2016) presented the first attempt to systematically evaluate the results produced by six popular computer applications: Aylien, DiscoverText, MeaningCloud, Semantria, Sentiment 140, and Sentistrength. The researchers collected a sample of 1,200 tweets about the 2016 U.S. presidential primaries and employed a traditional manual content analysis approach to code the valence (i.e., positive, neutral, and negative) and topic of each tweet (e.g., economy, gun control, education). The manual coding results were then compared with the results produced by each of the aforementioned programs. The finding is alarming in that none of the comparisons reached a minimum acceptable level of intercoder (machine-human) reliability, with none of them above 0.5 Krippendorff's alpha or 70 percent agreement. Note that in journalism and mass communication research, a robust intercoder reliability coefficient should reach at least 0.7 alpha or 90 percent agreement (Lombard, Snyder-Duch, & Bracken, 2002). In other words, the blind use of these analytical programs may create misleading or simply incorrect results that are significantly deviated from human reasoning, assuming the latter is the ground truth.

My own research also demonstrates the validity issue of some of these software programs. In Vargo, Guo, McCombs and Shaw (2014)'s Twitter analysis of 2012 U.S. presidential election, one research step was to determine the tweet sentiment in order to categorize the Twitter users into Obama or Romney supporters. The program we used was one of the six programs examined in Rohde and Wu (2016), SentiStrength, which claimed to have "human level accuracy for short social web texts in English" (Thelwall, 2010). The dictionary-based program mainly relies on its established wordlists to indicate positive and negative sentiment. For example, the word "love" indicates a positive sentiment, whereas the word "hate" indicates a negative one. The words and phrases come from sources outside of the text under analysis, which is termed as an "out of the box" approach. Like Rohde and Wu (2016), we collected a sample of tweets (n=380) and then compared the manual coding and machine coding results in terms of the tweet valence: positive, neutral and negative. It turned out the agreement reached 68.8%, a little over 63.4% found in Rohde and Wu (2016), but was still not acceptable.

Even a more sophisticated analysis may not be able to produce satisfactory results. Considering that the agreement level of 68.8% was far from robust, we further applied a machine-learning method in order to improve the accuracy of machine coding. The manually coded 380 tweets were used to train a machine-learning model through the program LightSIDE (Mayfield & Rose, 2013), and the model was used to predict the sentiment of a sample of new texts. A total of 133 and 189 additional terms for positive and negative affective dimensions, respectively, were added to the SentiStrength dictionary. Another sample of 380 tweets were manually coded and compared, and an agreement level of 82.8% was reached. While the human-machine reliability was significantly improved, it was not adequate according to most content analysis criteria.

Despite the problematic results these computer applications may produce, it is not unusual to see that some communication studies still applied these tools "as is" without validating the computer output or taking any remedy measures. Without a professional understanding of the "black box," the use of any available computer program may well misinform rather than inform political communication research, or research of any kind.

On the other hand, when communication researchers are aware of the "black box" issue, they may not necessarily have the expertise to "open" and "adjust" the "black box." Further, even if computer science or engineering experts are involved, it still does not guarantee validity and reliability of the results. The following is a case study that illustrates this concern.

A "Black Box" of Uncertainty: A Case Study

Unlike traditional communication research methods, many computational algorithms involve a large number of parameters for tuning, yet without an objective criterion or a "rule of thumb" to follow. For example, in using k-means clustering (MacQueen, 1967) to cluster objects into k groups, there is no single best way to determine an ideal k. Or, that ideal k simply does not exist. As Figure 4.1 illustrates, the same set of objects (e.g., text documents) may be partitioned into three or four groups. Imagine when the number of objects increases to millions or billions, it will become an even more challenging decision to select an appropriate k. To explicate this issue, I will use an analysis based on Guo et al. (2016) to demonstrate how changing variables and parameters in a topic-modeling algorithm throughout the research process may influence the final results.

To define, a typical topic model "explains" the observed word frequencies in a given document in terms of a suitably weighted mixture of topical word frequencies where the weights indicate the different proportions of topics that appear in

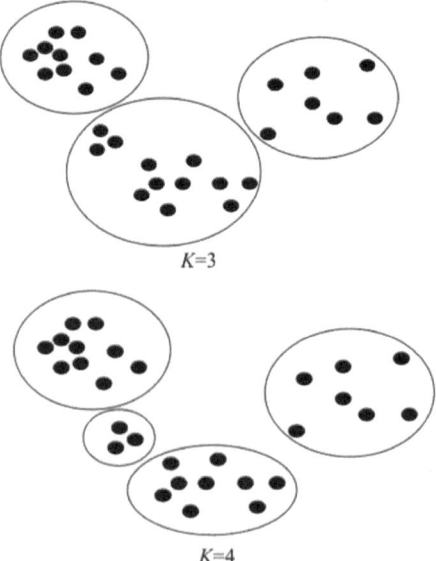

FIGURE 4.1 An Illustration of the K-means Cluttering Method

the document (Manning, Raghavan, & Schütze, 2009). For example, if an article contains the following words "gene," "dna," "evolve," "mutation," "data," "computational," and "statistics" in different proportions, then a topic model will view this article as a mixture of topics such as "genetics," "evolution," and "data science" with different proportions of words reflecting the article's topical emphasis. Guo et al.'s (2016) analysis employed the most widely used topic model, the Latent Dirichlet Allocation (LDA; Blei, Ng, & Jordan, 2003). One goal of the study was to identify "topics" in the 77 million tweets collected from the 2012 U.S. presidential election. Since we were interested in learning how Twitter users discussed the two political candidates differently, we further divided the dataset into Obama-only and Romney-only tweets. In total, 30,061,046 tweets about Obama authored by 1,631,095 unique Twitter users, and 18,677,277 tweets about Romney authored by 1,007,421 unique users were included in the analysis.

In conducting the LDA-based analysis, decisions such as the way to pre-process data, the number of "topics," whether to use an existing dictionary, and the number of passes are all to a great degree left to the researcher's discretion. In other words, different researchers may reach very different conclusions about how Twitter users discussed about the two political candidates. The results reported in Guo et al. (2016) were based on a careful research design, with the collaboration with two computer-engineering experts who specialize in the LDA algorithm. Here, I show how different decisions made in the study may change the final output.[1]

Data Preparation

Our approach of preparing the Twitter data is a unique component of the research design. There are LDA topic-modeling packages in R, Python and some other programing languages. However, applying the package as is without suitable pre-processing may not produce meaningful results. One reason is that the automated topic-modeling algorithms such as LDA have only been proved to work well with well-constructed data such as newspaper and academic journal articles (Tang, Zhang, & Mei, 2013). In other words, the unit of analysis for traditional LDA research is usually a formal, reasonably large text document. Tweets, on the other hand, are constrained to be much shorter pieces (no more than 140 characters) and are often terse, truncated, and quite "messy." In order to deal with unstructured data such as tweets, one option is to combine a certain number of tweets based on some common features such as authorship or time of posting (e.g., Hong & Davison, 2010; Zhao et al., 2011). However, no "rule of thumb" exists in terms of how to aggregate tweets. Ultimately, the various methods of aggregation deployed in different studies will influence the final topic matrices produced by the LDA analysis.

In our study, we chose to combine tweets that preserve both time- and user-resolution of topics by combining a certain number of consecutive tweets from the same user into one document. The assumption is that the same user may talk about a given political candidate in a similar way during a concentrated time period. Here, the number of tweets for combination is another uncertain variable and is subject to the researcher's decision. When n is too small, documents do not contain enough information to reliably estimate topics. When n is too large, on the other hand, tweets that contain many different subjects will be combined into one document, which may also influence the model performance. In order to find the "magic" number, we produced LDA topic matrices by combining different number of consecutive tweets (n=1–10) authored by the same user into a document. Due to the space limitation of this paper, Tables 4.1 and 4.2 illustrate the LDA topic matrices about Obama and Romney, respectively, generated by combining 4 (Approach A), 6 (Approach B), and 8 tweets (Approach C).

As the topic matrices in Table 4.1 show, the "topics"[2] generated about Obama are similar in most cases. It is clear that all the three approaches identified topics such as "Jobs/unemployment" (topic#5), "Foreign affairs—Bin Laden" (topic#9), "Michelle Obama's speech" (topic#13), and "Foreign affairs—Benghazi" (topic#14). In addition, important information such as Spanish (topic#3), incivility (topic#7), and background terms (topic#10) were also found in all the three topic matrices. On the other hand, the results also revealed some noticeable differences. For example, both Approach A and Approach C clearly showed "Hurricane Sandy" (topic#15) as a salient topic in the Twitter discussion about Obama, whereas Approach B failed to do so. In Approach A, topic#8 pointed to "Bush year legacy & federal debt"; however, neither Approach B nor C discovered this topic.

The LDA topic matrices about Romney (see Table 4.2) also showed similarities and differences when different numbers of tweets were combined. Topics such as "Hurricane Sandy" (topic#1), "Tax" (topic#2), and "the Republican's National Convention" (topic#11) were found in using all the three approaches. With respect to the discrepancies, for example, while Approach A and Approach C both identified the topic of Romney's business in China (topic#12), Approach B failed to generate a similar set of terms. The results also showed that the three approaches produced some completely unrelated information in some cases (see topic#9 and topic#15).

As Tables 4.1 and 4.2 illustrate, the choice of number for combining tweets will directly influence the results (i.e., "topics") in the final report. The impact of this one variable cannot be underestimated. In Guo et al. (2016), we made the decision by observing the coherence of the topic matrices. Topics are considered "coherent" if they are distinct from each other and semantically meaningful. We finally chose to combine every four consecutive tweets for the analysis. The decision was made by two communication researchers' careful reading and comparisons of all topic matrices. It turned out that the results (i.e., "topics") did provide important insights into the Twitter discussion about the two political candidates. Still, the lack of an objective criterion to determine the aggregation approach led to a number of limitations. First and foremost, researcher subjectivity is inevitable

TABLE 4.1 LDA topic matrices about Obama generated by aggregating different number of tweets

	A: 4 tweets as a document	B: 6 tweets as a document	C: 8 tweets as a document
1	term, second, ralli, campaign, unit, photo, nd, state, kati, fiscal	term, debat, bush, second, day, nd, year, presidenti, georg, fix	usa, di, il, presiden, et, sticker, les, est, dan, per
2	tax, cut, pay, busi, health, women, care, obamacar, student, gas	women, care, health, food, black, men, choic, decis, stamp, student	debate, women, health, care, student, fight, make, job, middle, class
3	de, la, que, el, en, un, di, president, se, para	para, president, su, las, di, presiden, dei, es, ha, estado	para, president, es, su, las, del, kati, lo, una, estado
4	debat, middl, presidenti, class, trump, jay, realdonaldtrump, offer, justin, donald	forward, four, middle, class, america, fight, work, ve, agao	gave, kill, troop, home, got, letter, want, back, better, els
5	job, offic, unemploy, creat, took, number, rate, dennisdmz, approv, month	job, tax, gop, cut, million, busi, creat, unemploy, economi, trump	job, tax, gop, cut, year, bush, debt, creat, unemploy, plan
6	poll, ohio, lead, voter, florida, earli, state, show, gop, among	poll, new, elect, campaign, news, endors, win, sandi, state, ohio	elect, win, poll, news, campaign, debat, victori, state, ohio, new
7	tcot, gop, teaparti, tlot, nigga, lnyhbt, slone, food, stamp, patdollard	fuck, nigga, win, shit, vote, ya, michell, bitch, black, ass	fuck, vote, win, nigga, shit, black, ya, michell, im, don
8	year, bush, economi, blame, four, gop, debt, econom, yrs, ago	war, state, unit, support, gay, sign, end, law, order, abort	iran, muslim, administer, Israel, new, anti, news, support, say, hous
9	youtub, seal, kill, bin, laden, home, navi, osama, movi, war	kill, bin, laden, home, gave, osama, shirt, wear, got, troop	kill, war, bin, laden, end, osama, Iraq, drone, peac, marijuana
10	vote, will, elect, can, get, go, like, say, just, win	like, just, get, will, say, peopl, vote, go, don, now	like, just, peopl, get, vote, say, go, will, don, think
11	news, white, hous, cnn, fox, msnbc, abc, gay, men, nbc	college, kid, set, letter, student, birth, accept, teacher, aid, financi	jay, video, beyoc, eastwood, clint, million, dinner, campaign, chair, dollar
12	campaign, anti, video, ad, big, new, donat, surpris, tv, bird	usa, walk, et, king, madonna, les, des, pour, est, plus	justin, im, follow, love, alien, yo, biever, niall, qu, belib
13	michell, speech, clinton, bill, dnc, ladi, convent, first, democrat, quot	michell, speech, clinton, dnc, bill, convent, ladi, first, democrat, watch	michell, dnc, speech, clinton, bill, ladi, first, wtch, convent, speak

(continued)

TABLE 4.1 (Cont.)

	A: 4 tweets as a document	B: 6 tweets as a document	C: 8 tweets as a document
14	benghazi, lie, american, libya, attack, us, call, administr, media	tcot, benghazi, attack, gop, libya, campaign, american, video, media, lie	tcot, benghazi, attack, lybia, lie, debat, American, media, campaign, video
15	sandi, hurrican, christi, storm, gov, endors, powel, new, chris, tour	follow, direct, im, style, song, jackson, fake, mr, sing, chavez	endors, sandi, trump, hurricane, new, christi, donald, bloomberg, powel, storm
16	new, endors, post, victori, elect, washington, reuter, york, blog, layoff	win, elect, tomorrow, earli, go, pleas, will, day, get	vote, elect, go, tomorrow, win, get, day, pleas, will, let

Note:
For each topic, top 10 words were included in the list. The words were ranked based on the probability estimated by the LDA model. The words were stemmed.

TABLE 4.2 LDA topic matrices about Romney generated by aggregating different number of tweets

	A: 4 tweets as a document	B: 6 tweets as a document	C: 8 tweets as a document
1	state, sandi, fema, relief, hurrican, disast, donat, moment, storm, use	sandi, fema, campaign, china, hurricane, relief, lie, ohio, disast, machin	sandi, fema, campaign, relief, hurricane, lie, disast, ad, auto, ohio
2	tax, pay, return, million, cut, paid, releas, hide, rais, rate	tax, plan, pay, return, cut, class, paid, middl, year, releas	tax, plan, pay, return, cut, say, paid, class, middl, year
3	video, new, ad, campaign, comment, post, youtub, percent, daili, washington	colleg, vote, even, said, nicki, parent, money, get, minaj, bitch	colleg, parent, money, get, said, mom, kid, make, teacher, birth
4	tcot, gop, endors, romneyryan, parti, teaparti, georg, tlot, republican, regist	pick, vp, run, presidenti, republican, mate, announc, candid, campaign, akin	usa, ha, video, republican, es, su, para, style, las, del
5	women, full, gay, binder, woman, pro, right, took, small, children	women, ann, gay, abort, right, woman, christi, want, poor, children	women, gay, binder, right, woman, want, abort, full, marriag, support
6	debat, plan, lie, big, fact, campaign, last, attack, media, check	debat, big, lie, last, night, bird, women, full, binder, tonight	debat, polici, video, say, big, foreign, lie, bird, attack, last

TABLE 4.2 (Cont.)

A: 4 tweets as a document	B: 6 tweets as a document	C: 8 tweets as a document
7 polici, de, foreign, la, el, en, un, que, candi, al	fuck, becom, gone, around, term, start, talk, read, might, like	car, poof, field, go, sticker, back, win, cotton, approv, crib
8 fuck, win, becom, bitch, make, ass, gone, colleg, bird, go	fuck, win, vote, shit, ass, get, nigga, black, peopl, don	fuck, win, nigga, vote, ass, like, will, gone, make, bitch
9 middl, machin, militari, tagg, class, war, vote, iran, fraud, secret	video, american, say, are, percent, secret, comment, mormon, campaign, middl	might, around, read, becom, term, start, condt, exist, pre, porn
10 news, fox, game, abc, leader, star, cbs, endors, trend, break	news, new, post, campaign, fox, endors, video, washington, poll, blog	news, campaign, video, new, republican, presidenti, fox, post, elect, blog
11 ann, speech, presidenti, pick, gop, republican, rnc, vp, christi, convent	speech, gop, rnc, ann, convent, street, eastwood, clint, republican, dnc	gop, ann, rnc, vp, pick, speech, run, republican, convent, will
12 job, bain, china, sensata, edshow, creat, auto, jeep, worker, compani	job, polici, million, foreign, create, attack, libya, war, bush, iran	job, bain, china, creat, company, machin, vote, capit, million, invest
13 white, black, hous, joke, rape, racist, control, shirt, birth, akin	slogan, keep, america, American, use, moment, kkk, realiz, awkward, akward	slogan, vote, american, nicki, America, minaj, keep, use, kkk, moment
14 poll, ohio, ralli, lead, state, voter, win, crowd, florida, endors	vote, tcot, will, poll, win, elect, elect, ohio, state, rally, romneyryan	tcot, poll, vote, win, will, ohio, endors, elect, romneyryan, state
15 governor, bill, breitbartnew, massachusett, john, clinton, sign, dnc, twitchyteam, mccain	make, will, car, poof, stamp, field, go, food, danc, band	like, just, think, get, one, look, say, go, will, peopl
16 vote, will, like, say, can, just, get, go, win	elect, like, just, vote, get, think, say, peopl, will, don, go	vote, peopl, don, win, want, get, will, go, elect, black

Note:
For each topic, top 10 words were included in the list. The words were ranked based on the probability estimated by the LDA model. The words were stemmed.

in this process. Further, even if other aggregation methods may not be able to produce as coherent topics, they may yield useful information that is not found in our approach. For example, in tweets about Obama (see Table 4.1), Approach B discovered "Education" (topic#11), a topic not discovered in the approach we used. In addition, the decision of combining four tweets from the same Twitter user excluded users who posted less than four tweets during the election. That is, the reported "topics" were extracted solely from tweets that were produced by relatively active Twitter users, a biased sample.

Another limitation comes from the time duration of the documents. The tweets were collected from August 1 to November 13, 2012, which covered a time period of almost four months. Combining any four consecutive tweets from the same user makes it possible to aggregate tweets that spanned a longer time period, which may increase the likelihood to include tweets about totally different subjects into one document. Figure 4.2 illustrates the time distribution for Obama-only tweets. The number of tweets increased first around early September when Obama and Biden were nominated for President and Vice President, respectively, at the 2012 Democratic National Convention, and then peaked around the Election Day (November 6). The number of tweets was scattered over the rest of time points. Figure 4.3 presents the distribution of time duration of each document. As the figure shows, while the majority of the documents spanned less than 10 days, a good number of them included tweets that were published several months apart.

This finding is worth noting. While all the tweets focused on the discussion about one presidential candidate in one election, the subject of conversation may have changed significantly from early August to the end of the election. In other words, our Twitter aggregation method would include potentially unrelated information into one document, which might—again—affect the final "topics" found in the study.

Other aggregation methods are not without problems either. For example, in order to ensure that documents include consistent information, some researchers attempted to combine tweets that follow the same hashtag into one document (Lim & Buntine, 2014; Mehrotra, Sanner, Buntine, & Xie, 2013). However, the approach is problematic in the case of tweets about one presidential election as a large number of users would use the same hashtags (e.g., #obama, #2012election, #tcot) while talking about varied subject matters. Further, not every tweet included a hashtag. Other researchers chose to combine tweets from similar users from a similar time frame (Bak, Lin, & Oh, 2014). While promising, this approach would exclude users that do not fit the criteria, and the decision to choose a "similar time frame" is another extremely challenging one especially considering the complexity of different political contexts.

The choices in pre-processing data are only one factor that can cause uncertainty in big data research. Some other aspects, as small as a single parameter in the algorithm, will also exert some significant effect on the results, as discussed in the following section.

The Number of Passes

In applying a complicated computer algorithm such as the LDA-based topic modeling, the change of any parameter in the model would potentially affect the final results. An example is the number of "passes," or the laps the model will take

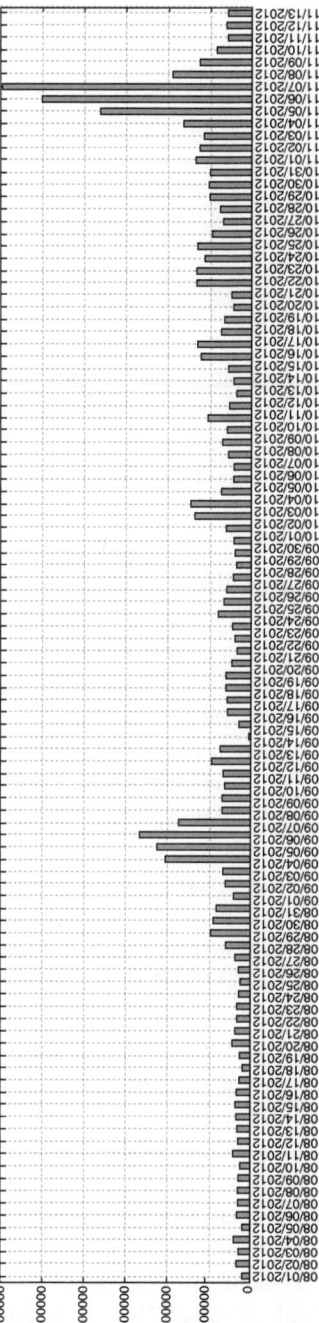

FIGURE 4.2 Time Distribution for Obama-only Tweets

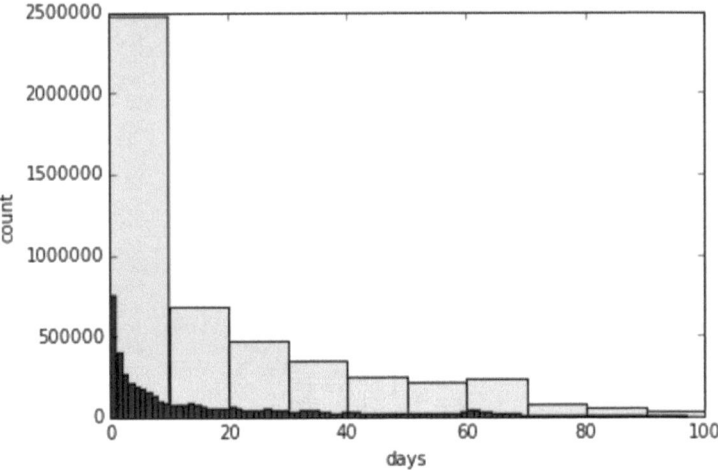

FIGURE 4.3 Document Time Duration Distributions for Obama-only Tweets

through corpus. One might assume that the machine is reliable and therefore the number of times a computer algorithm is applied to a dataset would not change the results. This, however, is not necessarily true for certain algorithms such as the LDA. Theoretically, the greater the number of passes, the more accurate the model is. As a compromise, adding passes will increase the algorithm's running time. In Guo et al. (2016), we used the Python package "Genism" with the default setting (pass=1). For a large corpus like 77 million tweets, a single pass is enough. Here, we tried different number of passes and explored the extent to which this choice would affect the generated topic matrices.

Table 4.3 presents the LDA topic matrices about Obama generated by using 2, 4 and 6 passes. In contrast to our expectation, the topic matrices did not become more stable as the algorithm ran more passes. In fact, Approach C (6 passes) even missed some information as discovered by the other two approaches. For example, while both Approach A and B clearly generated two foreign affairs topics, one dealing with the killing of Bin Laden (topic#8) and the other with the Benghazi's attack (topic#13), Approach C mixed the two subjects into one topic. Neither was an important topic "Jobs & tax cut" clearly identified by running 6 passes. Indeed, the results did show that the use of a different number of passes would result in the changes in the final topic matrices.

As the case study demonstrates, any variable and parameter in a computational algorithm may play an important role in determining the final results. *Machine* coding usually relies on a large number of *human* decisions; yet, oftentimes there is no objective criterion or "rule of thumb" by which a decision can be made. As a result, to what extent the algorithmic output can yield externally valid insight is rather uncertain. In Guo et al. (2016), we qualitatively examined a sample of tweets

TABLE 4.3 LDA topic matrices about Obama generated by using different number of passes

	A: 2 passes	B: 4 passes	C: 6 passes
1	debat, michell, night, last, tonight, jay, ladi, first, presidenti, beyonc	ralli, jay, ladi, michell, beyonc, million, wtf, eat, perform, kati	michell, speech, clinton, dnc, bill, ladi, convent, direction, first, eastwood
2	hous, usa, di, justin, white, teaparti, il, meet, da, direct	clinton, bill, justin, usa, direct, washington, niall, alien, direction, bieber	debat, hous, tonight, presidenti, jay, white, beyonc, watch, kid, eat
3	free, line, walk, hour, direction, king, car, song, mad, springsteen	es, di, para, president, las, est, da, il, qu, su	usa, justin, es, di, para, president, las, est, da, il
4	poll, voter, ohio, lead, florida, earli, state, republican, elect, latino	state, poll, voter, ohio, lead, florida, earli, unit, teaparti, messag	state, poll, ohio, lead, florida, earli, unit, voteobama, voter, endors
5	job, year, tax, bush, four, economi, blame, cut, million, creat	job, tax, cut, creat, gop, busi, million, debt, unemploy, plan	elect, win, term, second, victori, day, nd, celebr, pray, belieb
6	speech, clinton, bill, dnc, michell, convent, democrat, accept, watch, nation	bush, blame, hit, fix, year, mess, close, georg, critic, pari	barackobama, forward, fight, gay, teamobama, alien, ve, teacher, king, dream
7	new, sandi, hurricane, hit, york, christi, storm, declar, chris, day	sandi, realdonaldtrump, hurrican, new, york, storm, christi, visit, chris, declar	sandi, hurrican, hit, new, storm, christi, chris, critic, day, whitehous
8	fuck, bin, laden, ya, yo, es, para, president, kill, est	cnc, kill, bin, laden, home, gave, els, osama, got, back	will, year, now, america, one, say, time, american, support, make
9	news, campaign, ralli, fox, victori, washington, photo, elect, fire, post	term, elect, second, win, victori, readi, day, teamobama, nd, celebr	campaign, post, ralli, photo, stori, pictur, chicago, ballot, minut, visit
10	barackobama, forward, women, fight, health care, ve, student, colleg, class	women, care, health, gay, choic, men, king, decis, marriag, equal	women, tax, care, health, cut, class, middl, job, student, choic
11	video, state, youtub, unit, tv, busi, hoe, die, john, interview	campaign, news, new, video, endors, ad, youtub, anti, cnn, fox	video, tcot, new, gop, war, nation, ad, polici, youtub, administr
12	ad, anti, war, iran, muslim, israel, new, support, polici, big	barackobama, nigga, forward, move, class, fight, middl, colleg, student, ve	news, endors, fox, break, washington, new, york, answer, chang, abc

(continued)

TABLE 4.3 (Cont.)

	A: 2 passes	B: 4 passes	C: 6 passes
13	benghazi, tcot. lie, libya, attack, american, media, seal, cover, kill	tcot, benghazi, libya, attack, lie, administer, polici, muslim, war, american	benghazi, kill, libya, bin, laden, home, die, els, seal, osama
14	vote, elect, will, get, like, win, go, just, say, peopl	will, like, elect, get, just, say, peopl, go, now, know	vote, like, go, get, don, peopl, just, want, know, black
15	term, endors, realdonaldtrump, second, trump, chang, nd, record, donald, citi	white, hous, trump, black, surpris, donald, wear, go, shirt, daddi	realdonaldtrump, million, colleg, trump, dollar, letter, set, releas, donald, donat
16	campaign, gop, question, surprise, use, comment, answer, isn, never, slogan	vote, win, fuck, black, pleas, shit, lose, tomorrow, im, ya	fuck, big, name, ya, retweet, yo, lmao, niall, hoe, mama

Note:
For each topic, top 10 words were included in the list. The words were ranked based on the probability estimated by the LDA model. The words were stemmed.

and the topics assigned by the LDA approach. The study found that the approach did achieve decent performance by revealing nuanced details of the Twitter conversation about the two political candidates. However, it was also found that the LDA analysis produced quite a few false positives. That is, the computer-coded topics did not necessarily capture what the tweets actually meant.

Discussion: The "Black Box" Dilemma

The increasing size and richness of the data makes it possible to generate a holistic view about human behaviors and interactions. However, the "black box" dilemma as discussed in this chapter points out a series of potential problems this "holistic view" may have. To reiterate, the "black box" dilemma indicates that while the blind use of any big data analytics will lead to misleading results, spending efforts in tuning the algorithms does not guarantee external validity either. In fact, this is also the dilemma faced by many researchers in the field of computer science and engineering. To at least partly address this "big data" challenge, the following is a list of suggestions that communication researchers should consider.

(1) Communication researchers should be extremely cautious in using any unfamiliar computational programs and tools for conducting "big data" research. It is recommended that communication researchers should have at least a basic understanding of the rationale of computational algorithms before they decide to use them. It is important to know, for example, what is

the state of art of a particular methodological approach, what kind of data to which the approach is applicable, and the method's advantages and limitations. It is suggested to apply computational methods that have been used and systematically validated in social science contexts, or collaborate with computer science and engineering researchers with relevant expertise to explore new methods.

(2) Researchers should avoid reporting results from "click and run" computer programs when it is unknown how the results are generated. Such information (e.g., Twitter user gender in the aforementioned example) may be useful for researchers to obtain an exploratory overview of the data, but should not be used as variables to test any communication theories.

(3) For any big data analytics, communication researchers should manually and systematically evaluate the results using their own data because the performance of certain computational algorithms may vary by research context. It is essential to follow traditional manual content analysis procedure to assess inter-human-coder reliability first and then human-computer reliability (e.g., recall and precision). Notably, not all communication research analyses can be automated. For example, social data such as tweets often include irony and sarcasm, or nuances that can hardly be detected by machines. Under circumstances that human-computer comparison cannot achieve an acceptable level of consistency after a few iterations, researchers should consider other methods alternative to automated analysis.

It should also be noted that while human reasoning is often regarded as "ground truth," or "golden standard" in the research community, the decision made by several human coders might not always be externally valid. A recent development in computer science is to rely on a large number of crowdworkers to provide annotations for texts or visuals against which computer-generated results are compared (Sameki, Gentil, Mays, Guo, & Betke, 2016). This emerging approach is worth exploring, as it is likely that the wisdom of the crowd can be more valid than that of a few "expert coders."

(4) When researchers choose to tune certain parameters of an algorithm, they should try a set of values and look for recurring patterns. See Guo et al. (2016) and Freelon, McIlwain and Clark (2016) for how to decide LDA's topic matrices as examples. Again, it is vital to collaborate with computer science and engineering researchers in this process. Deciding which parameter(s) to tune—some parameters might be more important than others—and how to tune each of them often requires a specialized understanding of the given computational algorithm as well as research experience in coping with uncertainties the algorithm may cause.

(5) When reporting the results, researchers are encouraged to elaborate on the exact methodologies, validation approach, variables, parameters and any

relevant research procedure in their studies. It would also be part of reviewers' responsibilities to check all the relevant information about how researchers collect, prepare and analyze the data. The mere mention of a certain "big data" program will not justify the use of it in a study.

(6) Finally, in their writing it is important for researchers to discuss in detail the potential problems and limitations resulting from any decision made in the process of research design. Only by acknowledging that "big data" may *misinform* political communication research, or research of any kind, are we able to be *informed* by the benefits "big data" may bring us.

Notes

1 I would like to thank Prakash Ishwar, Weicong Ding, and Zixuan Pan for their help with data analysis and visualization presented in this section.
2 We chose to force the LDA to run 16 topics in order to make the "topics" comparable to those generated by the other "big data" method in the study. Here, the number of topics is another variable that researchers should decide.

References

Bak, J., Lin, C.Y., & Oh, A. (2014). Self-disclosure topic model for classifying and analyzing Twitter conversations. In *Proceedings of the 2014 Conference on Empirical Methods in Natural Language Processing* (pp. 1986–1996). Doha, Qatar: Association For Computational Linguistics.

Beyer, M. A., & Laney, D. (2012). *The importance of "big data": A definition.* Stamford, CT: Gartner.

Blei, D. M., Ng, A.Y., & Jordan, M. I. (2003). Latent Dirichlet Allocation. *Journal of Machine Learning Research, 3,* 993–1022.

Constine, J. (2015, July 8). Uber is now testing "suggested pickup points." Retrieved from https://techcrunch.com/2015/07/08/uber-suggested-pickup-points/

Freelon, D., McIlwain, C., & Clark, M. (2016). Quantifying the power and consequences of social media protest. *New Media & Society.*

Grimmer, J., & Steward, B. M. (2013). Text as data: The promise and pitfalls of automatic content analysis methods for political texts. *Political Analysis,* 1–31.

Guo, L., Vargo, C., Pan, Z., Ding, W., & Ishwar, P. (2016). Big social data analytics in journalism and mass communication: Comparing dictionary-based text analysis and unsupervised topic modeling. *Journalism & Mass Communication Quarterly, 93*(2), 332–359.

Hong, L., & Davison, B. D. (2010). Empirical study of topic modeling in Twitter. In *Proceedings of the First Workshop on Social Media Analytics* (pp. 80–88).

Kitchin, R. (2014). Big data, new epistemologies and paradigm shifts. *Big Data & Society, 1*(1).

Laney, D. (2001). 3D data management: Controlling data volume, velocity and variety (META Group Research Note). Retrieved from http://blogs.gartner.com/doug-laney/files/2012/01/ad949-3D-Data-Management-Controlling-Data-Volume-Velocity-and-Variety.pdf

Lim, K.W., & Buntine, W. (2014). Twitter opinion topic model: Extracting product opinions from tweets by leveraging hashtags and sentiment lexicon. In *Proceedings of the 23rd ACM*

International Conference on Conference on Information and Knowledge Management (pp. 1319–1328). New York, NY: ACM.

Lombard, M., Snyder-Duch, J., & Bracken, C. C. (2002). Content analysis in mass communication: Assessment and reporting of intercoder reliability. *Human Communication Research, 28*(4), 587–604.

MacQueen, J. B. (1967). Some methods for classification and analysis of multivariate observations. In *Proceedings of 5th Berkeley Symposium on Mathematical Statistics and Probability* (Vol. 1, pp. 281–297). Berkeley, CA: University of California Press.

Manning, C., Raghavan, P., & Schütze, H. (2009). Flat clustering. In *Introduction to information retrieval* (pp. 349–374). New York, NY: Cambridge University Press.

Mayfield, E., & Rose, C. P. (2013). LightSIDE: Open source machine learning for text accessible to non-experts. In M. D. Shermis & J. Burnstein (Eds.), *Handbook of automated essay evaluation* (pp. 124–135). New York, NY: Routledge.

Mehrotra, R., Sanner, S., Buntine, W., & Xie, L. (2013). Improving LDA topic models for microblogs via tweet pooling and automatic labeling. In *Proceedings of the 36th International ACM SIGIR Conference on Research and Development in Information Retrieval* (pp. 889–892). New York, NY: ACM.

Riffe, D., Lacy, S., & Fico, F. (2014). *Analyzing media messages: Using quantitative content analysis in research*. New York, NY: Routledge.

Rohde, J., & Wu, D. (2016). Agreement between humans and machines? – A reliability check among computational content analysis programs. Presented at the AEJMC, Minneapolis, MN.

Sameki, M., Gentil, M., Mays, K. K., Guo, L., & Betke, M. (2016). Dynamic allocation of crowd contributions for sentiment analysis during the 2016 US presidential election. Presented at the Association for the Advancement of Artificial Intelligence, Austin, Texas.

Sebastiani, F. (2002). Machine learning in automated text categorization. *ACM Computing Surveys (CSUR), 34*(1), 1–47.

Tang, J., Zhang, M., & Mei, Q. (2013). One theme in all views: Modeling consensus topics in multiple contexts. In *Proceedings of the 19th ACM SIGKDD International Conference on Knowledge Discovery and Data Mining* (pp. 5–13).

Thelwall, M. B. (2010). Sentiment detection in short informal text. *Journal of the American Society for Information Science and Technology, 61*, 2544–2558.

Vargo, C., Guo, L., McCombs, M., & Shaw, D. L. (2014). Network issue agendas on Twitter during the 2012 US presidential election. *Journal of Communication, 64*(2), 296–316.

Zhao, W. X., Jiang, J., Weng, J., He, J., Lim, E. P., Yan, H., & Li, X. (2011). Comparing Twitter and traditional media using topic models. In P. Clough, C. Foley, C. Gurrin, G. Jones, W. Kraaij, H. Lee et al. (Eds.), *Advances in information retrieval* (pp. 338–349). Berlin Heidelberg: Springer.

5

WHY DON'T TWEETS CONSISTENTLY TRACK ELECTIONS?

Lessons from Linking Twitter and Survey Data Streams

Josh Pasek and Jake Dailey

If its proponents are to be believed, the tools of data science stand poised to upend our political, social, and economic worlds. Companies that exploit "big data" will gain new insights that help them optimize their supply chains and better sell their products (e.g., Waller & Fawcett, 2013), physicians will soon identify and prevent medical ailments before they become life-threatening through wearable medical technology (cf. Steinhubl, Muse, & Topol, 2015), and computational social scientists will be able to rely on user-generated data that allow us to observe social phenomena unobtrusively, in real time, and at a vast scale (Lazer et al., 2009). These benefits are expected to accrue from the ability to passively collect and analyze trace data generated by our increasingly digital lives.

Before we can reap the rewards of large-scale passive data collection, however, we need to reach a fundamental understanding of what the data we observe can tell us about society at large. That is, if we don't know what it is we are observing, we are unlikely to recognize what we should be learning from those observations. Many of the principal datasets that scholars are using to dig into the social world are measures of social processes that we are only beginning to understand (boyd & Crawford, 2012). Scholarship examining posts on online social network sites and Google searches—which constitute much of the literature to date—are measuring the product of occurrences from social environments (Marwick & boyd, 2011). Further, because they are produced organically in social contexts that we do not necessarily observe, we can easily misinterpret the information we gather (boyd & Crawford, 2012).

The potential to make incorrect inferences from socially generated data is compounded by the way these data are often collected and analyzed. Because social media data are generated at scale, and thus include a very large number of data points, many analytic approaches either use machine learning tools or run a number of models to find the best fit between the observational data and the world (Dietterich, 2000). This set of methods is valuable given that the large N of the datasets guarantees that almost all relations we examine are likely to reach statistical significance. This means that the interesting challenge is not one of finding statistically significant results, but instead requires identifying the most important relations (Dietterich, 1995). Although data-driven approaches constitute a powerful way to identify connections, they are also prone to spurious results (Leinweber, 2015). Many of the correlations that are observed and even highlighted when comparing models in this way are not actually causal and may be inflated by correlated forms of measurement error (Fan, Han, & Liu, 2014; Lazer, Kennedy, King, & Vespignani, 2014). Further, inaccurate large findings may be prone to propagate more than accurate smaller ones due to publication biases (Ferguson & Heene, 2012; Franco, Malhotra, & Simonovits, 2014).

The risks of misunderstanding new sources of data are perhaps nowhere more apparent than in attempts to predict elections using Twitter data. Many researchers have presumed that some combination of the volume and sentiment of tweets should be useful for estimating either the relative vote share of candidates in an election or trends in the performance of the candidates (e.g., DiGrazia, McKelvey, Bollen, & Rojas, 2013; Franch, 2013; Sang & Bos, 2012). And a number of early studies appeared to suggest that this was indeed the case (e.g., DiGrazia et al., 2013; O'Connor, 2010; Tumasjan, Sprenger, Sandner, & Welpe, 2011). But in a few widespread attempts to replicate the findings that have been published, scholars contend that initial successes were either fleeting or artefactual (Gayo-Avello, 2013; Huberty, 2015; Jungherr, Jürgens, & Schoen, 2012). As one recent attempted replication concludes, "Twitter ... neither indicates public opinion at large nor allows inferences on the electoral chances of parties mentioned in tweets" (Jungherr, 2015, p. 208).

If we hope to use trace data and data science tools as a new window into the social world, we must not limit our study to the circumstances under which successful prediction has been demonstrated. Instead, we must interrogate conditions of failure such that we understand *why* so many of our models have not panned out. Here, the literature critical of these observed relations points to two key aspects of social media data that could render inaccurate predictions about political phenomena: social media data are gleaned from an unrepresentative set of site users through a set of social processes that may differ from those of more typical methods for social prediction (see Schober, Pasek, Guggenheim, Lampe, & Conrad, 2016). Presumably, if we can account for the impact of these differences, we may be able to extract meaningful population inferences.

In the rest of this chapter, we attempt to identify conditions that discriminate election predictions derived from Twitter data with those from more traditional survey-based analysis. Comparing tweets about Obama and McCain in 2008 with data on candidate favorability from a large rolling cross-sectional survey, we test four potential explanations for the discrepancies that emerged in earlier studies.

These include the proposals 1) that distinctions in results are principally a function of demographic differences between Twitter users and survey respondents, 2) that Twitter data may capture trends in perceptions of the candidates rather than absolute levels of support, 3) that the sentiment of tweets may operate independently in predicting favorability for each candidate, and 4) that tweets and survey metrics may only come to align toward the end of the election cycle, once there is more general attention to the campaign. To accomplish this, we first discuss a rationale for each of these expectations, describe a series of tests we use to assess each possibility, illustrate the results of these tests, and finally discuss what the results tell us about future attempts to predict elections using tweets and other social media data.

Concerns About User Representativeness

Students of survey statistics are well aware that the generalizability of conclusions from a sample can only be assured if every individual in society has some definite, nonzero probability of being sampled (Lohr, 2009; Neyman, 1934). Despite the fact that around one in five Americans appear to use Twitter (see Perrin, 2015; Twitter, 2016), Twitter users are hardly a microcosm of the American public; users differ from nonusers on a variety of demographic and behavioral attributes. Using Twitter requires that someone has internet access, for instance, and around 16% of American adults still do not use the internet (Perrin & Duggan, 2015). Twitter use, like engagement with other social media sites, is also concentrated among younger and more urban individuals, though demographic differences between users and nonusers have shrunk considerably over the last decade (Perrin, 2015).

Beyond differences between users and nonusers more generally, patterns of use of Twitter are far from equitably distributed. A small set of individuals post an overwhelming proportion of the content on Twitter and a related subset of individuals are also retweeted far more frequently than the average user (Kwak, Lee, Park, & Moon, 2010). Compounding these effects, individuals on Twitter are nested within social networks; for any given topic of conversation, individuals in some networks will post about the subject whereas individuals in other networks will not do so (Chen, Wang, & Sheth, 2012; Conover et al., 2011). Because of these dynamics, the set of posts about a particular topic on Twitter are wildly different from what might be expected if tweets emerged randomly from across the entire population.

A large literature on the differences between probability and nonprobability samples in survey research implies that differences between Twitter posters and the public will hinder the accuracy of conclusions derived from tweets. Survey methodologists regard these distinctions as "coverage errors" (Groves & Lyberg, 2011; Weisberg, 2005); the concern is that Twitter data may describe only the kinds of people who post on Twitter. Some scholars have attempted to reconcile this distinction by estimating the demographic attributes of Twitter users and then weighting posts such that these estimated demographics mirror those of the public (e.g., Choy, Cheong, Laik, & Shung, 2012). There are three central challenges with this approach, however. First, the collection of Twitter users sometimes radically underrepresents certain subsets of users, which means the resulting estimates rely heavily on the few individuals in certain categories that can be found. Second, estimates of the demographic attributes of Twitter users are often problematic, both because little profile information can be found that reliably indicates this for many users (Burger, Henderson, Kim, & Zarrella, 2011; Rao, Yarowsky, Shreevats, & Gupta, 2010; Zamal, Liu, & Ruths, 2012), and because they may be systematically inaccurate (see Freelon's chapter in this volume). And third, demographic differences between posters and the public may not account for the substantive covariates that influence whether people use Twitter and how often they post. That is, there may be substantive distinctions between users and nonusers that cannot be corrected by reconciling demographic differences (see Baker et al., 2013; Japec et al., 2015; Murphy et al., 2014).

Notably, distinctions between Twitter users and nonusers may not necessarily undermine the representativeness of tweets. Many scholars that have advocated for the use of Twitter data contend that these data capture essential features of society and thus may be fit for the purpose of societal description even if they do not come from a set of users that represent the public. This could be the case because tweets track media content (Phuvipadawat & Murata, 2010), or because the performative aspect of generating tweets for an audience leads to content that is more reflective of society than the base of Twitter users (Marwick & boyd, 2011; Schober et al., 2016).

The current study leverages an approach to reconciling the differences between users and nonusers of Twitter that simplifies this process somewhat. Instead of trying to make Twitter data look like the population (as e.g., Diaz, Gamon, Hofman, Kıcıman, & Rothschild, 2016), we explore whether correspondence between nationally representative survey data and Twitter data would improve if the survey data were limited to the types of individuals who report using Twitter. Twitter users are decently represented in national survey samples and can be predicted (as some surveys ask about whether people use Twitter). By estimating the likelihood of Twitter use among survey respondents, we can assess how likely it is that differences between Twitter users and nonusers account for failures in election predictions. Hence, we test the following hypothesis:

> H1 – *Correspondence between electoral survey and Twitter data will be stronger when both reflect the same underlying population of individuals.*

Levels of Support or Electoral Trends?

Many studies have used the volume of tweeting about candidates or parties to estimate the absolute levels of support that candidates or parties have (e.g., DiGrazia et al., 2013). This type of analysis makes an implicit assumption that the individuals who are tweeting about a topic are engaged in arbitrarily-timed expressions of their political preferences. This assumption is unquestionably wrong—tweets about elections are closely linked to election-related events (Lin, Keegan, Margolin, & Lazer, 2014) and many mentions of particular parties and candidates are negatively valenced (Mohammad, 2013). Some scholars have recognized these challenges and instead suggested that amounts of tweeting index political attention, and that attention to candidates or parties is what corresponds with political support (Tumasjan et al., 2011). On some highly aggregated level, this is likely true— candidates and parties that are poised to get a miniscule amount of the vote are unlikely to be discussed—but this mechanism is not likely to operate for the principal contenders in a given contest. As critics note in response to these studies, the lack of some theoretical justification for linking tweet volume with electoral performance makes this sort of analysis difficult to defend (Gayo-Avello, 2012; Huberty, 2015).

A more sophisticated approach has used the sentiment surrounding candidate-related tweets as a metric for support. Here, the notion is that people who speak positively about a candidate support that candidate and people who speak negatively about a candidate do not. This premise is likely true. But proponents of this approach may err if they presume that the relative ratio of positive and negative statements about various choices will provide an estimate of aggregate behavior (also see Chung & Mustafaraj, 2011). Such a leap is problematic because it can gloss over the cognitive and social processes that lead individuals to produce their tweets in the first place. That is, people likely don't express positive sentiment about somebody on Twitter simply because they have that sentiment; they express positive sentiment on Twitter because they are motivated to express that sentiment to their followers. Treating aggregated sentiment as a measure of attitudes is akin to presuming that positive and negative sentiments about political actors in all parties appear at relatively equitable rates. There is little reason to expect this sort of equity.

A serious consideration of why people post election-related tweets and when they do so is necessary if we hope to understand what tweets can tell us about election performance. Here our theoretical expectations are somewhat different from much of the past literature. Specifically, we believe that tweets about elections are principally an indicator of substantive election-related events (Guggenheim & Pasek, 2013; Hu, John, Seligmann, & Wang, 2012). When events happen in the political world, people respond to those events and express their sentiments toward the actors involved. Individuals thus have a motivation to post when events happen because that affords an opportunity to shape or express opinions about salient political matters. If this expectation is correct, then the aggregated opinions at those moments of mass expression should not be expected to tell us about the *state* of political perceptions, but rather about how new events are shifting the political landscape. Thus, the presence of highly valenced information about one candidate on a particular day seems likely to correspond with proximal changes in election polls. We therefore hypothesize that:

> *H2 — Twitter sentiment will correspond more closely with changes in electoral survey data than with absolute levels of support for various candidates.*

Disaggregating Competition

To the extent that Twitter data tell us about the interpretation of newsworthy events as they reflect on particular candidates and parties, the influence of these processes may differ depending on what people already know about these objects (cf. Zaller, 1992). Negative information about a well-known candidate is likely to have less of an impact than negative information about a political newcomer. By treating vote share as the outcome in many analyses, scholars may be blinding themselves to differential responsiveness across parties or candidates and obscuring the relations that exist. Instead, by treating the favorability of each candidate or party as a separate object of prediction, we could potentially find that social media sentiment and public opinion are consistently related. This leads to the expectation that:

> *H3 — Twitter sentiment about candidates will correspond more closely with the favorability of those candidates than with estimates of relative candidate vote share.*

The Electoral Cycle

U.S. Presidential Elections display notable trends over each election cycle. These trends have a clear impact on how individuals view the major party candidates and how they respond to survey questions about their vote intention (Erikson & Wlezien, 2012). Both John McCain and Barack Obama announced their respective runs for the presidency in February of 2007. It took more than a year for either of these individuals to assume the status of their party's presumptive nominees. As late as March 3, 2008 for McCain and June 2, 2008 for Obama, the principal opponents of these candidates were members of their own parties running in primary elections. Because primary elections can be deeply divisive (Atkeson, 1998), much of the sentiment observed on Twitter during this period may be a function of intra-party competition rather than inter-party contestation. Unusual patterns in this period may be further fueled by the fact that individuals who pay attention to and vote in primaries are a selective, hyper-partisan subset of the electorate (Brady, Han, & Pope, 2007; Norrander, 1991). Hence, we might expect sentiment on Twitter to track general election preferences only after this volatile period has ended and possibly only once the general election has commanded national attention.

One strong relevant trend is an increase in attention to the election as the campaign cycle goes on. Whereas many people appear to have weak electoral preferences early in a campaign, their preferences tend to solidify as Election Day draws near (Erikson & Wlezien, 2012). This means both that survey responses become a better predictor of respondents' actual behavior (Moore, 2008; Pasek, 2015) and that an ever-larger group of individuals might be interested in tweeting about the candidates. That the elicited preferences of survey respondents early in the cycle are similar to final election results is likely a product of patterns induced by partisan preferences in a two-party system rather than a meaningful expression of future preferences (Erikson & Wlezien, 2008; Moore, 2008). By limiting the analysis to the heart of the general election period—typically regarded as running from Labor Day through Election Day—we might expect to maximize the extent to which both data streams capture popular sentiment toward the candidates. This yields our final hypothesis that:

> H4 —*Twitter sentiment about candidates will correspond more closely with the favorability and vote share of those candidates in the final three months of the campaign than over the full range of the pre-election period.*

The Current Study

To test these hypotheses, we juxtapose Twitter and survey data on candidates prior to the 2008 U.S. Presidential Election. Leveraging both tweets and a continuous rolling cross-sectional survey of the American Public, we assess how the sentiment surrounding mentions of the presidential candidates in 2008 related to perceptions of those candidates as reported in national surveys. We then test whether four types of alternate specifications improved correspondence. One involves limiting survey data to the "kinds of people" who used Twitter, as estimated by data from a contemporaneous Pew survey. Another compares Twitter data with changes in survey responses over time. A third approach looks at each candidate's favorability instead of predicted vote choices. And a fourth involves limiting our examination to the final few months of the campaign. We compare correspondence for each permutation of the aforementioned strategies.

Methods

Twitter Data

Twitter data for the current study were gathered using Topsy. Topsy was a service that allowed users to download all historical tweets matching particular search parameters—it was purchased by Apple in 2013 and is no longer available.[1] Unlike many Twitter data services, Topsy provided access to the full Twitter "firehose"— all tweets ever tweeted—rather than either the unrepresentative sample accessible via the Twitter API or the more limited systematic sample available using so-called "gardenhose" access tools (see Morstatter, Pfeffer, Liu, & Carley, 2013). Topsy provided data that were ostensibly cleaned of spam and searches conducted for the current study were limited to tweets that the service identified as coming from the United States and being written in English. To download the Twitter data, daily searches were conducted for each day from January 1, 2008 through November 3, 2008 using the keywords "Obama" and "McCain." In total, 635,442 tweets were collected during this time period that contained the word "Obama" and 521,603 tweets were collected that contained "McCain." The distribution of these tweets over time is shown in Figure 5.1a.

A random sample of 150 tweets was drawn from the *Obama* and *McCain* datasets to identify whether or not these tweets actually pertained to presidential candidates Barack Obama and John McCain. These tweets were then analyzed based on their content; mentions of the election, campaigns, media coverage, other candidates or other relevant political issues were deemed to indicate a tweet about a given candidate. The sample revealed ~5% of tweets containing *"McCain"* and ~4% of tweets containing *"Obama"* were found to lack features that would identify them as being about the respective presidential candidates. This high proportion of tweets pertinent to the election led us to conclude that tweets with the selected keywords were generally on topic.

Tweets collected from Topsy were run through the Lexicoder sentiment dictionary using Lexicoder 3.0. The Lexicoder sentiment dictionary provides a list of

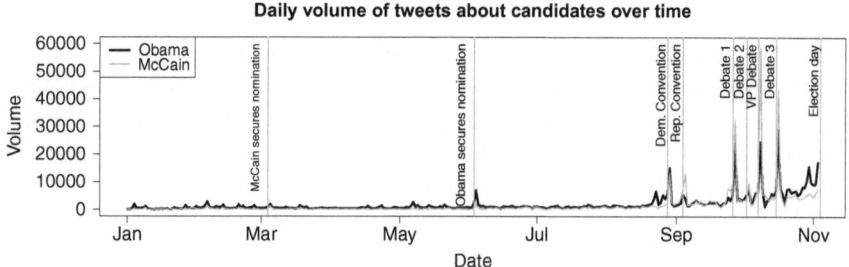

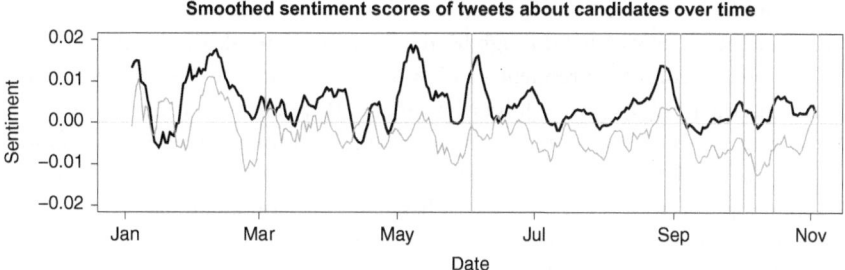

FIGURE 5.1 Daily Volume and Sentiment of Tweets about Obama and McCain Over Time, Smoothed Over 7 Days

positively and negatively valenced words (see Young & Soroka, 2012). Using this dictionary thus allows us to assign positive and negative sentiment scores to each day's corpus of tweets. These scores are output in the form of count variables. This output was then used to create a more intuitively interpretable measure, which is the percentage of all words that were positive minus the percentage of all words that were negative averaged across all tweets on each day. Daily sentiment estimates for both candidates are shown in Figure 5.1b.

The decision to use Lexicoder for the current analysis stems from a desire for consistency in identifying positive and negative sentiment. As the most comprehensive dictionary-based sentiment coding approach (Young & Soroka, 2012), Lexicoder should provide reasonably unbiased estimates of the relative positivity of tweets about each candidate. Although machine learning methods tend to produce far greater objective accuracy in coding individual cases, we are interested in comparing daily estimates across candidates and over time. For our purposes, then, it is more important that the quality of the classifications is unbiased than that any given classification is correct (cf. Hopkins & King, 2009). Because dictionary-based approaches are designed to compare multiple corpuses, they are less likely to systematically err in different ways across candidates and time.

Survey Data

Survey data for the current study come from the 2008 National Annenberg Election Survey (NAES) National Rolling Cross-Section. The NAES National Rolling Cross-Section was a telephone survey conducting between 40 and 313 interviews daily between December 17, 2007 and November 3, 2008.[2] In total, 57,967 respondents were interviewed via either landline or cellular telephones during this period. Additional information on the 2008 NAES is available from the Annenberg Public Policy Center at the University of Pennsylvania (2008). The response rate for the study was 19% (AAPOR RR3).

Vote Choice

Respondents were asked one of a few questions about their vote choice in 2008. Respondents from March 7 through March 27, 2008 were asked, "Thinking about the general election for president in November 2008, if that election were held today and the candidates were John McCain, the Republican, and Barack Obama, the Democrat, for whom would you vote?" As information became available about third-party candidates and vice presidential candidates, the question wording and response options to this question were changed correspondingly.

After September 26, 2008, respondents were first asked, "Some states allow individuals to vote before Election Day, that is vote early at a polling station or by filling out an absentee ballot. How about you? Have you already voted in this year's presidential election, or not?" Respondents who said they had already

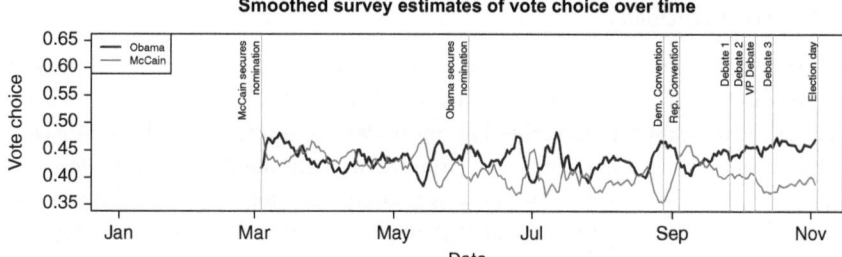

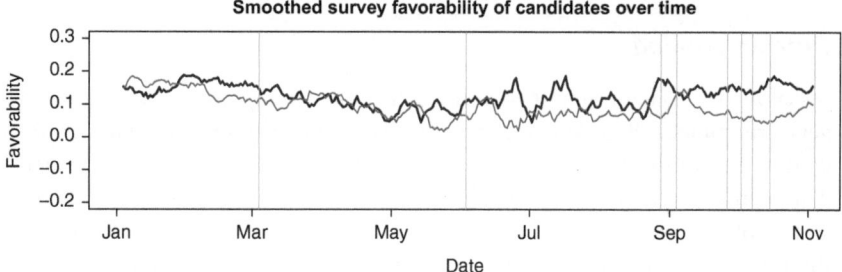

FIGURE 5.2 Survey Estimates of Vote Choice and Candidate Favorability Over Time, Smoothed Over 7 Days

voted were asked, "In the 2008 presidential election who did you vote for: John McCain and Sarah Palin, the Republicans; Barack Obama and Joe Biden, the Democrats; Ralph Nader and Matt Gonzalez, the Independent candidates; Bob Barr and Wayne Allyn Root, the Libertarians; or Cynthia McKinney and Rosa Clemente, the Green Party candidates?"[3]

Across both types of questions, responses were coded "McCain" for responses that indicated a preference for John McCain or John McCain and Sarah Palin. They were coded "Obama" for responses that indicated a preference for Barack Obama or Barack Obama and Joe Biden. All other responses were coded as, "Something Else," including volunteered "don't know" answers and responses indicating that the respondent would not be voting. Smoothed estimates of preferences for each of the two candidates are shown in Figure 5.2a.

Obama Favorability

Respondents were asked, "For the following person, please tell me if your opinion is favorable or unfavorable using a scale from zero to 10. Zero means very unfavorable, and 10 means very favorable. Five means you do not feel favorable or unfavorable toward that person. Of course you can use any number between zero and 10... On a scale of zero to 10, how would you rate Barack Obama?" Responses were divided by 10 to create a scale that ranged from 0 to 1. Estimates of Obama's favorability are shown with the darker line in Figure 5.2b.

McCain Favorability

Respondents were asked, "For the following person, please tell me if your opinion is favorable or unfavorable using a scale from zero to 10. Zero means very unfavorable, and 10 means very favorable. Five means you do not feel favorable or unfavorable toward that person. Of course you can use any number between zero and 10... On a scale of zero to 10, how would you rate John McCain?" Responses were divided by 10 to create a scale that ranged from 0 to 1. Estimates of McCain's favorability are shown with the lighter line in Figure 5.2b.

Data Smoothing

Social media data are subject to considerable periodicity in the ways individuals generate content. Posts on weekdays and weekends, for instance differ in their content and in the volume of information created (see e.g., Jang & Pasek, 2015). These processes have the potential to introduce spurious patterns into the data and to obscure meaningful trends over time. Further, there are good reasons to think that social media data and survey data may sometimes respond to similar information in ways that are asynchronous (Diaz et al., 2016). This means that the substantive relations may also be obscured by small and varying autocorrelations between data streams. One way to address these issues is to smooth data from both survey and social media streams over a longer period of time. For the purposes of the current study, both types of data are smoothed over a period of seven days to reduce the potential impacts of both periodicity and these small autocorrelations. This is achieved by averaging the values from three days prior to the date of interest to three days after the date in question. This also has the ancillary benefit of preventing us from making conclusions that are too heavily dependent on the relatively low number of tweets at the beginning of our examination period. Because we extract standard errors and p values from smoothed data, we also correct for the overreliance on each day by multiplying the standard errors of smoothed comparisons by the square root of the length of the smoothing period (in this case, 7 days).

Matching Survey and Social Media Coverage

As noted above, one dominant theory contends that social media data fail to forecast elections due to coverage errors (Couper, 2013; Langer Research Associates, 2013). That is, people on social media do not "look like" the population and thus report different preferences. To the extent that this explanation accounts for failed predictions, we should find that methods of electoral prediction that do not have coverage errors will yield results similar to the social media estimates if those coverage errors are introduced. To assess this possibility, we generated an estimate of how likely it is that any given individual in the probability sample survey used

Twitter. Presumably, if we weighted the survey data by these probabilities, we would end up with a sample that looked considerably more like the social media results.

To generate estimates of each individual's probability of using Twitter, we introduced data from a 2008 Pew survey that asked respondents, "Please tell me if you ever use the internet to do any of the following things. Do you ever use the internet to use Twitter or another 'micro-blogging' service to share updates about yourself or to see updates about others?" We then identified every question that could be matched between the Pew survey and the NAES dataset. Responses from the Pew survey question were predicted using a regularized logistic regression. A lasso-penalized logistic regression was run using the *glmnet* R package to ensure that the model was not over-specified.[4]

The model generated for the Pew data could then be applied to each individual's survey response in the NAES to yield a predicted probability that those individuals would use Twitter. Although the average individual was assigned a 5.1% chance of using Twitter, probabilities of Twitter use based on this model ranged from 0% to 99.9% (s.d.=8.5%). By subsequently weighting the NAES data by these probabilities, we could generate an estimate of the average favorability of each of the two candidates and vote choice among the types of individuals who would be expected to use Twitter. Original and weighted favorability and two-party vote choices can be found in Figure 5.3 and Appendix Figure 5.A1.

Change Scores

To test the second hypothesis, that Twitter data might inform us about changes in the state of an election, we generated a measure of the marginal change in the survey measures over a period of seven days. We did this by measuring the differences between the mean survey value three days before a target date and the mean survey value in the three days following a target date. These change scores were then compared to the absolute sentiment scores in the Twitter data to see if levels of Twitter sentiment were associated with changes in favorability or relative vote share.

Results

Full Time Period

Over the full period from January 1, 2008 until Election Day, smoothed sentiment on Twitter was associated with favorability toward John McCain, but was not significantly related to either favorability toward Barack Obama or electoral preferences. Sentiment toward Obama was unrelated to the overall level of favorability toward Obama, as gleaned from the survey data (Pearson's r=.14, p=.34, first panel in the top row of Figure 5.4). Sentiment toward McCain,

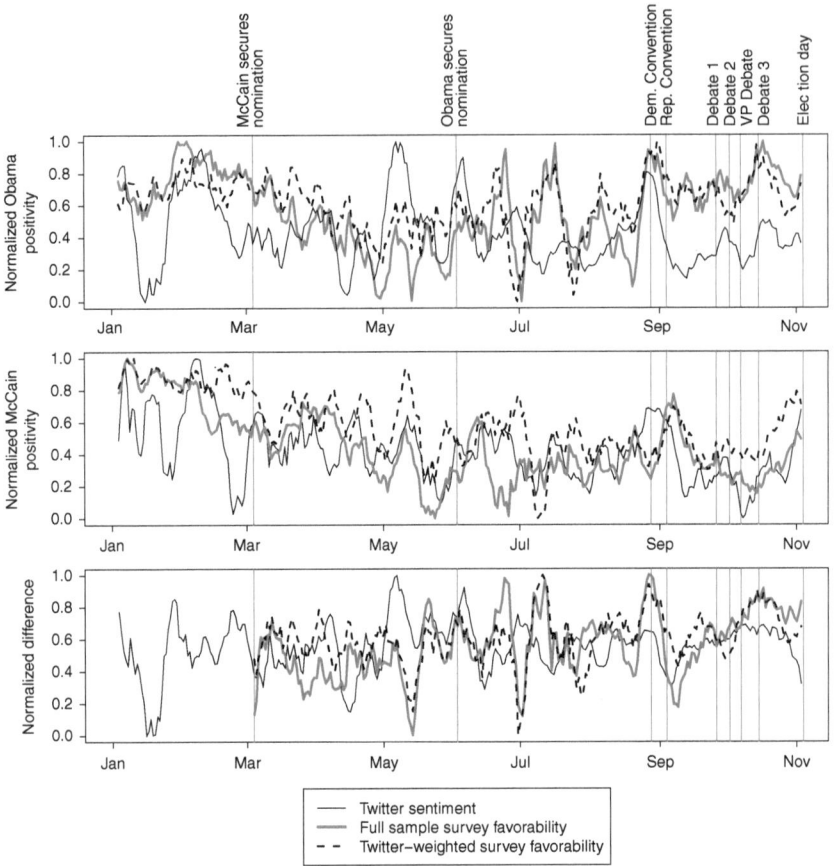

FIGURE 5.3 Normalized Twitter Sentiment, Survey Opinions, and Weighted Survey Opinions Over Time, Smoothed Over 7 Days

however, was closely associated with measures of McCain's favorability among all survey respondents (r=.51, p<.001, first panel in middle row). And differences between Obama and McCain's sentiment were unrelated to electoral preferences (r=.10, p=.54). These results echo the seemingly contradictory evidence in the prior literature, where significant positive and null results emerged regularly using the same methods. Unsmoothed comparisons yielded similar results and can be found in Appendix Figure 5.A2.

Subsetting survey respondents on the types of people who would be expected to use Twitter did nothing to improve correspondence between survey and social media metrics. The favorability of Obama among survey respondents modeled to look like Twitter users was again unrelated to Twitter sentiment about Obama

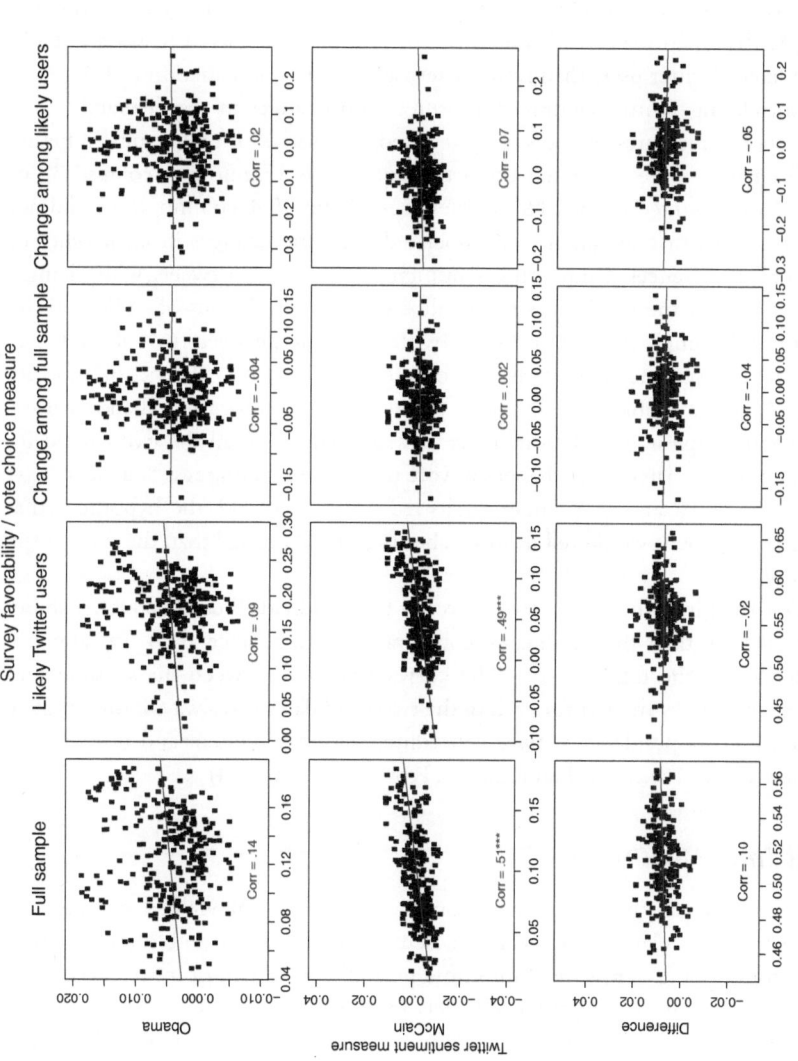

FIGURE 5.4 Correspondence between Twitter Sentiment and Survey Metrics for All Survey Dates, Each Smoothed Over a Period of 7 Days with Significance Corrected for Smoothing

(Pearson's r=.09, p=.54, second panel in the top row of Figure 5.4). McCain's favorability among survey respondents projected to use Twitter was again closely related to sentiment, though this relation was no stronger than before (r=.49, p<.001, second panel in middle row). And preferences between the candidates were not associated with differences between the sentiment of tweets about Obama and McCain (r=-.02, p=.89, second panel in bottom row). These findings suggest that sentiment on Twitter was no more closely related to survey results from likely Twitter users than from society at large, in contradiction to H1.

Correlating Twitter sentiment measures with changes in the favorability and vote choice measures of the survey resulted in a series of null results. Whether these changes were generated using the full sample (Figure 5.4, column 3), or the subset weighted to look like Twitter users (Figure 5.4, column 4), we did not find evidence that sentiment was associated with any changes in favorability or electoral preferences. Comparing sentiment about Obama tweets with changes in measures of the candidate's favorability yielded correlations of -.004 and .02 for the full sample and set of likely Twitter users respectively (p=.98 and .92). Sentiment about McCain tweets was completely unrelated to changes in measures of McCain's favorability (r=.002 and .07, p=.99 and .66 for the full and Twitter-weighted samples). And the difference in sentiment between the two candidates was also unassociated with changes in vote preferences among respondent (r=-.04 and -.05, p=.82 and .77). These results led us to reject H2, the hypothesis that Twitter sentiment would tell us more about electoral change than the state of the election.

Our final hypothesis, that tweets would track individual candidate favorability more closely than the candidates' comparative performance (H3) was also not evidenced in the full year data. The correspondence between the sentiment of tweets and survey metrics for each of the two candidates was always more negative than the correspondence between the difference in sentiment and relative vote choice (Rows 1 and 2 of Figure 5.4 vs. Row 3 of Figure 5.4).

Last Three Months

Limiting data to the final three months of the election yielded considerably more positive relations between the sentiment of tweets and survey metrics than comparisons across the entire time period. Strong significant relations were observed linking the sentiment of tweets about Obama with survey ratings of his favorability (Pearson's r=.59, p=.03, first panel in the top row of Figure 5.5). Nearly identical relations were observed linking the sentiment of tweets about McCain with favorability ratings (r=.64, p=.02). And the difference between sentiments expressed about the two major party candidates was also strongly associated with electoral preferences (r=.64, p=.02). Hence, we find strong support for the notion that Twitter metrics track election results more effectively later in the campaign cycle (H4).

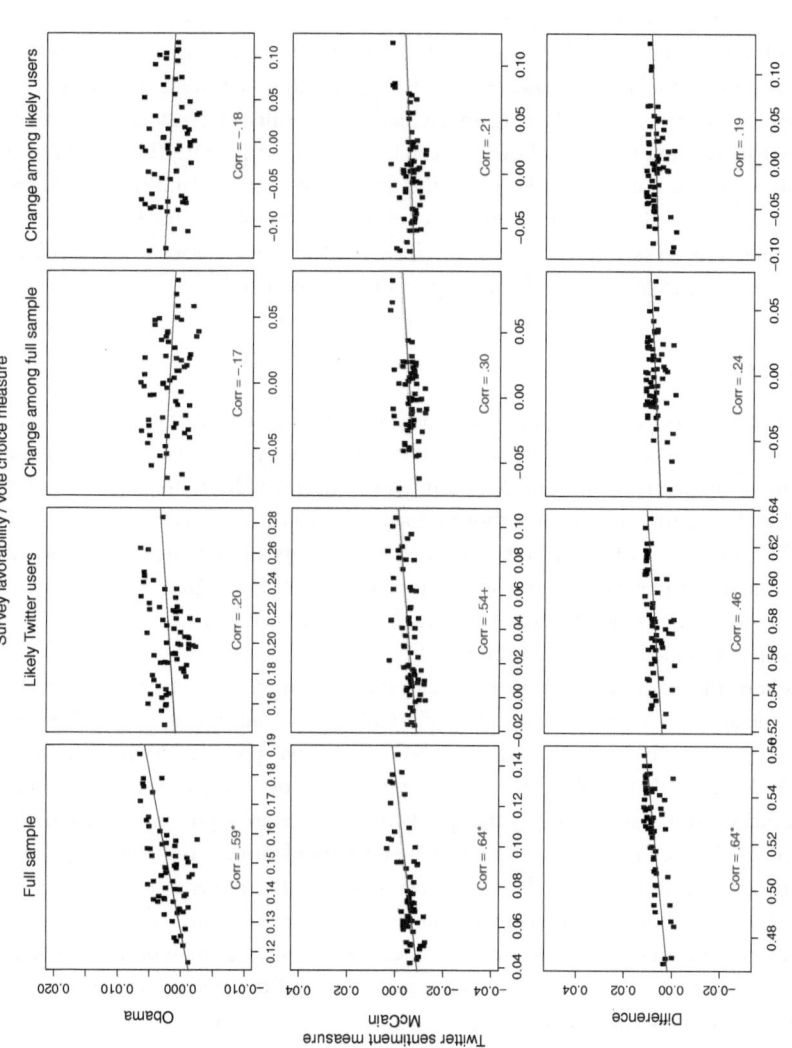

FIGURE 5.5 Correspondence between Twitter Sentiment and Survey Metrics for the Last Three Months Before Election Day, Each Smoothed Over a Period of 7 Days with Significance Corrected for Smoothing

Despite the greater correspondence observed between Twitter sentiment and survey measures in this later period, we continued to reject our hypotheses about other conditions that would maximize correspondence. Weighting the survey data to provide estimates of favorability among likely Twitter users produced data streams that were not as strongly associated with sentiment as the full survey samples (H1; column 2 of Figure 5.5). None of these relations reached conventional levels of statistical significance—though they were not significantly worse than the full population measures. Comparing Twitter sentiment measures with changes in survey favorability again yielded null results, suggesting that tweets did not in fact tell us more about electoral change than its state (H2; columns 3 and 4). Finally, a comparison between the favorability metrics and the vote share metric did not indicate that either approach was preferable for tracking electoral dynamics (H3; rows 1 and 2 vs row 3). These results were less robust to the use of daily data instead of smoothed data (Appendix Figure 5.A3).

Discussion

In many respects this study can be seen as yet another example of the inconsistent results that emerge when comparing Twitter and survey data. We found that the sentiment of tweets about John McCain tracked his favorability throughout 2008, but that the sentiment of tweets about Barack Obama did not track his favorability for the same time period. In this vein, we join a variety of esteemed colleagues in our conclusion that Twitter and survey metrics sometimes match and sometimes do not, even when using the same analytical strategies (see e.g., Gayo-Avello, 2013; Metaxas, Mustafaraj, & Gayo-Avello, 2011).

Where this study builds on prior analyses is through a variety of attempts to theoretically determine why social media and survey data match when they do, and do not match when they do not. Specifically, we provide empirical tests of four hypotheses that might explain the conditions under which tweets sometimes track elections. These include 1) that predictive failures are a product of systematic differences between Twitter users and the voting population, 2) that tweets are capturing seminal moments of change, rather than running preferences, 3) that sentiment surrounding tweets might be measuring the favorability of candidates or parties, rather than relative vote preferences, and 4) that survey and sentiment metrics may only attend to the same patterns toward the end of the election campaign.

Although these theories are all grounded in a social scientific understanding of both Twitter use and electoral behavior, they do not all improve correspondence in the run-up to the 2008 U.S. Presidential Election. We see no improvement in the correspondence of Twitter and survey metrics when survey results are focused to match the population of likely Twitter users. Electoral tweets also do not seem to track changes in the favorability levels of the various candidates any more than they track the absolute levels of favorability. And favorability measures do not appear to perform notably better or worse than vote choice.

Evidence from the current study does, however, suggest that the correspondence between the sentiment of tweets and survey measures of favorability improved toward the end of the election cycle. This result fits nicely given what might be expected from greater attention to the candidates as Election Day drew closer (Erikson & Wlezien, 2012). As a larger proportion of the electorate—and also presumably of U.S. Twitter users—engaged with the campaign, both data streams appeared to respond to events in similar ways.

Explaining Differences between Candidates

One of the more surprising results of the current study is the extent to which Twitter sentiment corresponded closely with McCain favorability through the entire pre-election period of 2008 but only with Obama favorability as the election drew near. A closer look at how the correspondence between these data streams itself trended over time is presented in Figure 5.A4 of the Appendix. Although both candidates typically experienced positive correspondences at similar times, Obama's insignificant correlation appears attributable to moderate negative relations between Twitter sentiment and reported favorability throughout July and August of 2008. It is not clear why this might have been the case.

Interpreting Failed Predictions

Many of the theoretically derived hypotheses in this study failed to improve correspondence between candidates' sentiment on Twitter and their favorability in surveys. These failures to predict are important for honing our understanding of how survey and social media data relate. We therefore discuss some of the substantive implications of each of the failed predictions.

Perhaps the most notable failure in the current study is the lack of improvement in correspondence when weighting survey data to mirror the types of individuals who reported using Twitter. The rationale for this corrective is the assumption—made by many—that the nonprobability nature of tweets is a core reason that they sometimes fail to predict (see e.g., Couper, 2013; Langer Research Associates, 2013). Although the weighting strategy employed was somewhat crude, given the need to rely on a third-party dataset that measured Twitter use, we would still expect improvement in correspondence if this constitutes one of the major differences between data streams. Given the lack of improvement, we could reach one of three conclusions: It is possible that 1) Twitter users are surprisingly similar to the public at large on the measures of interest, 2) that Twitter posting is sufficiently different from use that we are adjusting to the wrong metric, or 3) that the conditions that lead to correspondence do not depend on tweets that represent the opinions of their posters. This third possibility is, in the view of the authors, the most likely. Because tweeting is a social process performed for an audience, posts may be more reflective of societal trends than individual attitudes and beliefs (Conrad et al., 2015; Schober et al., 2016).

Given the social process involved in posting to Twitter (Marwick & boyd, 2011), it seems odd that tweets would track the state of the election more than they corresponded with electoral change. We imagine a few alternative hypotheses that might account for this. One possibility is that much of what was generated on Twitter was strategic communication on behalf of the campaigns rather than individual expressions of attitudes and beliefs. Under such a scenario, the sentiment of tweeting—and possibly even its volume—may have captured the relative organizational capacity of the two campaigns. It is unlikely under this scenario that what was being posted was solely news content, as news about the candidates would be expected to result in substantive changes in attitudes (cf. Sides & Vavreck, 2013).

It is less clear what we should make of the fact that candidate favorability was not generally better or worse in its correspondence with Twitter metrics than electoral preferences.

Limitations and Future Studies

The 2008 U.S. Presidential Election is in various ways both an ideal and a problematic contest for assessing the predictive capacity of social media metrics. The case is ideal in that neither of the two major parties had an incumbent candidate running, which means that the election campaign served as a key opportunity for both individuals to introduce themselves to the public. Further, events during the campaign—rather than reflections on prior performance in office—were likely to dominate the learning that occurred. In contrast, though, the 2008 U.S. Presidential Election occurred early in the history of Twitter, which meant that many of the norms and habits guiding user behaviors on the site may not have been well established. Whether the results of this study would replicate for the candidates in another election year thus remains an open question.

A variety of the features of the comparison presented here were suboptimal. Use of Twitter in early 2008 was relatively rarified, making trends in this period more difficult to identify and potentially clouding the results we observed. The need for an external dataset to identify likely Twitter users undermined our ability to effectively estimate the opinions of these individuals, at least in comparison to a survey that asked this question more directly. It also meant that our measure of likely Twitter use was constrained to demographic covariates, and necessarily could not include other, unmeasured factors that distinguished users and nonusers of the site. Finally, the need to smooth the data led to clearer time trends at the cost of overlapping periods of analysis. Corrections for this overlap reduced the functional sample size from 308 days to a mere 44 unique time periods, and from 63 to 9 when analyses were limited to the final three months of the campaign.

Notably, we weighted the survey data to match the demographic profile of Twitter users, not necessarily those who posted on Twitter and certainly not those who posted political content on the site. It is hard to imagine that a truly random subsample of users decides to post about politics, meaning that these weights would likely only account for part of the variance in posting about Twitter. This was a sizable limitation due to data availability. That said, it stands to reason that people who post about candidates on Twitter should be more similar to Twitter users than to the public at large. Hence, it is still surprising that we found no improvement with this metric.

As with many studies comparing social media metrics with electoral results, we are again considering only a single electoral context. It is imperative that we replicate in other contexts to ensure that what we observed here was not the function of some idiosyncrasy of the data or the period examined.

Conclusion

The results of the current study suggest that social scientific theories may have an important role to play in understanding why the correspondence between tweets and electoral surveys has proven fickle. By recognizing the dynamics of election campaigns, we are able to identify consistent results linking social media sentiment with the favorability of both major party candidates in the 2008 election. These correspondences, however, were only consistent in the most intense part of the campaign and were not apparent earlier in the election season. Notably, however, not all attempts to identify theoretical links between these two data streams produced corresponding results. In contrast to what many have argued, the evidence presented here does not indicate that the biggest problem with Twitter is the nonprobability nature of its users. Instead, it seems as if tweets track elections—when they do—through a mechanism that differs from that of survey response (cf. Schober et al., 2016).

Appendices

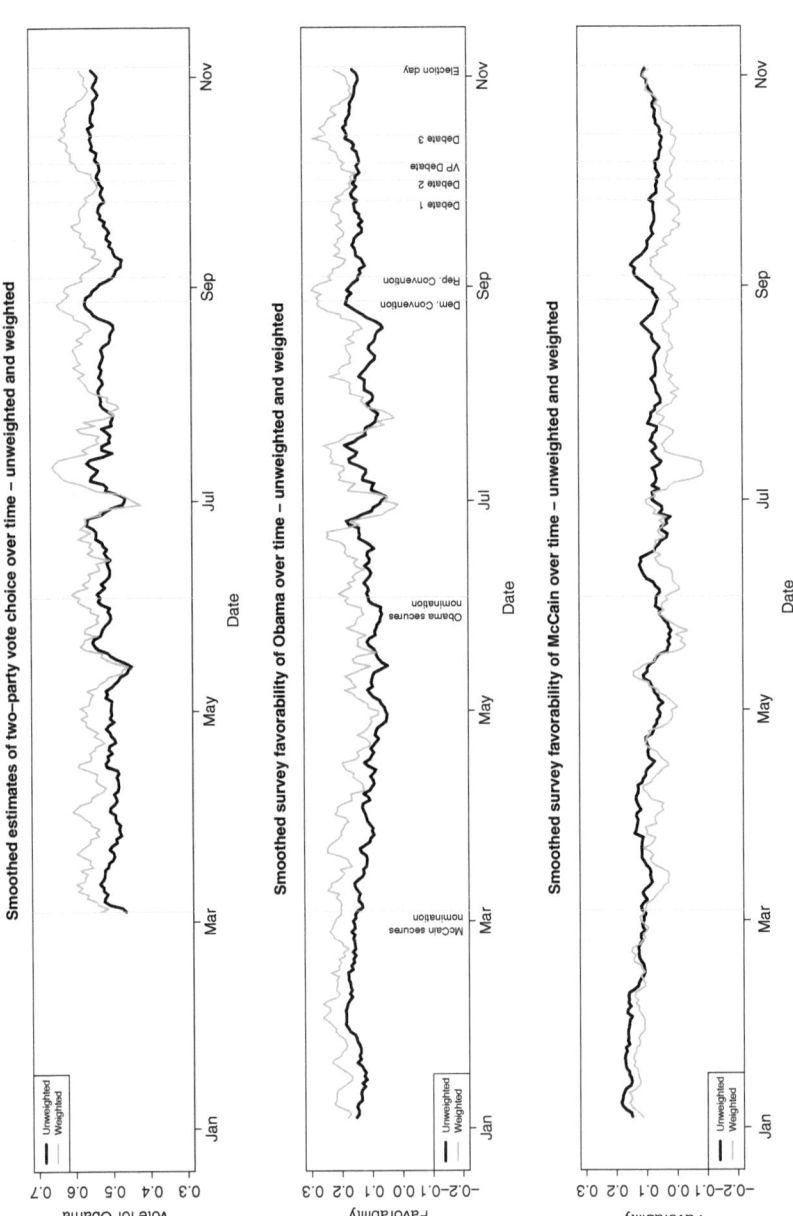

FIGURE 5.A1 Raw Unweighted and Weighted Estimates

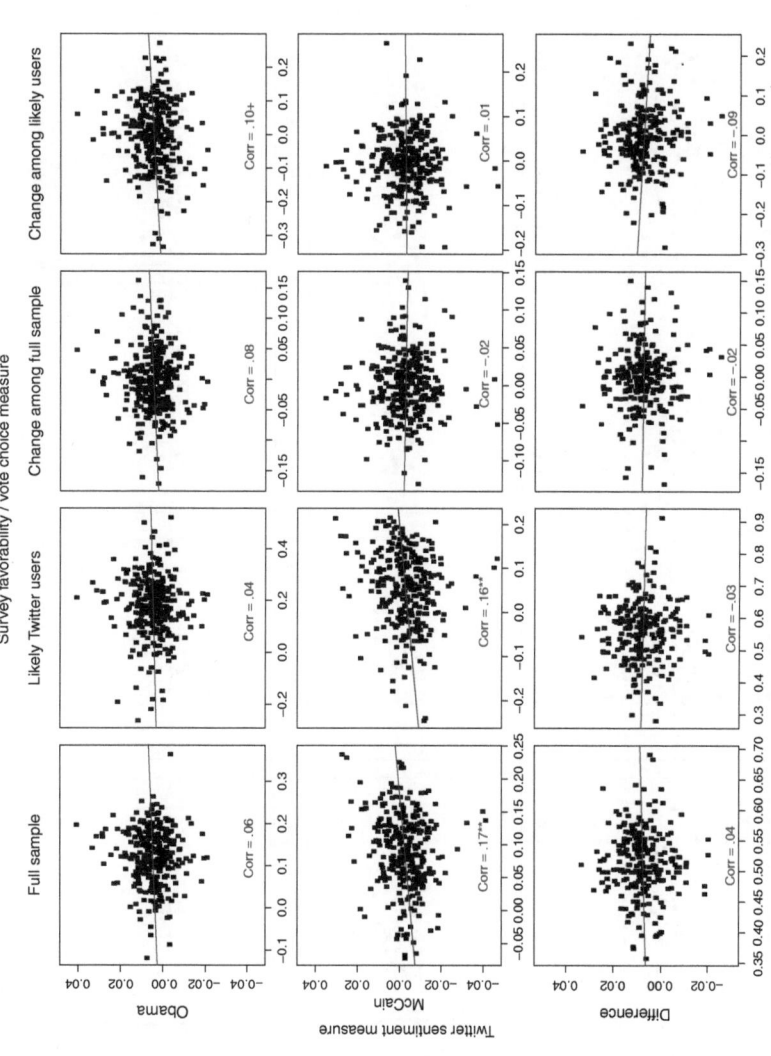

FIGURE 5.A2 Replication of Figure 5.4 Using Daily Data Instead of Smoothed Data

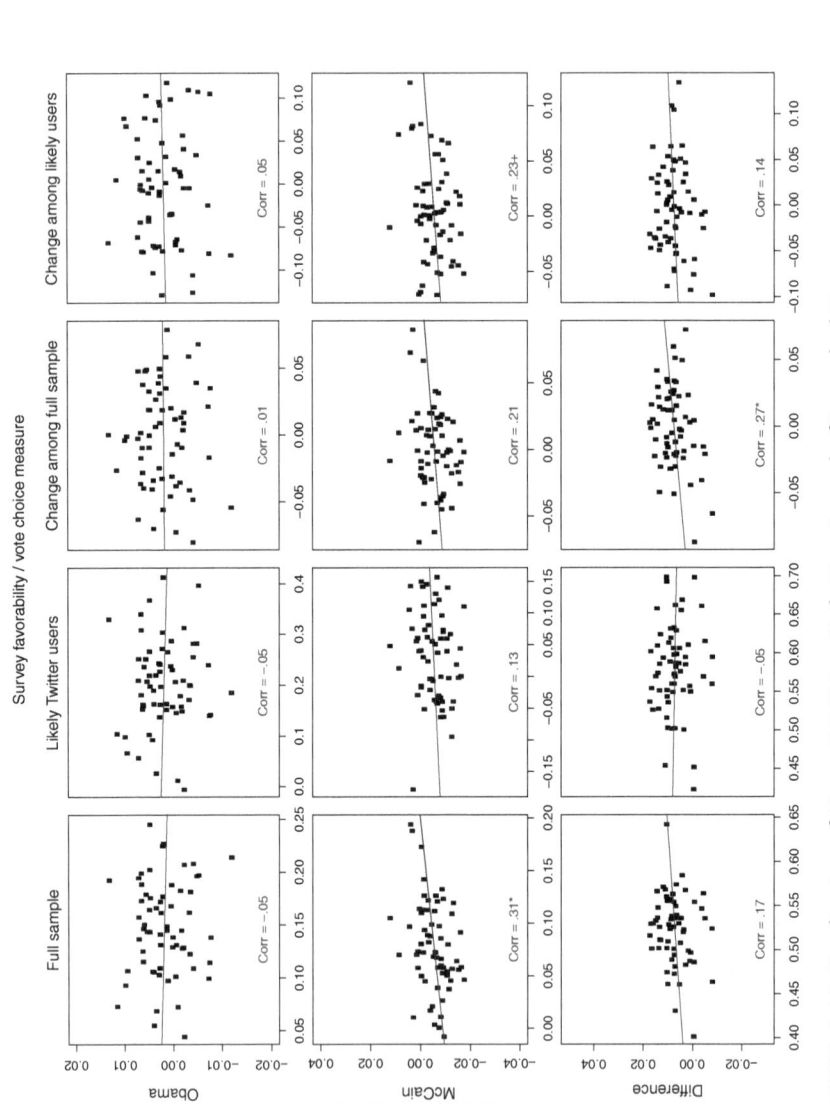

FIGURE 5.A3 Replication of Figure 5.5 Using Daily Data Instead of Smoothed Data

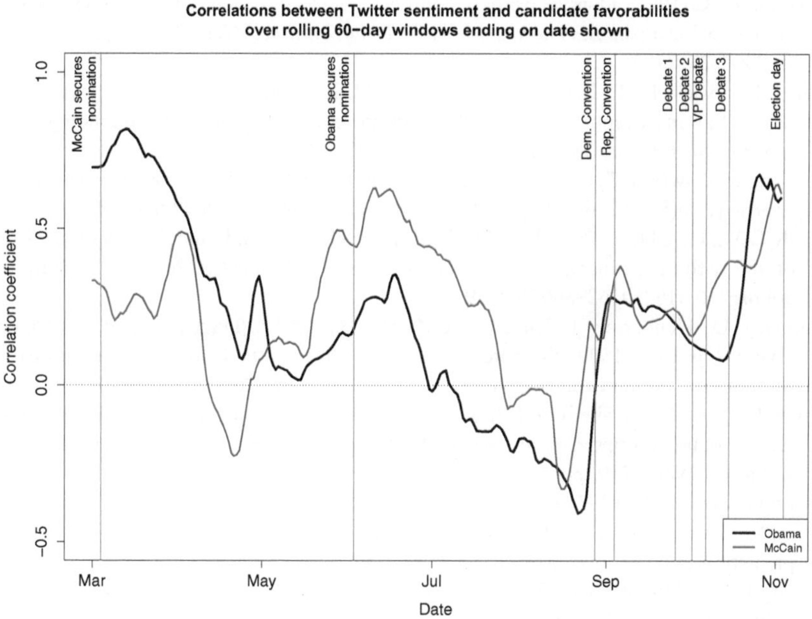

Correlations between Twitter sentiment and candidate favorabilities
over rolling 60-day windows ending on date shown

FIGURE 5.A4 Correlations between Twitter Sentiment and Survey Favorability Over Rolling 60-Day Windows

Notes

1 We recognize that the inability of current researchers to gather the same data poses important replication challenges. This is a large-scale challenge of relying on corporate actors as a source of social science data. Although we are happy to work with individuals hoping to replicate these analyses, we consider the situation suboptimal.

2 No interviews were conducted on the following dates: 12/24/2007, 12/25/2007, 12/31/2007, 1/1/2008, 3/23/2008, 7/4/2008, and 10/7/2008.

3 Between September 18 and September 25, 2008, this question did include not third party vice presidential candidates or either Libertarian candidate.

4 The model was fit by predicting Twitter use with the following equation: *Twitter Use ~ Sex x Age + Marital Status + Employment Status + Education x Race + Party + Income + Internet Use + Religiosity*. Each level of each predictor was treated as an independent covariate, with all levels of each interaction predicted uniquely. These variables were used because they were coded similarly in the Pew data and NAES and we thought that they might account for some features of likely Twitter use. Diagnostic tests on the *glmnet* model indicated that the model did not appear to overfit the data when generated on the Pew dataset.

References

Annenberg Public Policy Center. (2008). *National Annenberg election survey 2008 phone edition (NAES08-Phone) codebook*. Philadelphia, PA: University of Pennsylvania.

Atkeson, L. R. (1998). Divisive primaries and general election outcomes: Another look at presidential campaigns. *American Journal of Political Science, 42*(1), 256. http://doi.org/10.2307/2991755

Baker, R., Brick, J. M., Bates, N. A., Battaglia, M. P., Couper, M. P., Dever, J. A., et al. (2013). Summary report of the AAPOR task force on non-probability sampling. *Journal of Survey Statistics and Methodology, 1*(2), 90–143.

boyd, d., & Crawford, K. (2012). Critical questions for big data. *Information, Communication & Society, 15*(5), 662–679. http://doi.org/10.1080/1369118X.2012.678878

Brady, D. W., Han, H., & Pope, J. C. (2007). Primary elections and candidate ideology: Out of step with the primary electorate? *Legislative Studies Quarterly, 32*(1), 79–105. http://doi.org/10.3162/036298007X201994

Burger, J. D., Henderson, J., Kim, G., & Zarrella, G. (2011). Discriminating gender on Twitter (pp. 1301–1309). Presented at the Proceedings of the Conference on Empirical Methods in Natural Language Processing, Association for Computational Linguistics.

Chen, L., Wang, W., & Sheth, A. P. (2012). Are Twitter users equal in predicting elections? A study of user groups in predicting 2012 U.S. republican presidential primaries. In *Social Informatics* (Vol. 7710, pp. 379–392). Berlin, Heidelberg: Springer Berlin Heidelberg. http://doi.org/10.1007/978-3-642-35386-4_28

Choy, M., Cheong, M., Laik, M. N., & Shung, K. P. (2012). US presidential election 2012 prediction using census corrected Twitter model. *ArXiv E-Prints.*

Chung, J. E., & Mustafaraj, E. (2011). Can collective sentiment expressed on Twitter predict political elections? Presented at the Proceedings of the Twenty-Fifth AAAI Conference on Artificial Intelligence.

Conover, M. D., Ratkiewicz, J., Francisco, M., Goncalves, B., Flammini, A., & Menczer, F. (2011). Political polarization on Twitter (pp. 89–96). Presented at the Proceedings of the Fifth International AAAI Conference on Weblogs and Social Media.

Conrad, F. G., Schober, M. F., Pasek, J., Guggenheim, L., Lampe, C., & Hou, E. (2015). A collective-vs-self hypothesis for when Twitter and survey data tell the same story. Presented at the 6th Conference of the European Survey Research Association, Reykjavik, Iceland.

Couper, M. P. (2013). Is the sky falling? New technology, changing media, and the future of surveys. *Survey Research Methods, 7*(3), 145–156.

Diaz, F., Gamon, M., Hofman, J. M., Kıcıman, E., & Rothschild, D. (2016). Online and social media data as an imperfect continuous panel survey. *PLoS ONE, 11*(1), e0145406. http://doi.org/10.1371/journal.pone.0145406

Dietterich, T. G. (1995). Overfitting and undercomputing in machine learning. *ACM Computing Surveys (CSUR), 27*(3), 326–327. http://doi.org/10.1145/212094.212114

Dietterich, T. G. (2000). Ensemble methods in machine learning. In *Multiple Classifier Systems* (Vol. 1857, pp. 1–15). Berlin, Heidelberg: Springer Berlin Heidelberg. http://doi.org/10.1007/3-540-45014-9_1

DiGrazia, J., McKelvey, K., Bollen, J., & Rojas, F. (2013). More tweets, more votes: Social media as a quantitative indicator of political behavior. *PLoS ONE, 8*(11), e79449. http://doi.org/10.1371/journal.pone.0079449

Erikson, R. S., & Wlezien, C. (2008). Are political markets really superior to polls as election predictors? *Public Opinion Quarterly, 72*(2), 190–215. http://doi.org/10.1093/poq/nfn010

Erikson, R. S., & Wlezien, C. (2012). The timeline of presidential elections. Chicago, IL: University of Chicago Press.

Fan, J., Han, F., & Liu, H. (2014). Challenges of big data analysis. *National Science Review, 1*(2), 293–314. http://doi.org/10.1093/nsr/nwt032

Ferguson, C. J., & Heene, M. (2012). A vast graveyard of undead theories publication bias and psychological science's aversion to the null. *Perspectives on Psychological Science,* 7(6), 555–561. http://doi.org/10.1177/1745691612459059

Franch, F. (2013). (Wisdom of the crowds) 2: 2010 UK election prediction with social media. *Journal of Information Technology & Politics,* 10(1), 57–71. http://doi.org/10.1080/19331681.2012.705080

Franco, A., Malhotra, N., & Simonovits, G. (2014). Publication bias in the social sciences: Unlocking the file drawer. *Science,* 345(6203), 1502–1505.

Gayo-Avello, D. (2012). No, you cannot predict elections with Twitter. *IEEE Internet Computing,* 16(6), 91–94. http://doi.org/10.1109/MIC.2012.137

Gayo-Avello, D. (2013). A meta-analysis of state-of-the-art electoral prediction from Twitter data. *Social Science Computer Review,* 31(6), 649–679. http://doi.org/10.1177/0894439313493979

Groves, R. M., & Lyberg, L. (2011). Total survey error: Past, present, and future. *Public Opinion Quarterly,* 74(5), 849–879. http://doi.org/10.1093/poq/nfq065

Guggenheim, L., & Pasek, J. (2013). Binders full of tweets: Stimulus-response curves in Twitter reactions to news events. Presented at the 11th Annual American Political Science Association Preconference on Political Communication, Chicago, IL.

Hopkins, D. J., & King, G. (2009). A method of automated nonparametric content analysis for social science. *American Journal of Political Science,* 54(1), 229–247. http://doi.org/10.1111/j.1540-5907.2009.00428.x

Hu, Y., John, A., Seligmann, D. D., & Wang, F. (2012). What Were the tweets about? Topical associations between public events and Twitter feeds (pp. 154–161). Presented at the Proceedings of the Sixth International AAAI Conference on Weblogs and Social Media.

Huberty, M. (2015). Can we vote with our tweet? On the perennial difficulty of election forecasting with social media. *International Journal of Forecasting,* 31(3), 992–1007. http://doi.org/10.1016/j.ijforecast.2014.08.005

Jang, S. M., & Pasek, J. (2015). Assessing the carrying capacity of Twitter and online news. *Mass Communication and Society,* 18(5), 577–598. http://doi.org/10.1080/15205436.2015.1035397

Japec, L., Kreuter, F., Berg, M., Biemer, P., Decker, P., Lampe, C., et al. (2015). Big data in survey research AAPOR task force report. *Public Opinion Quarterly,* 79(4), 839–880. http://doi.org/10.1093/poq/nfv039

Jungherr, A. (2015). Twitter use in election campaigns: A systematic literature review. *Journal of Information Technology and Politics,* 13(1), 72–91. http://doi.org/10.1080/19331681.2015.1132401

Jungherr, A., Jürgens, P., & Schoen, H. (2012). Why the Pirate Party won the German election of 2009 or the trouble with predictions: A response to Tumasjan, A., Sprenger, T. O., Sander, P. G., & Welpe, I. M. "Predicting elections with Twitter: What 140 characters reveal about political sentiment." *Social Science Computer Review,* 30(2), 229–234. http://doi.org/10.1177/0894439311404119

Kwak, H., Lee, C., Park, H., & Moon, S. (2010). What is Twitter, a social network or a news media? *Proceedings of the 19th International Conference on World Wide Web,* 591–600. http://doi.org/10.1145/1772690.1772751

Langer Research Associates. (2013). *Briefing paper: Social media and public opinion* (pp. 1–12).

Lazer, D., Kennedy, R., King, G., & Vespignani, A. (2014). The parable of Google flu: Traps in big data analysis. *Science,* 343(6176), 1203–1205. http://doi.org/10.1126/science.1248506

Lazer, D., Pentland, A., Adamic, L., Aral, S., Barabási, A.-L., Brewer, D., et al. (2009). Computational social science. *Science, 323*(5915), 721–723. http://doi.org/10.1126/science.1167742

Leinweber, D. J. (2015). Nerds on Wall Street. *Nerds on Wall Street* (pp. 135–148). Hoboken, NJ, USA: John Wiley & Sons, Inc. http://doi.org/10.1002/9781119201113.ch6

Lin, Y.-R., Keegan, B., Margolin, D., & Lazer, D. (2014). Rising tides or rising stars?: Dynamics of shared attention on Twitter during media events. *PLoS ONE, 9*(5), e94093. http://doi.org/10.1371/journal.pone.0094093

Lohr, S. (2009). *Sampling: Design and analysis* (2nd ed.). Boston, MA: Cengage Learning.

Marwick, A. E., & boyd, d. (2011). I tweet honestly, I tweet passionately: Twitter users, context collapse, and the imagined audience. *New Media & Society, 13*(1), 114–133. http://doi.org/10.1177/1461444810365313

Metaxas, P. T., Mustafaraj, E., & Gayo-Avello, D. (2011). How (not) to predict elections (pp. 165–171). Presented at the Privacy, Security, Risk and Trust (PASSAT) and 2011 IEEE Third International Conference on Social Computing (SocialCom).

Mohammad, S. (2013). Identifying purpose behind electoral tweets (pp. 1–9). Presented at the Proceedings of the Second International Workshop on Issues of Sentiment Discovery and Opinion Mining – WISDOM '13, New York, NY: ACM Press. http://doi.org/10.1145/2502069.2502070

Moore, D. W. (2008). *The opinion makers: An insider exposes the truth behind the polls.* Boston, MA: Beacon Press.

Morstatter, F., Pfeffer, J., Liu, H., & Carley, K. M. (2013). Is the sample good enough? Comparing data from Twitter's streaming API with Twitter's firehose. Presented at the Seventh International AAAI Conference on Weblogs and Social Media.

Murphy, J., Link, M. W., Childs, J. H., Tesfaye, C. L., Dean, E., Stern, M., et al. (2014). *Report of the emerging technologies task force of the American Association for Public Opinion Research.* Washington, DC: American Association for Public Opinion Research. Retrieved from www.aapor.org/Social_Media_Task_Force_Report.htm

Neyman, J. (1934). On the two different aspects of the representative method: The method of stratified sampling and the method of purposive selection. *Journal of the Royal Statistical Society, 97*(4), 558–625.

Norrander, B. (1991). Explaining individual participation in presidential primaries. *The Western Political Quarterly, 44*(3), 640–655.

O'Connor, B. (2010). From tweets to polls: Linking text sentiment to public opinion time series (Vol. 11, pp. 122–129). Washington, DC. Retrieved from www.scopus.com/inward/record.uri?partnerID=HzOxMe3b&scp=84890614558&origin=inward

Pasek, J. (2015). Predicting elections: Considering tools to pool the polls. *Public Opinion Quarterly, 79*(2), 594–619. http://doi.org/10.1093/poq/nfu060

Perrin, A. J. (2015). *Social media usage: 2005–2015.* Washington, DC: Pew Research Center.

Perrin, A. J., & Duggan, M. (2015). *Americans' internet access: 2000–2015.* Washington, DC: Pew Research Center.

Phuvipadawat, S., & Murata, T. (2010). Breaking news detection and tracking in Twitter (Vol. 3, pp. 120–123). Presented at the Web Intelligence and Intelligent Agent Technology (WI-IAT), 2010 IEEE/WIC/ACM International Conference on IS – SN -, IEEE. http://doi.org/10.1109/WI-IAT.2010.205

Rao, D., Yarowsky, D., Shreevats, A., & Gupta, M. (2010). Classifying latent user attributes in Twitter (pp. 37–44). Presented at the 2nd international workshop, New York, NY: ACM. http://doi.org/10.1145/1871985.1871993

Sang, E.T. K., & Bos, J. (2012). Predicting the 2011 Dutch senate election results with Twitter (pp. 53–60). Presented at the Proceedings of the 13th Conference of the European Chapter of the Association for Computational Linguistics, Avignon, FR: Association for Computational Linguistics.

Schober, M. F., Pasek, J., Guggenheim, L., Lampe, C., & Conrad, F. G. (2016). Social media analyses for social measurement. *Public Opinion Quarterly, 80*(1), 180–211. http://doi. org/10.1093/poq/nfv048

Sides, J., & Vavreck, L. (2013). The gamble: Choice and chance in the 2012 presidential election. Princeton, NJ: Princeton University Press.

Steinhubl, S. R., Muse, E. D., & Topol, E. J. (2015). The emerging field of mobile health. *Science Translational Medicine, 7*(283), 283rv3–283rv3.

Tumasjan, A., Sprenger, T. O., Sandner, P. G., & Welpe, I. M. (2011). Election forecasts with Twitter: How 140 characters reflect the political landscape. *Social Science Computer Review, 29*(4), 402–418. http://doi.org/10.1177/0894439310386557

Twitter. (2016, June 30). Company | About. Retrieved August 24, 2016, from https:// about.twitter.com/company

Waller, M. A., & Fawcett, S. E. (2013). Data science, predictive analytics, and big data: A revolution that will transform supply chain design and management. *Journal of Business Logistics, 34*(2), 77–84.

Weisberg, H. F. (2005). *The total survey error approach: A guide to the new science of survey research.* Chicago, IL: University of Chicago Press.

Young, L., & Soroka, S. N. (2012). Affective news: The Automated coding of sentiment in political texts. *Political Communication, 29*(2), 205–231. http://doi.org/10.1080/ 10584609.2012.671234

Zaller, J. (1992). *The nature and origins of mass opinion.* Cambridge, UK; New York, NY: Cambridge University Press.

Zamal, Al, F., Liu, W., & Ruths, D. (2012). Homophily and latent attribute inference: Inferring latent attributes of Twitter users from neighbors (pp. 387–390). Presented at the ICWSM.

6

INFERRING INDIVIDUAL-LEVEL CHARACTERISTICS FROM DIGITAL TRACE DATA

Issues and Recommendations

Deen Freelon

The digital age has generated innumerable new data sources for scholars of communication. Political communication researchers have probably benefited from this bonanza more than some subfields (interpersonal and organizational, for example) due to the public nature of many of its objects of study. From social media and websites to digitized versions of offline texts, digital data sources allow us to explore political communication research questions in unprecedented ways. Thus far we have only scratched the surface of the methodological possibilities afforded by the many datasets now available to us through a few clicks.

One important category of digital data for our subfield is *digital traces*. These are the records of online activity recorded by the servers that undergird all internet-based communication (Freelon, 2014). Traces can be created manually or generated automatically: user-generated text, hyperlinks, social media follows, "likes" and "favorites," and timestamps are all examples. (Not included are analog media content that is later digitized for preservation; in other words, traces are necessarily native to digital contexts.) These records collectively contain enormous empirical potential to answer all manner of politically relevant questions.

One of the greatest challenges for researchers interested in digital traces is managing the gap between their research's conceptual focus and the set of readily available traces. Not every type of trace will be equally valuable from a particular research standpoint, and not every interesting concept will be measurable using the traces to which we have access. Researchers should never assume without support that a given trace or trace-derived construct indicates a given underlying concept, however intuitive it may seem. Some traces may require only brief explanations of how and why they relate to their theoretical referents. For others, more elaborate arguments and data transformations may be necessary to suffi-ciently justify particularly theoretical uses.

The purpose of this chapter is to contribute to the development of a frame-work for assessing the construct validity of theoretical inferences drawn from digital traces. Most high-quality trace-based empirical research does this to some extent, but what is missing is an abstract set of standards and heuristics by which the quality of its inferences may be assessed. This will help ensure the rigor of such research, which is especially important given that it is still in its infancy. I define four nested, platform-independent domains that researchers should bear in mind when choosing traces for analysis: technical design, terms of service (TOS), social context, and the potential for misrepresentation. I demonstrate the value of this framework in discussions of three general categories of techniques for trace infer-ence: *direct indication, proper names,* and *speech patterns.* I apply the framework to these techniques by drawing examples from three individual-level characteristics of great interest to political communication researchers: gender, race/ethnicity (R/E), and geographical location. Each of these has seen a diverse range of empir-ical attempts to infer them from traces in the relevant literature.

Four Domains Affecting the Construct Validity of Trace Data

The well-known dictum that "raw data is an oxymoron" (Bowker, 2005, p. 184; Gitelman, 2013) is rarely illustrated more clearly than in the case of digital traces. Their use is so common in contemporary social science research that authors rarely bother pointing out that they were not generated with research in mind (Howison, Wiggins, & Crowston, 2011). Unlike survey or experimental data, which are constructed to optimize the quality of the research based on them, trace data are created incidentally through everyday internet use. Because their fitness as research data is not guaranteed for any particular purpose, researchers should argue convincingly that particular inferences can be drawn from them.

When deciding whether to infer a specific characteristic from a specific trace, four domains warrant close consideration: technical design, terms of service, social context, and the potential for misrepresentation. These are hierarchically nested (see Figure 6.1) in that the outer domains constrain the range of choices available within the domains they enclose. The outermost domain, technical design, defines the absolute limits of what can and cannot be done within a sociotechnical system. Proceeding inward, a platform's terms of service designate which technically possible behaviors may result in official punishment, including account suspension and deletion. Social contexts can only be built upon behaviors that operate within a platform's terms of service, and misrepresentation is a char-acteristic of certain social contexts. Together, these domains provide a compre-hensive foundation for arguments about the relationships between traces and their ostensible referents.

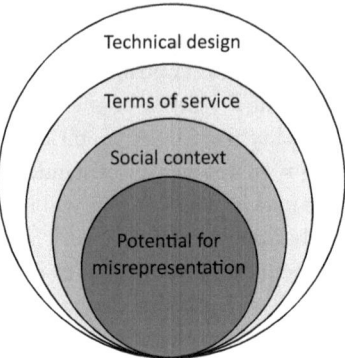

FIGURE 6.1 Four Nested Domains Affecting the Construct Validity of Digital Traces

The following subsections discuss each in turn. They rely heavily on examples drawn from social media, which offer many diverse examples of theoretically valuable traces.

Technical Design

The design of a communication system determines the kinds of communications it can support (Freelon, 2010, 2015a; Sack, 2005; Wright & Street, 2007). Almost none of the 20th century's mass media allowed their audiences to respond, so their channels were dominated by elites. Online media permit such responses, which grants ordinary users an unprecedented menu of communication options. Every platform's menu is unique: for example, Twitter allows its users to unilaterally "follow" one another by default, while Facebook requires its users to approve each "friend" request. Snapchat deletes messages as soon as the recipients have viewed them, and the now-defunct social network This allowed users to share just one hyperlink per day. Design features such as these set the absolute boundaries of digital behavior.

This general point is fairly well understood by most students of communication technologies, so I will not belabor it here. However, before continuing it is worth briefly discussing how the official labels of some design features invite specific inferences. One example of this is "likes" as implemented by Facebook and Twitter, which allow users to mark individual posts with a thumbs-up or heart icon, respectively. A researcher could infer positive sentiment toward "liked" posts on the basis of the feature label alone. But such an argument would not be satisfactory, because "likes" can convey much more than just positive sentiment, which is not a monolithic concept in any case (Gerlitz & Helmond, 2013). This example demonstrates that even in the most seemingly obvious of cases, researchers should not take traces at face value. "Likes" may reliably indicate positive sentiment in some or even most cases, but we need more evidence than the platform creators' intentions to soundly argue as much.

Terms of Service (TOS)

Terms of service are the lengthy documents we all must agree to (without necessarily reading) before registering as users on most social media platforms. They specify the platforms' rules and the consequences of violating them. Unlike the descriptive rules of technical design, which forcibly forbid or require certain behaviors, terms of service are often prescriptive rules that must be voluntarily obeyed. Many TOS can be broken fairly easily in the normal course of using a platform, whereas the restrictions imposed by technical design cannot. For example, notwithstanding a few exceptions I cannot post a tweet of more than 140 characters or befriend more than 5,000 Facebook users. I can, however, create a pseudonymous profile on Facebook or reveal another private user's personal information on Twitter or Facebook, both TOS violations punishable by account suspension. Most platforms' TOS require users to obey the laws of the countries in which they live in addition to whatever other rules they choose to set.

When widely known and enforced, a TOS's provisions can influence user behavior, which in turn affects how traces can be interpreted. Facebook's real-name policy has cultivated a norm of real name use on the platform, which has important implications for inferences of gender and race, as I discuss below. But because Twitter's TOS does not require its users to tweet under their real names, comparable inferences cannot always be made for that platform. In a very different example, researchers interested in TOS violations such as hate speech or advocacy of violence must account for the fact that platforms often remove such content quickly. Such vigilance, while laudable from most users' perspectives, complicates the task of measuring the prevalence of such behavior. However, researchers may be able to effectively track certain TOS violations that are not vigorously enforced by the platform (e.g. Matias et al., 2015).

Social Context

As both boyd et al. (2010) and Gerlitz and Helmond (2013) attest, traces can contain multitudes. It therefore stands to reason that a single trace cannot assume all of its possible meanings in any given instance. Social context can help researchers decide whether a given trace interpretation is plausible for the study at hand. For example, reporters often warn that retweets should not be construed as endorsements (Metaxas et al., 2015), which implies a tendency to assume that they are considered as such in at least some contexts. In contrast, several studies have shown that retweets are valid indicators of ideology among communities of users that discuss politics (Aragón, Kappler, Kaltenbrunner, Laniado, & Volkovich, 2013; Conover et al., 2011; Freelon, Lynch, & Aday, 2015; Freelon, McIlwain, & Clark, in press). Thus we have emic evidence that agreement should not be inferred from retweets in one context, and etic evidence that it should in a different context. Such empirical evidence should be adduced whenever possible to support trace-based inferences.

Researchers should strive to understand the social contexts of their research as thoroughly as possible, obvious as that may sound. Unfortunately, trace-based research conducted using computational methods does not always reflect such understanding (Freelon, 2015b). One task for which this is especially important is the inference of certain identity characteristics (e.g. gender and race) from first names. One widely accepted means of inferring gender from first names is to use a dictionary of popular first names keyed to the genders they most often predict. Twitter poses a problem for this method because it allows its users to post under whatever pseudonym they like, as noted above. Most importantly from the standpoint of social context, available evidence suggests that pseudonym use may not be evenly distributed across social groups. Participants in "Black Twitter," for example, have been known to choose sui generis screen names that cleverly allude to pop culture figures and media (see Clayton, 2013). LGBTQ individuals also frequently adopt nontraditional names to express their identities. Such pseudonyms may confound tools for inferring identity characteristics specifically for those social groups who do not typically use their given names, or whose given names are unique. This in turn may lead to disproportionately high levels of "unknown" categorizations for members of these groups. Understanding such social contexts can help researchers address the methodological challenges they present.

Potential for Misrepresentation

In a perfect world, every digital trace would directly index a specific action committed by a specific human being. Needless to say, they do not, and a key reason for that is willful misrepresentation by duplicitous parties. Thieves and fraudsters have created false traces whenever and wherever they can profit from doing so, with varying levels of success. Machine-generated spam promising wealth, health, beauty, love, and other human desiderata will almost certainly be familiar to anyone with an email account. Some politicians and other would-be notables have purchased non-human followers for themselves on Twitter and other social network sites to cultivate the illusion of popularity (Cresci, Di Pietro, Petrocchi, Spognardi, & Tesconi, 2015; Stringhini et al., 2013). These are just two digital examples of Campbell's law, which holds that valuable social metrics will inevitably be gamed and distorted (Campbell, 1979; cf. Karpf, 2012).

Campbell's law implies that not every trace will be subject to the same degree of pressure toward misrepresentation. The greater the opportunity for tangible benefit, the greater the potential for misrepresentation. Commercial spammers who target social media mostly focus on a particular range of businesses, including finance, dietary and health products, marketing, and consumer electronics (Lee, Eoff, & Caverlee, 2011; Sridharan, Shankar, & Gupta, 2012). Other things being equal, datasets devoted to such commercial topics should exhibit more of a spam problem than those covering other topics. One major exception is episodes of contentious politics in some non-Western countries, which have seen unknown parties inundating political conversations with machine-generated nonsense (Thomas, Grier, & Paxson, 2012; Verkamp & Gupta, 2013). Bot-detection methods and region-specific expertise can help researchers discern when automated conversation hijacking will be a more or less serious concern.

Individual-Level Characteristics

In the following sections, I will evaluate three general types of traces from which individual-level characteristics are often inferred. These trace types do not have established names, so here I refer to them as *direct indication, proper names,* and *speech patterns*. Each of these is common in sociotechnical systems and has been analyzed by a substantial body of work. Further, each is relevant to multiple individual-level characteristics, of which I discuss three: gender, R/E, and geographical location. I chose these particular characteristics for several reasons: first, each harbors clear value for one or more political communication theories. Second, and accordingly, empirical attempts to detect each from text are common in the communication, political science, sociology, and/or social computing literatures. Third, each of these characteristics has an objective answer known to someone somewhere, even if discovering it is prohibitively difficult for researchers. Everyone has a gender identity, an ethnic identity, and a physical location. In contrast, there are no objective ways of judging whether something is (for example) funny, racist, or attractive. An exploration of how best to infer such subjective characteristics from digital traces is beyond the scope of the current chapter.

Direct Indication

One of the simplest methods of inferring individual characteristics from digital traces is simply to take users at their word. One important way platforms allow researchers to do so is through *direct indication*, by which I mean dedicated fields through which users can (or must) declare specific facts about themselves. Facebook, for example, offers users a mandatory open-text box into which users can enter whatever gender label(s) fits them best.[1] Instagram offers direct indication for gender, but the only three options are "Male," "Female," and "Not Specified" (the default). Twitter's design does not permit direct indication of gender, and none of the three permit direct indication of R/E. Because Facebook requires users to indicate a gender while Instagram does not, direct indication is a superior source of gender information for the former than it is for the latter.[2] Facebook enacts its real-identity TOS requirement in part by requiring users to indicate their gender as a condition of account creation, and Instagram enacts its looser identity policy by not requiring it. Social context is likely to be a major issue for platforms in which users can choose to hide their gender. Facebook's terms of service require gender indication uniformly across all social contexts, but on Instagram it may be less customary in some contexts (e.g. politically-charged ones) than in others. For the same reason, systematic gender misrepresentation is less likely on Facebook than it is on Instagram.

Many sociotechnical systems also permit the direct indication of location information. For social media, this usually means either GPS-generated location data or text strings that may or may not correspond to identifiable physical locations. There are at least four key design considerations here: first, whether the system offers a dedicated location field; second, if such a field exists, whether location indication is opt-in or opt-out; third, whether the field supports GPS; and fourth, whether the field supports auto-complete for locations. An opt-out policy obviously makes a location field much more useful from a research perspective than opt-in, ethical considerations notwithstanding. Studies of Twitter, whose location field is opt-in, have found substantial numbers of users for whom locations cannot be determined (Hecht, Hong, Suh, & Chi, 2011; Leetaru, Wang, Padmanabhan, & Shook, 2013; Mislove, Lehmann, Ahn, Onnela, & Rosenquist, 2011). This is because they either left the field blank or entered a string that did not match a known place name. Where available, GPS is the gold standard for location data, as it can estimate a user's physical location to within several feet. But GPS is rarely enabled by default, and when it is not (as with Facebook, Twitter, and Instagram), very few users bother to turn it on (Leetaru et al., 2013; Morstatter, Pfeffer, Liu, & Carley, 2013). Thus, studies that include only users who have turned on GPS location run a high risk of systematically omitting certain types of users. One study that investigated this question directly on Twitter found that younger, urban, higher-income, Black, and Hispanic users were more likely to opt in to GPS (Malik, Lamba, Nakos, & Pfeffer, 2015). The same is likely true for textual locations: certain groups may be more likely to use official place names, while others may more often use informal location names or nonstandard abbreviations that cannot be resolved by automated location-guessing systems. Users can also misrepresent their locations, either intentionally or unintentionally. Among other reasons, intentional misrepresentation can occur as an act of solidarity, as when Twitter users around the world changed their locations to "Tehran" in an attempt to stymie the Iranian authorities' attempts to surveil local protesters' tweets (Mueller & van Huellen, 2012). Since location fields are usually static, but people move around quite a bit, researchers may find discrepancies between users' listed and actual locations. Though unintentional, these discrepancies may reduce the validity of trace inferences drawn in studies of major protests, concerts, conferences, and other events to which many people travel.

Proper Names

People's names can convey a wide range of relevant facts about them. In English and many other widely-spoken languages, most given names are overwhelmingly used by either males or females (Flowers, 2015). Thus, gender can usually be inferred from a person's given name (e.g. Burger, Henderson, Kim, & Zarrella,

2011; Freelon, Becker, Lannon, & Pendleton, 2016; Liu & Ruths, 2013; Mislove et al., 2011; Sloan et al., 2013). Most platforms have one or more fields through which users can or must name themselves, but as discussed above, not all require the use of official names. Even some sites that do not require real names have strong social norms toward real name usage (Google Plus, for example). For such sites, researchers can use simple dictionary-based gender-guessing programs for some populations such as Genderize (https://genderize.io/), Genderator (https://github.com/bmuller/genderator), and Gender API (https://gender-api.com/). These programs contain large dictionaries of common names, each of which is indexed to the gender it most often indicates: male for "John," female for "Mary," etc. Gender-guessing programs typically assign the corresponding gender for each name present in its dictionary and "Unknown" values to all names not present or that indicate maleness about as often as femaleness. Real-name requirements that are strictly enforced reduce the potential for misrepresentation, since misrepresentation risks negative consequences. So as long as the names in your gender-guessing program largely match those in your population, you would have a strong case for using it.

But this is not always the case. Gender-guessing programs reflect their creators' social backgrounds, and often skew toward traditional English and American names (e.g. Muller, 2012). Online social contexts that lie beyond the programmers' familiarity may therefore not be the best match for such programs. Services such as Genderize and Gender API attempt to overcome this limitation by using dictionaries of hundreds of thousands or millions of names across dozens of languages. But these particular services' dictionaries are closed and proprietary, preventing users from seeing for themselves how comprehensive they are (see Guo's chapter in this volume for more discussion of this issue). And even the most expansive and open dictionary will not suffice for populations that favor unique names and spellings, such as African Americans. Handling non-Latin character sets effectively is another major issue for inferring gender from names written in those scripts. Of course, in spaces where pseudonym use is the norm, none of these methods may provide acceptable levels of accuracy.

Several major differences in inferring R/E vs. gender from proper names become apparent immediately. First, few if any major social media platforms even permit, let alone require, users to indicate R/E directly. Most of the time it can only be inferred indirectly, with users' family names (rather than given names) being a popular data source (Chang, Rosenn, Backstrom, & Marlow, 2010; Fiscella & Fremont, 2006; Mislove et al., 2011). As with gender, the overall efficacy of this method for inferring R/E depends on the availability of the user's full name, which in turn depends on the four domains. Design-wise, the number and label(s) of the "name" field(s) is a major consideration. Facebook offers "first name" and "last name" fields as well as a field for "other names" including nicknames, maiden names, former names, and the like. Twitter offers two name-related fields: one simply labeled "Name," the other labeled "Username." Both of these can be easily altered at will, unlike Facebook's primary name fields, which can be changed only once every 60 days and are subject to multiple content restrictions. Thus, Twitter's technical environment is more hospitable to creative pseudonyms, from which gender is more difficult to infer. Some will take more advantage than others of opportunities to create pseudonyms, for example those interested in sensitive content such as drugs, guns, pornography, and racial hatred (Peddinti, Ross, & Cappos, 2014). Social contexts in which impersonation is relatively common, such as politics and entertainment (Freelon & Karpf, 2015; Highfield, 2016), should also receive extra scrutiny. But even given the presence of a credible full name, dictionary-based gender-guessing techniques are not equally effective for all races and ethnicities. It works better for Latinos and Asians than for African Americans, women, and individuals of higher socio-economic status (Fiscella & Fremont, 2006). Generally, it appears that the more heterogeneous the sample, the worse this technique is likely to perform on it.

Speech Patterns

A third trace-based inference technique exploits group-level differences in speech patterns. The idea here is that people who share a certain trait (gender, R/E, location, etc.) will tend to speak in ways that distinguish them from those who do not possess the trait. From a design standpoint, as long as a system allows users some degree of free textual expression (as all social media do), it will always offer the researcher something to analyze. However, the method's viability may depend on the extent to which the design restricts users' expressive latitude, for example through limitations on the number of posts or characters per post permitted (Burger et al., 2011; Peersman, Daelemans, & Van Vaerenbergh, 2011). Terms of service play a similar role: prohibitions on certain forms of expression could potentially affect a researcher's ability to infer certain characteristics from speech. For example, both Twitter and Facebook's terms forbid users from engaging in abusive behavior, which could potentially include words that predict membership in gender, racial, or affinity groups. But social context is probably the most consequential domain for this method, especially as it applies to R/E and gender. The predictive value of speech patterns for identity characteristics relies on the strength of the correlation between group membership and social context. In other words, speech pattern-based inference techniques assume that women will talk in distinctly "female" ways, men will talk in "male" ways, Blacks will talk in "Black" ways, etc. The truer this assumption, the more valid the results will be. It has long been known that men and women tend to speak differently in the aggregate, and speech-based studies of gender detection have exploited this fact to achieve gender classification rates of 70–90% (Bamman, Eisenstein, & Schnoebelen, 2014; Burger et al., 2011; Sap et al., 2014). While these rates are indeed high, they mask the fact that these methods may systematically misclassify certain subsets of individuals—those with heterogeneous social networks, for example (Bamman et al., 2014). Therefore, researchers should use the empirical record and expert knowledge about the population under study to ascertain whether speech-based classification will perform adequately for any given case. This would of course include any group-level proclivities toward identity tourism (Nakamura, 1995), which could prove misleading.

Several studies have also used the full text of user posts to identify their physical locations (e.g. Cheng, Caverlee, & Lee, 2010; Li, Wang, Deng, Wang, & Chang, 2012; Mahmud, Nichols, & Drews, 2012; Stefanidis, Crooks, & Radzikowski, 2013). In platforms that lack direct indication, this may be the only means of location identification available. Most of the technical design and TOS constraints are the same as for detection R/E and gender, so I will not reprise those here; the most substantial differences lie in the social domains. Simply put, the tendency to talk about one's physical location is probably not evenly distributed across a given platform's user population. The issue here is similar to GPS opt-in, with the main difference being that it is very easy to determine when someone has opted out of GPS. But it's much more difficult to determine when people regularly mention places they have been. A typical approach would process a corpus of social media posts through a dictionary of location names and analyze the matches (see Leetaru et al., 2013). But users will likely differ greatly in the volume of identifiable locations they post. Moreover, while some users' hits may represent places they've been, others might be places they want to go, places they've visited in the past, or places in the news. This could be seen as a form of misrepresentation, albeit one created as an unavoidable side effect of this technique's basic assumptions. The solution is the same: expert knowledge and a full consideration of the extent to which deviations from the assumptions might harm the analysis.

Conclusion

As we have seen, the value of trace data inference techniques depends on differences between cases that can be expressed in terms of the four domains of technical design, TOS, social context, and potential for misrepresentation. The type of pre-research analysis demonstrated here will help researchers judge when particular techniques will be more and less effective. Unfortunately, there is no quantitative threshold to cleanly separate "effective" and "ineffective" research applications. Instead, researchers will have to make their cases based on the specifics of each situation and on prior research practice.

I hope I have made it clear that in many cases inferring individual characteristics from trace data will *not* be a straightforward affair. The staggering multiplicity of ways users can express gender, race/ethnicity, and location presents nontrivial challenges for both manual and computational methods. Moreover, in some research contexts none of the available methods will yield sufficient classification rates or levels of validity. There are no guarantees in research, especially when using data that was not created for that purpose. Only through shared empirical standards and frameworks will we be able to recognize the differences between higher- and lower-quality trace inferences.

The four dimensions of trace inference offer a useful framework for evaluating the construct validity of trace-based inferences. Each contributes independently to the quality of the argument that a given trace reliably and validly indicates a given concept within a given context. Clearly the technical design must enable the provision of certain traces for researchers to be able to analyze them, and so much the better if the design actively encourages it. A platform's TOS is almost as powerful in this regard, although its relevance depends upon how strictly it is enforced. Social context reminds us that inferential validity depends to a large extent on use: inferences that are valid in one context may not be in another. The same goes for the potential for misrepresentation, which is technically a special case of social context, but recurs frequently enough to warrant its own category.

While this chapter analyzed three types of trace inference techniques individually, I should point out that many studies base their inferences on multiple trace indicators. In studies that use machine-learning classification, multiple indicators are additive: the more of them point toward a particular category, the stronger the confidence that that category is the correct one. For example, using speech patterns and proper names together has been demonstrated to increase the percentage of correct gender classifications (Burger et al., 2011). But the framework introduced in this chapter suggests that inferences based on some traces may be inherently more valid than those based on others. Consider the difference in validity between classifying an individual as a woman, or Black, or in New York City because 1) she stated as much directly, 2) her name is disproportionately common among members of the first two categories, or 3) she tends to speak in ways typical of people in those categories. Per the previous section, it is possible, and likely in some cases, that the subsets of individuals given incorrect and "unknown" judgments will differ systematically across these three techniques. But perhaps even more importantly, we should ask ourselves: are the outcomes of each of these inference techniques really epistemologically equivalent?

This should direct us to think not only about how to maximize classification rates, but also about the reasons behind our misclassifications and the extent to which certain groups may be excluded from analysis. We already know that most social media platforms (aside from perhaps Facebook in some cases) are not representative of any broader offline population. Ignoring possible bias in our classification techniques may skew social media datasets even further. It seems important to know, for example, if a given technique works twice as well for one subpopulation as it does for another. To address this issue, we must understand how it applies to our particular datasets and introduce methods that include all the sub-populations relevant to our study.

The discussions above demonstrate the four dimensions' value for the specific characteristics of gender, R/E, and location, but it is not limited to them.

Articulating the dimensions at such a high level of abstraction allows them to be applied to other characteristics and platforms. They will almost certainly prove useful for the study of subjective concepts, which are not addressed in this chapter. And as platforms inevitably rise and fall in popularity and digital communication technologies continue to advance, these dimensions will retain their relevance because they are not tied to any single platform.

Methods, too, will continue to develop. As computational researchers, we find ourselves in something of an arms race with platform developers: as soon as methodological best practices for widely used traces begin to solidify, new traces emerge from which new inferences might be drawn. For example, in early 2016 Facebook expanded its menu of one-click reaction indicators from one (the "like" button) to six (new buttons for "love," "haha," "wow," "sad," and "angry"). Facebook executives may well intend and believe that these buttons transparently convey the sentiments on their labels across all users and contexts. But as I hope I have sufficiently argued here, such claims should only be established on a foundation of solid conceptual and empirical substantiation.

Notes

1 When users first sign up for a Facebook account, they must indicate that they are "Male" or "Female." They can access the more inclusive open-text option only after their account has been created.
2 Facebook's API does not grant access to this gender information, although it is visible to a user's friends and can also be accessed by Facebook apps with the user's permission.

References

Aragón, P., Kappler, K. E., Kaltenbrunner, A., Laniado, D., & Volkovich, Y. (2013). Communication dynamics in Twitter during political campaigns: The case of the 2011 Spanish national election. *Policy & Internet, 5*(2), 183–206. https://doi.org/10.1002/1944-2866.POI327

Bamman, D., Eisenstein, J., & Schnoebelen, T. (2014). Gender identity and lexical variation in social media. *Journal of Sociolinguistics, 18*(2), 135–160. https://doi.org/10.1111/josl.12080

Bowker, G. C. (2005). *Memory practices in the sciences.* Cambridge, MA: MIT Press.

Burger, J. D., Henderson, J., Kim, G., & Zarrella, G. (2011). Discriminating gender on Twitter. In *Proceedings of the Conference on Empirical Methods in Natural Language Processing* (pp. 1301–1309). Stroudsburg, PA, USA: Association for Computational Linguistics. Retrieved from http://dl.acm.org/citation.cfm?id=2145432.2145568

Campbell, D.T. (1979). Assessing the impact of planned social change. *Evaluation and Program Planning, 2*(1), 67–90. https://doi.org/10.1016/0149-7189(79)90048-X

Chang, J., Rosenn, I., Backstrom, L., & Marlow, C. (2010). ePluribus: Ethnicity on social networks. *ICWSM, 10,* 18–25.

Cheng, Z., Caverlee, J., & Lee, K. (2010). You are where you tweet: a content-based approach to geo-locating Twitter users. In *Proceedings of the 19th ACM International Conference on*

Information and Knowledge Management (pp. 759–768). New York, NY: ACM. https://doi.org/10.1145/1871437.1871535

Clayton, T. (2013, July 28). Black Twitter's best screen names. Retrieved from www.theroot.com/blog/the-grapevine/black_twitter_the_best_screen_names/

Conover, M. D., Ratkiewicz, J., Francisco, M., Goncalves, B., Flammini, A., & Menczer, F. (2011). Political polarization on Twitter. In *Proceedings of the 5th International Conference on Weblogs and Social Media* (pp. 89–96). Barcelona, Spain: AAAI.

Cresci, S., Di Pietro, R., Petrocchi, M., Spognardi, A., & Tesconi, M. (2015). Fame for sale: Efficient detection of fake Twitter followers. *Decision Support Systems, 80*, 56–71. https://doi.org/10.1016/j.dss.2015.09.003

Fiscella, K., & Fremont, A. M. (2006). Use of geocoding and surname analysis to estimate race and ethnicity. *Health Services Research, 41*(4p1), 1482–1500.

Flowers, A. (2015, June 10). The most common unisex names in America: Is yours one of them? Retrieved from http://fivethirtyeight.com/features/there-are-922-unisex-names-in-america-is-yours-one-of-them/

Freelon, D. (2010). Analyzing online political discussion using three models of democratic communication. *New Media & Society, 12*(7), 1172–1190.

Freelon, D. (2014). On the interpretation of digital trace data in communication and social computing research. *Journal of Broadcasting & Electronic Media, 58*(1), 59–75.

Freelon, D. (2015a). Discourse architecture, ideology, and democratic norms in online political discussion. *New Media & Society, 17*(5), 772–791. https://doi.org/10.1177/1461444813513259

Freelon, D. (2015b). On the cutting edge of big data: Digital politics research in the social computing literature. In S. Coleman & D. Freelon (Eds.), *Handbook of digital politics* (pp. 451–472). Northampton, MA: Edward Elgar.

Freelon, D., Becker, A. B., Lannon, B., & Pendleton, A. (2016). Narrowing the gap: Gender and mobilization in net neutrality advocacy. *International Journal of Communication, 10*(0), 5908–5930.

Freelon, D., & Karpf, D. (2015). Of big birds and bayonets: Hybrid Twitter interactivity in the 2012 presidential debates. *Information, Communication & Society, 18*(4), 390–406. https://doi.org/10.1080/1369118X.2014.952659

Freelon, D., Lynch, M., & Aday, S. (2015). Online fragmentation in wartime: A longitudinal analysis of tweets about Syria, 2011–2013. *The ANNALS of the American Academy of Political and Social Science, 659*(1), 166–179. https://doi.org/10.1177/0002716214563921

Freelon, D., McIlwain, C. D., & Clark, M. D. (in press). Quantifying the power and consequences of social media protest. *New Media & Society.*

Gerlitz, C., & Helmond, A. (2013). The like economy: Social buttons and the data-intensive web. *New Media & Society, 15*(8), 1348–1365. https://doi.org/10.1177/1461444812472322

Gitelman, L. (2013). *Raw data is an oxymoron.* Cambridge, MA: MIT Press.

Hecht, B., Hong, L., Suh, B., & Chi, E. H. (2011). Tweets from Justin Bieber's heart: The dynamics of the location field in user profiles. In *Proceedings of the SIGCHI Conference on Human Factors in Computing Systems* (pp. 237–246). New York, NY: ACM. https://doi.org/10.1145/1978942.1978976

Highfield, T. (2016). News via Voldemort: Parody accounts in topical discussions on Twitter. *New Media & Society, 18*(9), 2028–2045. https://doi.org/10.1177/14614448 15576703

Howison, J., Wiggins, A., & Crowston, K. (2011). Validity issues in the use of social network analysis with digital trace data. *Journal of the Association for Information Systems, 12*(12), 767–797.

Karpf, D. (2012). Social science research methods in internet time. *Information, Communication & Society, 15*(5), 639–661. https://doi.org/10.1080/1369118X.2012.665468

Lee, K., Eoff, B. D., & Caverlee, J. (2011). Seven months with the devils: A long-term study of content polluters on Twitter. In *Fifth International AAAI Conference on Weblogs and Social Media*. Retrieved from www.aaai.org/ocs/index.php/ICWSM/ICWSM11/paper/view/2780

Leetaru, K., Wang, S., Padmanabhan, A., & Shook, E. (2013). Mapping the global Twitter heartbeat: The geography of Twitter. *First Monday, 18*(5). https://doi.org/10.5210/fm.v18i5.4366

Li, R., Wang, S., Deng, H., Wang, R., & Chang, K. C.-C. (2012). Towards social user profiling: Unified and discriminative influence model for inferring home locations. In *Proceedings of the 18th ACM SIGKDD International Conference on Knowledge Discovery and Data Mining* (pp. 1023–1031). New York, NY: ACM. https://doi.org/10.1145/2339530.2339692

Liu, W., & Ruths, D. (2013). What's in a name? Using first names as features for gender inference in Twitter. In *AAAI Spring Symposium: Analyzing Microtext* (Vol. 13, p. 1). Retrieved from https://pdfs.semanticscholar.org/b60d/04043a60e46670f182b2debb4 85e9d17ce46.pdf

Mahmud, J., Nichols, J., & Drews, C. (2012). Where is this tweet from? Inferring home locations of Twitter users. In *Sixth International AAAI Conference on Weblogs and Social Media*. Retrieved from www.aaai.org/ocs/index.php/ICWSM/ICWSM12/paper/view/4605

Malik, M. M., Lamba, H., Nakos, C., & Pfeffer, J. (2015). Population bias in geotagged tweets. In *Ninth International AAAI Conference on Web and Social Media*. Retrieved from www.aaai.org/ocs/index.php/ICWSM/ICWSM15/paper/view/10662

Matias, J. N., Johnson, A., Boesel, W. E., Keegan, B., Friedman, J., & DeTar, C. (2015). *Reporting, reviewing, and responding to harassment on Twitter* (SSRN Scholarly Paper No. ID 2602018). Rochester, NY: Social Science Research Network. Retrieved from http://papers.ssrn.com/abstract=2602018

Metaxas, P., Mustafaraj, E., Wong, K., Zeng, L., O'Keefe, M., & Finn, S. (2015). What do retweets indicate? Results from user survey and meta-review of research. In *Ninth International AAAI Conference on Web and Social Media*. Citeseer. Retrieved from http://citeseerx.ist.psu.edu/viewdoc/download?doi=10.1.1.713.6936&rep=rep1&type=pdf

Mislove, A., Lehmann, S., Ahn, Y.-Y., Onnela, J.-P., & Rosenquist, J. N. (2011). Understanding the demographics of Twitter users. *ICWSM, 11*, 5th.

Morstatter, F., Pfeffer, J., Liu, H., & Carley, K. M. (2013). Is the sample good enough? Comparing data from Twitter's streaming api with Twitter's firehose. *Proceedings of ICWSM*. Retrieved from www.public.asu.edu/~fmorstat/paperpdfs/icwsm2013.pdf

Mueller, P. S., & van Huellen, S. (2012). A revolution in 140 characters? Reflecting on the role of social networking technologies in the 2009 Iranian post-election protests. *Policy & Internet, 4*(3–4), 184–205. https://doi.org/10.1002/poi3.16

Muller, B. (2012). *Genderator*. Python. Retrieved from https://github.com/bmuller/genderator

Nakamura, L. (1995). Race in/for cyberspace: Identity tourism and racial passing on the internet. *Works and Days, 25*(26), 13.

Peddinti, S. T., Ross, K. W., & Cappos, J. (2014). "On the internet, nobody knows you're a dog": A Twitter case study of anonymity in social networks. In *Proceedings of the Second ACM Conference on Online Social Networks* (pp. 83–94). New York, NY: ACM. https://doi.org/10.1145/2660460.2660467

Peersman, C., Daelemans, W., & Van Vaerenbergh, L. (2011). Predicting age and gender in online social networks. In *Proceedings of the 3rd International Workshop on Search and Mining User-generated Contents* (pp. 37–44). New York, NY: ACM. https://doi.org/10.1145/2065023.2065035

Sack, W. (2005). Discourse architecture and very large-scale conversation. In R. Latham & S. Sassen (Eds.), *Digital Formations: IT and New Architectures in the Global Realm*, 242–282.

Sap, M., Park, G., Eichstaedt, J. C., Kern, M. L., Stillwell, D., Kosinski, M., … Schwartz, H. A. (2014). Developing age and gender predictive lexica over social media. In *Proceedings of the 2014 Conference on Empirical Methods in Natural Language Processing (EMNLP)* (pp. 1146–1151).

Sloan, L., Morgan, J., Housley, W., Williams, M., Edwards, A., Burnap, P., & Rana, O. (2013). Knowing the tweeters: Deriving sociologically relevant demographics from Twitter. *Sociological Research Online, 18*(3), 7.

Sridharan, V., Shankar, V., & Gupta, M. (2012). Twitter games: How successful spammers pick targets. In *Proceedings of the 28th Annual Computer Security Applications Conference* (pp. 389–398). New York, NY: ACM. https://doi.org/10.1145/2420950.2421007

Stefanidis, A., Crooks, A., & Radzikowski, J. (2013). Harvesting ambient geospatial information from social media feeds. *GeoJournal, 78*(2), 319–338.

Stringhini, G., Wang, G., Egele, M., Kruegel, C., Vigna, G., Zheng, H., & Zhao, B. Y. (2013). Follow the green: Growth and dynamics in Twitter follower markets. In *Proceedings of the 2013 Conference on Internet Measurement Conference* (pp. 163–176). New York, NY: ACM. https://doi.org/10.1145/2504730.2504731

Thomas, K., Grier, C., & Paxson, V. (2012). Adapting social spam infrastructure for political censorship. Presented as part of the 5th USENIX Workshop on Large-Scale Exploits and Emergent Threats. Retrieved from www.usenix.org/conference/leet12/workshop-program/presentation/thomas

Verkamp, J.-P., & Gupta, M. (2013). Five incidents, one theme: Twitter spam as a weapon to drown voices of protest. Presented as part of the 3rd USENIX Workshop on Free and Open Communications on the Internet. Retrieved from www.usenix.org/conference/foci13/workshop-program/presentation/verkamp

Wright, S., & Street, J. (2007). Democracy, deliberation and design: The case of online discussion forums. *New Media & Society, 9*(5), 849.

7

THE TECHNICAL, THE PERSONAL, AND THE POLITICAL

Understanding Journalists and News Users' Engagement in *The New York Times* Comments Section

Ashley Muddiman

Ever since The New York Times and other news organizations began allowing comments on their sites, journalists have been concerned about the amount and level of discourse that appears in comment sections. Clark Hoyt (2007), the public editor of The New York Times when the paper launched comments on news stories, summed up this concern well when he stated, "How does the august Times, which has long stood for dignified authority, come to terms with the fractious, democratic culture of the Internet, where readers expect to participate but sometimes do so in coarse, bullying and misinformed ways?" Nearly ten years after Hoyt first asked his question, many questions remain about comment section behavior as media organizations attempt to balance the desire for engagement with their site visitors and the desire to keep some element of control over comment content.

This chapter examines the influences of commenting behavior. Specifically, the chapter raises three questions: How does the discourse architecture of a news comment section affect engagement with that comment section? How does interaction with commenters influence future commenting behavior? And does a political context influence any of these patterns?

Dataset: New York Times Comments

To answer these questions, I used a dataset of 9.6 million comments from The New York Times website. These comments made up all of the comments posted to The New York Times website between October 30, 2007—when The New York Times opened up comments to news stories instead of only blogs and entertainment pieces (Hoyt, 2007)—and August 13, 2013. The data are unique not only in size but also in the breadth of information provided. The timeline of the comments included a redesign of The New York Times comment section in late-November 2011, which allowed me to examine how the technical characteristics of a comment section can influence the comments. The dataset also included both behavioral information and the full text content for each comment. These characteristics of the dataset are described below.

Behavioral Variables

The data included behavioral information that indicated when a news user or a journalist interacted with a comment. When news users visit The New York Times comment section, each comment provides two user interaction buttons: a recommendation button in one corner of a comment and a flag button in a different corner. The recommendation button allows site visitors to signal their approval of a comment whereas the flag button allows site visitors to signal their disapproval with a comment that they feel is abusive in some way. Throughout this chapter, I approach these variables as either present—that is, a comment received at least one recommendation or at least one abuse flag for a comment—or absent—that is, a comment did not receive a recommendation or did not receive an abuse flag. Overall, 78.8 percent of the comments that were approved for publication on the site received at least one recommendation, and 2.1 percent of the comments that were approved received at least one abuse flag.

Journalist interaction variables also were included. Unlike many news sites, The New York Times has an active community editing team made up of journalists who moderate the comment section. The team uses pre-moderation, meaning that journalists screen comments *before* they are posted online, and also engages with comments after they are approved. Journalists could interact with the comments in a number of ways. First, The New York Times dataset was unique in part because it included both comments that were approved for the site—and thus became part of the public commenting record—*and* comments that were rejected from the site by the journalist moderating team—and thus never became public. Examining the rejection data allows me to determine the characteristics of the comments that journalists did not consider suitable for publication on The New York Times comment section. Further, journalists could read the comments approved for publication and decide to prominently feature some of the comments that are representative of the discussion in the comment section (Sullivan, 2013). These prominently featured comments are known as NYT Picks. Finally, journalists had the option of posting a reply to a comment thread below a news article in response to another comment. Thus, journalists had the opportunity to disapprove of a comment (by rejecting it from the site), to approve of a comment (by selecting it as a NYT Pick), or to interact with the individuals participating in a comment thread (by replying to a comment on the site). Overall, 14.4 percent of the comments posted to The New York Times comment section were rejected from the site by a journalist, 2.1 percent of the comments were selected as NYT Picks, and 0.1 percent of the comments were replies from journalists.

These five behavioral variables—user recommendations, user abuse flags, journalist rejections, journalist NYT Picks, and journalist replies—provide rich data to investigate the many ways news organizations and news users engage with comment sections.

Comment Content

The New York Times dataset also included the full text of every comment posted to the site. Of interest for this project were two sets of content: political content and uncivil content. These two comment types were chosen due to their centrality in scholarly research that investigates comment sections. Specifically, comment sections often are decried for including content that is too partisan (see, for description, Freelon, 2015) or too uncivil (Coe, Kenski, & Rains, 2014). Comments are feared to lack the respectful tone necessary for deliberative discussions (e.g., Fishkin & Luskin, 2005; Stromer-Galley, 2007). By examining this content in The New York Times comments, I determine whether political and uncivil comments are treated differently by site visitors and journalists.

Given the expansive dataset, human coding of all of the comments was not an option; but, since incivility is difficult to code even when it is possible to use human coders, computer-aided content analysis alone would likely not provide a valid measure of incivility. Thus, I took a two-step approach, which is presented in detail in Appendix A. In short, I, first, I developed two dictionaries—one that included political words and one that included uncivil words—and used human coding to determine whether each word should be included in each dictionary. Second, I ran computer-aided content analysis to determine whether each dictionary was present in each of the 9.6 million comments in the dataset. The political dictionary included any words signaling that the comment mentioned politics, for instance terms related to politics in general (e.g., mayor, veto), partisanship (e.g., partisan, extremist, Obama, Bush, dems, repubs), citizenship (e.g., citizen, voter), and political extremes (e.g., Stalin, Hitler). Forty-two percent of the comments in the dataset included a reference to at least one word in the political dictionary.

Presence of uncivil content is trickier to determine, and many researchers note the difficultly in defining the concept (e.g., Coe et al., 2014; Maisel, 2012). For the purposes of the current study, incivility is a mix of words that violate both politeness norms, such as namecalling and swearing (Mutz, 2015), and democratic norms, such as discrimination and threatening democratic rights (Papacharissi, 2004). The incivility dictionary included words related to profanity (e.g., BS, damn), namecalling (e.g., dumb, insane), discrimination (e.g., racist, bigotry), threats to democracy (e.g., treason, traitor), misinformation (e.g., deceive, mislead), dysfunction (e.g., unconstitutional, obstructionist), and other terms related to incivility (e.g., disrespect, yell). Notably, the comments could be uncivil themselves *or* they could be describing the incivility of someone else. Either way, the comment references incivility. Eleven percent of the comments in the dataset included at least one of the words in the incivility dictionary. Using the behavioral variables and the content variables present in the dataset, I am able to examine the technical affordances of the comment section, the effects of comment interaction, and the different patterns that appear for political/nonpolitical and uncivil/civil comments.

The Technical: Effects of a Comment Section Redesign

Technical characteristics of comment sections can influence how users engage with comments. Comment sections that allow anonymous commenting, for instance, may include more incivility than comment sections that do not allow anonymous commenting (Santana, 2014). Changing an engagement button from "Like" or "Recommend" to "Respect" can prompt comment section users to become less partisan in their use of online buttons (Stroud, Muddiman, & Scacco, 2017). Most closely related to the current project, Freelon (2015) found that the way in which a comment section structures discussion through an assemblage of technical features—or its discourse architecture—is related to the norms present in the comment section. For example, Twitter, with its promotion of short messages and hashtags that allow users to follow a discussion of specific issues, encourages different types of comments than news organizations that typically allow commenters to post individual thoughts directly under news articles and provide little structure to promote community building. Freelon (2015) determined that Twitter's discourse architecture encouraged comments that aligned with communitarian norms, like acknowledging a political in-group and using calls to action, whereas the architecture of news site commenting sections' promoted comments that aligned with deliberative (e.g., asking cross-cutting questions) and liberal individualistic norms (e.g., posting monologues).

In sum, the technical affordances present in a comment section may affect commenting practices. Yet previous research generally has compared the comment content posted to two or more different comment spaces that have different technical designs. The New York Times dataset, since it includes comments posted to the site across a seven year period, offers a novel context: investigating how changes to the design of a comment section relate to changes in commenting behavior on the *same* website. Essentially, I ask, what happens to commenting when the discourse architecture of a comment section is altered?

In November 2011, The New York Times launched a redesigned comment section. Before the change, commenters were only able to make comments on website content by clicking on a "comments" link below an article or blog, which opened the comment section on a new webpage. After the redesign, the comment section was placed directly below the article text, allowing commenters to more

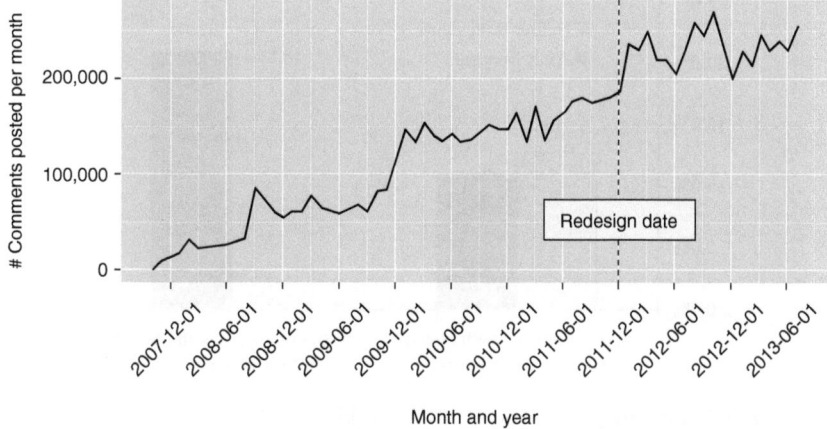

FIGURE 7.1 Number of Comments Posted Each Month from November 2007 to July 2013

easily make comments without leaving the article page. Additionally, although abuse flag buttons were included in the comment section both before and after the redesign, the button was always visible before the redesign whereas after the redesign the button was hidden unless a user hovered a cursor over the correct spot on a comment.[1] In this first set of analyses, I examine whether the changes in the discourse architecture of The New York Times comment section altered the number of comments posted, the content and moderation of the comments, and the way news users interacted with recommendations and abuse flags.

The redesign affected the number of comments posted to the site. News users took advantage of the new design. As illustrated in Figure 7.1, the number of comments posted to The New York Times website per month generally increased over time. Important for the current study, there was a notable uptick in the number of comments posted per month after the November 2011 redesign. After the redesign, there was no month in which the number of comments posted dipped below the number of comments posted a month prior to the redesign, suggesting that the ease of access prompted users to post more comments to the site.[2]

Although it is important to determine whether technical affordances influence the *amount* of engagement with a comment section, the *content* of that engagement also is important to consider.[3] The increase in number of comments on the site could overwhelm human moderators and make it more difficult for them to filter out comments that do not meet the standards a news organization sets out in its commenting policy.

At least for The New York Times, however, this fear was not justified. The percentage of all comments posted to the site that included at least one uncivil word decreased slightly after the redesign (see Figure 7.2).

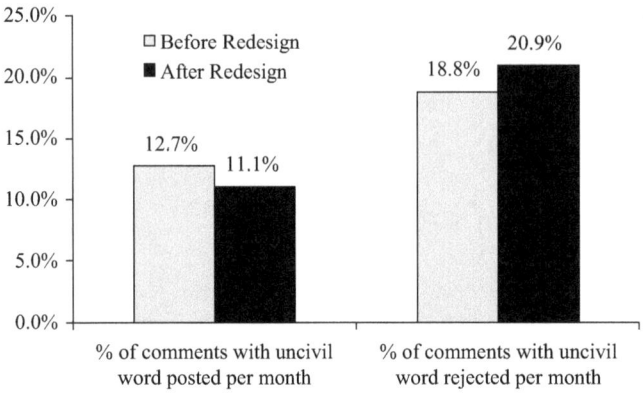

FIGURE 7.2 Percentage of Comments with Uncivil Word Posted and Rejected per Month

The modest decrease in uncivil comment content raises a further question—did the journalists moderating the comment section begin to reject a smaller percentage of comments as well? Fortunately, The New York Times dataset included comments that were rejected by the journalist moderators who evaluated the appropriateness of each comment. In total, comments that contained uncivil words were rejected 20 percent of the time whereas comments that did not contain words from the uncivil dictionary were rejected 14 percent of the time. Even though the percentage of comments that contained uncivil language decreased after the redesign, the percentage of comments with uncivil words that were rejected by moderators *increased* after the redesign (see Figure 7.2).

Overall, the redesign prompted site visitors to post a smaller percentage of comments with uncivil words and journalists to reject a larger percentage of comments with uncivil words. The change in discourse architecture of The New York Times website prompted a modestly more civil commenting space.

The New York Times discourse architecture also influenced how site visitors used recommendations and abuse flags in the comment section. These buttons allow visitors to express their approval or disapproval of any comment. The popularity of online content can affect individuals' willingness to pay attention to that content (Knobloch-Westerwick, Sharma, Hansen, & Alter, 2005; Messing & Westwood, 2012), making it important to understand how people engage with interaction tools like these in the first place.

It is helpful to compare the potential effects of a technological structure that changed—here, the abuse flag button— to a structure that did not—here, the recommendation button. After the comment section redesign, there was a nearly 2 percent decrease in the percentage of comments that received an abuse flag (see Figure 7.3). Visibility, or in this case lack of visibility of the abuse flag button, may have reduced the use of abuse flags slightly.

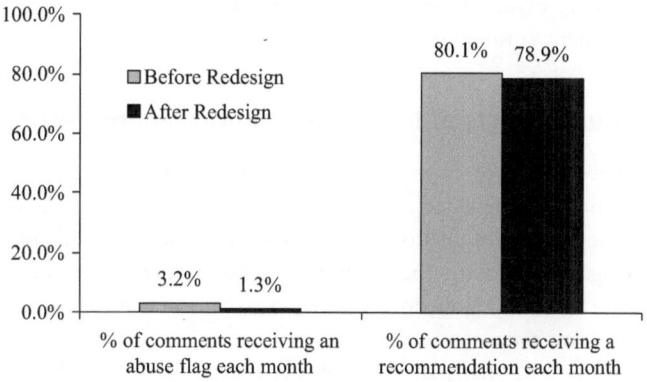

FIGURE 7.3 Percentage of Comments Receiving Abuse Flags or Recommendations

However, even though the recommendation button did not change dramatically after the site redesign, there also was a slight decrease of approximately 1 percent in the percentage of comments that received a recommendation (see Figure 7.3). The decrease in recommendation button use nearly mirrored the decrease in abuse flag use, although a 2 percent decrease in abuse flag use made up a greater *percentage* decrease (66.7%) than the 1 percent recommendation use decrease (1.2%). This result deserves more attention in future research. It may be the case that the redesign simply prompted site visitors to engage with buttons slightly less than they did prior to the redesign. Alternatively, the design features related to visibility could have discouraged use of the abuse flag specifically.

This analysis of The New York Times comment section redesign demonstrates that choices about the technical aspects of a comment section affect site visitor engagement with a comment section. By examining engagement with a news comment section both before and after a technical redesign of a comment section of a website, the results provide evidence to support Freelon's (2015) discourse architecture approach to comment sections.

The comment section itself became more visible after the redesign. The number of comments posted to the website increased after the redesign, likely because the comments themselves moved from a separate webpage to the space directly under the news story. As visibility of the comment section increased, so did the number of comments posted to the site. Abuse flags, alternatively, decreased slightly after the redesign, perhaps because the abuse flag was not automatically visible on a comment after the redesign. The redesign seemed to prompt a lower percentage of uncivil comments, as well, compared to the percentage posted prior to the redesign. The New York Times did not dramatically change the format of the comment section—for instance, it did not switch to a social media format—but the changes in the technical design of the site led to different commenting patterns, providing evidence that even small differences in discourse architecture can affect comment content and behavior (Freelon, 2015).

The Individual: Effects of Interactivity in Comment Sections

Thus far, I have discussed how a change in the discourse architecture of The New York Times comment section influenced site visitor and journalist engagement with the comment section. I now flip the question and ask whether (and how) engagement with the comment section affects the individuals who comment. In other words, how do commenters react when another user or a journalist interacts with their comments?

Interactivity is a hallmark attribute of the internet generally (Eveland, 2003) and comment sections specifically (Ziegele, Breiner, & Quiring, 2014). News organizations, which are not always keen to release control of their content to their audiences, commonly include interactive elements on their sites, ranging from interactive polls to social media sharing tools (Stroud, Muddiman, & Scacco, 2015).

Stromer-Galley's (2004) approach to interactivity is helpful in the context of a comment section. Much of the interactivity on news sites is what Stromer-Galley (2004) calls interactivity-as-product, meaning that the interaction is between a person and a technology rather than directly with another person. For instance, clicking on a hyperlink or taking an online news poll could be considered interactivity-as-product. Comment sections also are capable of interactivity-as-process, which Stromer-Galley (2004) describes as person-to-person communication that happens to use technology as a mediating process. For instance, the replies that journalists make to comments posted to commenting threads after an article count as interactivity-as-process because a journalist responds to a commenter and indicates to other commenters that a human is involved in the commenting process.

Yet where some interactive tools stand in this dichotomous approach to interactivity is unclear. Recommendations and NYT Picks on The New York Times site, in particular, involve interaction with an interactive tool rather than directly with another person. Indeed, it is possible that a person who writes a recommended or NYT Pick comment never even finds out that someone has interacted with that comment. These buttons, then, could be considered interactivity-as-product. Yet some element of person-to-person interactivity occurs even with the interactive buttons in a comment section because a person wrote the comment and another person recommended the comment or chose it as a NYT Pick.

The focus of this section is to investigate whether interactivity-as-product and interactivity-as-process lead to more engagement with a comment section in the future. Specifically, do recommendations and NYT Picks prompt commenters to post more comments in the future? Additionally, does a journalist's reply in a comment thread relate to more or less commenting and more or less uncivil content in that comment thread? Answering these questions will help determine whether site tools and human engagement in comment sections should be approached as examples of interactivity-as-process.

First, I explore what happens when site visitors and journalists interact with commenters via the interactive tools available on The New York Times website by asking: Does a commenter who receives a first recommendation or a first NYT Pick post more comments after that interaction than before? In the analysis, I focus on the *first* time a commenter posted a comment that received at least one recommendation or a NYT Pick. I found each person's first comment that received a recommendation or a NYT Pick. Then I computed the number of comments the person posted in the 30 days before posting that comment and compared it to the number of comments the person posted in the 30 days after.

When a commenter received the first recommendation, the interaction prompted an increase in commenting behavior over the next 30 days.[4,5] Similarly, when a commenter received a first NYT Pick, that commenter posted more comments to the site in the 30 days after the NYT Pick than in the 30 days before (see Figure 7.4).[6]

A site visitor or journalist who engaged with comments through technology—either by clicking a "recommendation" button or moving a comment to a featured "NYT Picks" section of an article's commenting space—encouraged commenters to engage in the comment space more often in the future. Although neither of these behaviors involves two people directly communicating through a comment section, they did spark more interactivity from commenters, suggesting that they may represent more than interactivity-as-product.

I now turn to a clearer type of interactivity-as-process: journalist replies to comments. Journalist engagement in comment sections has become a topic of heated debate. On one hand, some argue that comment spaces are the domain of

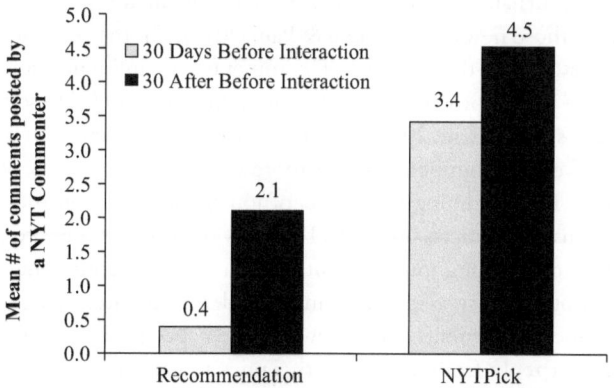

FIGURE 7.4 Mean Number of Comments Posted 30 Days Before and After a First Recommendation or a First NYT Pick

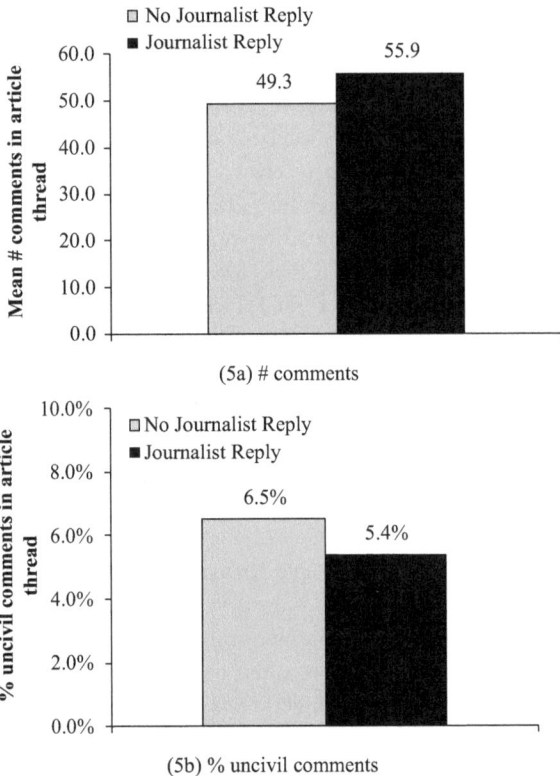

(5a) # comments

(5b) % uncivil comments

FIGURE 7.5 Mean Number of Comments and Mean Percentage of Uncivil Comments Posted to Article's Comment Section Threads

news users, and journalists who encroach on this domain are threatening the free speech rights of those news users (Chen & Pain, 2016). On the other hand, studies have demonstrated that the content of comments can influence how individuals interpret an article posted above the comment section (Anderson, Brossard, Scheufele, Xenos, & Ladwig, 2014) and that journalist interaction in a comment section can make that comment section more civil (Stroud, Scacco, Muddiman, & Curry, 2015). By examining the effects of journalist replies on the content of comment streams after articles posted to The New York Times website, I both add to the literature concerning journalist interaction with the comments *and* determine whether interactivity-as-process can engender more interactivity-as-process by promoting more comments after a news article. I specifically examine whether the presence of a reply from a New York Times journalist is related to various comment thread differences. Does a reply from a journalist occur in comment section threads with more or fewer comments in general and with more or fewer uncivil comments specifically in a comment thread after an article?

As Figure 7.5 demonstrates, comment threads with journalist replies were longer—that is, they had more comments—than comment threads without journalist replies.[7] Additionally, journalist replies occurred in comment threads with slightly fewer uncivil comments than threads with no reporter replies. Causality cannot be determined here, but previous research suggests that the presence of a journalist in a comment section can cause a decrease in incivility on a site (Stroud, Scacco, Muddiman, & Curry, 2015). The New York Times dataset provides longer-term evidence that this may be the case on news sites. Journalist replies may behave as interactivity-as-process by prompting more, and more civil, interactions among site visitors in the comment section.

The Political: Differences between Political and Nonpolitical Comments

The New York Times dataset included all comments posted to the site between 2007 and 2013. This means that the comments were posted to all types of article content on the New York Times website, including news, blogs, entertainment, and any other type of article that was open to commenting. Yet it is not clear whether site visitors and journalists behave similarly when engaging with political and nonpolitical content. Partisanship has become a prominent social identity for many individuals (Iyengar, Sood, & Lelkes, 2012), and there is evidence that political partisans use online buttons in ways that align with their partisan identity (Stroud, Muddiman, & Scacco, 2017). Thus, site visitors may interact differently with political than nonpolitical comments.

Journalists, similarly, may treat political and nonpolitical comments differently. Comment sections often are evaluated based on the prevalence of uncivil comment content (e.g., Coe et al., 2014; Stroud, Scacco, Muddiman, & Curry, 2015; see, for exception, Freelon, 2015). Yet established news values for political coverage, such as emphasis on conflict and support of political free speech (e.g., Gans, 2004/1979; Semetko & Valkenburg, 2000), may make the decision to reject incivility in comments more difficult for journalists. Journalists may allow more incivility—which centers on conflict with interpersonal and political norms—in political comments compared to nonpolitical comments.

For these reasons, the final question of this chapter asks: are patterns of political and nonpolitical commenting different? Potential differences between political and nonpolitical content could arise in three areas: discourse architecture, comment interaction, and comment incivility.

Political Content and Discourse Architecture

Technical affordances influenced political and nonpolitical comment content differently. Examining a baseline measure of engagement with comments—number of comments posted before and after the comment section redesign—demonstrated

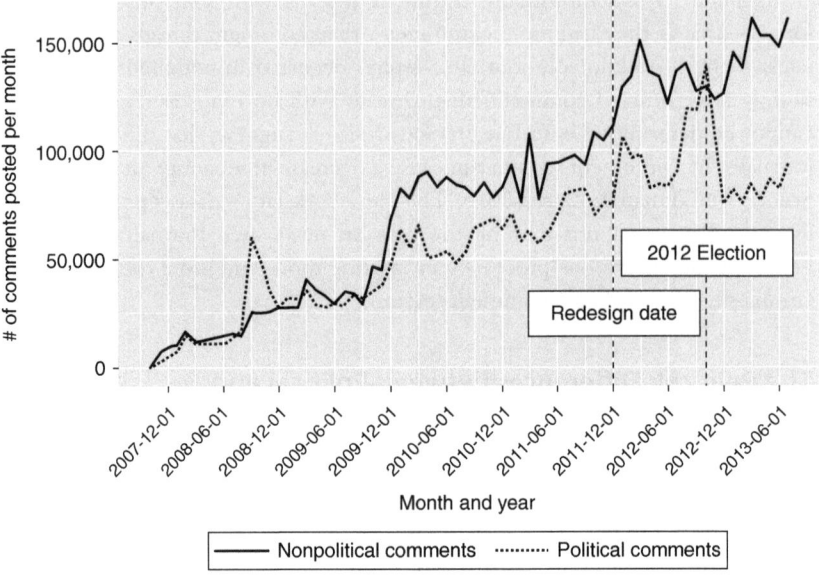

FIGURE 7.6 Number of Political and Nonpolitical Comments Posted Each Month from November 2007 to July 2013

that the redesign affected different types of content in unique ways (see Figure 7.6). Although comments with political terms and comments without political terms generally increased over time, it was comments *without* political terms that saw the most drastic increase after the redesign. Political comments, even though the redesign occurred just before the 2012 election year, increased immediately after the redesign, spiked again in the months leading up to the 2012 election, then decreased considerably after the election.

There are at least two possibilities for the difference in number of political and nonpolitical comments before and after the redesign, though neither can be tested directly with the current dataset. First, it may be that commenters posting political material are more motivated to comment. Political partisans tend to be more likely to participate in a number of political behaviors, including voting (Bartels, 2000) and sharing news on social media (Weeks & Holbert, 2013). In comment sections, people interested in posting a political comment also may be determined to participate no matter whether a comment section is on a separate page from a news story. Thus, the movement of a comment thread to a location directly below site content may have prompted more people who were less politically motivated to take advantage of an easy-to-access comment section.

Second, the difference may be due to the content of the articles where the comment sections were located. In order to keep the number of comments posted per day manageable for the group of journalists who moderate the comment section, comments are not open on every New York Times news story (Etim,

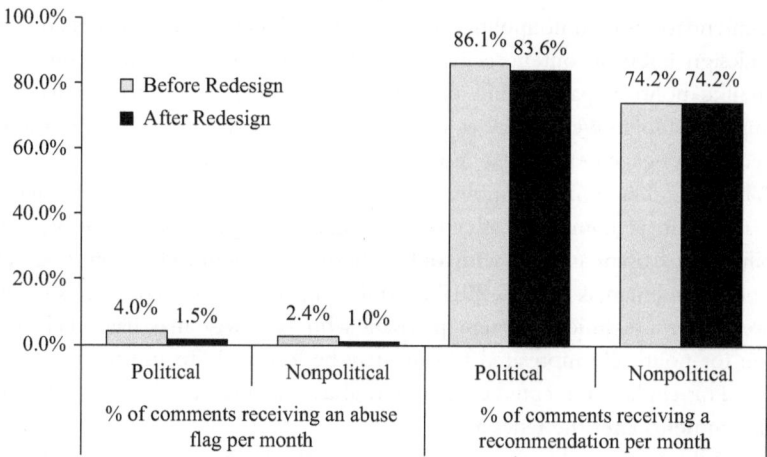

FIGURE 7.7 Mean% of Political and Nonpolitical Comments that Received an Abuse Flag per Month and that Received a Recommendation per Month Before and After NYT Redesign

n.d.). Therefore, it is possible that there was something about the articles that included comments after the redesign compared to the articles that included comments prior to the redesign. Although both of these suggestions are possible, The New York Times dataset did not include information about the type of article posted (e.g., science, politics) or about the individual differences (e.g., partisan identities) of its commenters.

The redesign affected user interactions with political and nonpolitical content slightly differently as well. In the dataset overall, 2 percent of nonpolitical comments and 3 percent of political comments received an abuse flag. For both political and nonpolitical content, the percentage of comments that received an abuse flag was higher before the redesign than after (see Figure 7.7). Political comments saw a slightly larger reduction in abuse flag usage (decrease of 2.5%) than nonpolitical comments (decrease of 1.4%), making the percentage of comments with abuse flags nearly equal for political and nonpolitical comments after the redesign.

Similarly, the redesign affected recommendations for political more than nonpolitical comments. Overall, 74 percent of comments without politics received at least one recommendation and 85 percent of comments with political content received at least one recommendation. The average percentage of nonpolitical comments that received recommendations each month remained the same before and after the redesign (see Figure 7.7). Political comments showed a slightly different pattern, such that the average percentage of comments that received recommendations each month decreased by about 2.5 percent after the redesign.

The data demonstrate that political comments prompted more interactivity overall from site visitors. Political comments received more abuse flags and more recommendations than nonpolitical comments, both before the redesign and after the redesign. Political content seems to prompt more engagement with comments, much like political partisanship prompts more voting and social media news sharing (Knobloch-Westerwick et al., 2005; Messing & Westwood, 2012), though that edge in engagement shrank modestly after the redesign.

Why did interactions with political comments decrease more than interactions with nonpolitical comments after the redesign? One potential reason is, again, visibility. If partisans engage with online buttons in politically motivated ways (Stroud, Muddiman, & Scacco, 2017), and if a digital button becomes less visually apparent after a technical redesign, partisans who otherwise may have clicked the button for politically motivated reasons may be less likely to use the less visible button. This explanation could explain why abuse flag use decreased most for political comments after the redesign.

If visibility is the only explanation, however, the finding that political content *recommendation* use decreased is surprising since the recommendation button did not change substantially. Perhaps the redesign was disorienting and made people less likely to engage with a comment simply because everything looked a little different. However, if this were the case, recommendations should have decreased similarly for both political and nonpolitical comments. Instead, there likely is something different about the political comments that changed after the redesign but that also was not captured in the current dataset.

In sum, the redesign prompted an increase in nonpolitical comments compared to political comments and a decrease in percentage of political comments that received abuse flags and recommendations. The analysis suggests that the redesign differently influenced commenting behavior related to nonpolitical and political comments. Future research can examine exactly *why* this was the case.

Political Content and Effects of Interaction

Although the redesign differently influenced interactions with political and nonpolitical comments, the effects of that interaction did not differ for political and nonpolitical comments. A commenter's first recommendation on either type of comment prompted an increase in commenting behavior (see Figure 7.8). After a commenter posted a comment that received the commenter's first recommendation, commenting behavior increased in the next 30 days for both political and nonpolitical comments. Similarly to the recommendation results, commenters who made a comment that was selected as a NYT Pick posted more comments to the site in the 30 days after the NYT Pick than in the 30 days before (see Figure 7.8). This effect was consistent across political and nonpolitical comments. Thus, it appears that when a commenter receives a recommendation or a NYT Pick for a comment, no matter whether the comment is political or nonpolitical, that commenter may be encouraged to post more comments on The New York Times website in the near future.

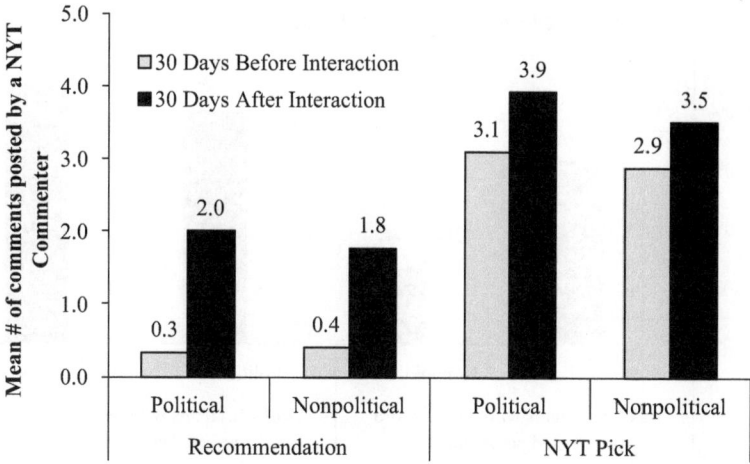

FIGURE 7.8 Mean Number of Political and Nonpolitical Comments Posted 30 Days Before and After a First Recommendation or a First NYT Pick

Political Content and Comment Incivility

Similar to the redesign and in contrast to comment interactions, differences appeared between political and nonpolitical comments when incivility was included in the analysis. Uncivil words were more prevalent in comments that included political words than in comments that did not include political words. Uncivil words appeared in 7 percent of comments without political words and in 17 percent of comments with political words. Comments without politics were rejected at a slightly higher rate (15%) than comments with politics (14%). When uncivil and political words both appeared in a comment, the difference between rejected comments and non-rejected comments grew larger. Comments that mentioned politics *and* at least one uncivil word were rejected at a rate of 19 percent whereas comments that included at least one uncivil word but no political words were rejected at a rate of 21 percent.

The redesign of The New York Times comment section affected both political and nonpolitical comments that included incivility, though the effects were differently sized for different types of content. For both political and nonpolitical comments, the percentage of posted comments that included the incivility dictionary decreased after the redesign (see Figure 7.9). The decrease was slightly larger for political comments. The percentage of nonpolitical comments with uncivil words decreased by 1.4 percent per month, slightly less than the 2.5 percent per month decrease in political comments that contained the uncivil dictionary. The decreases were modest but, considering that there were not a large percentage of comments with incivility in the first place, notable. The decrease in political comments with incivility, for instance, translated to 91,406 fewer uncivil comments posted after the redesign.

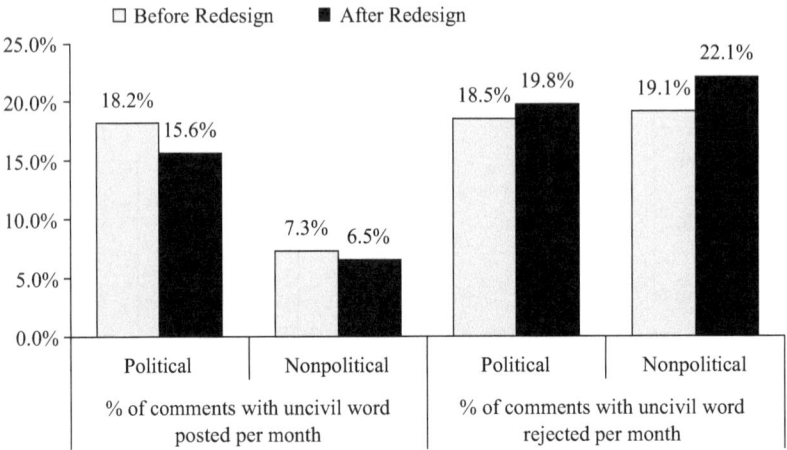

FIGURE 7.9 Mean% of Political and Nonpolitical Comments that Included an Incivility Word per Month and Mean% of Political and Nonpolitical Uncivil Comments Rejected per Month Before and After NYT Redesign

To determine whether the redesign affected journalist decisions in moderating comments that included incivility, I examined the percentage of political and nonpolitical comments that included uncivil words that were rejected from the site each month before and after the redesign. The increase in rejection of uncivil comments was greatest for comments that did not contain political content (see Figure 7.9). The change between the percentage per month that were rejected before and after the redesign was 3 percent, another small change but one that was twice as large as the change in rate of rejection (1.3%) before and after the redesign for comments with uncivil and *political* language.

Similarly, the comment threads in which journalists engaged were different when political rather than nonpolitical comments appeared in the thread. When a comment thread on an article included no political comments but included at least one reply from a journalist, the mean number of comments posted on that thread was substantially higher than the mean number of comments posted on a nonpolitical thread that did not include a journalist reply (see Figure 7.10a). Contrastingly, for comment threads that had at least one political comment, a reply from a journalist had nearly no effect on the number of comments posted to the thread. In sum, it seems that comment threads with journalist replies have more comments than threads with no journalist replies but only when the comment thread is nonpolitical.

Journalist replies also related to patterns of uncivil political and nonpolitical comments (see Figure 7.10b). In comment threads with no political comments, the presence of a journalist reply decreased the likelihood of a presence of uncivil comments by less than 1 percent. Article comment threads that contained at least

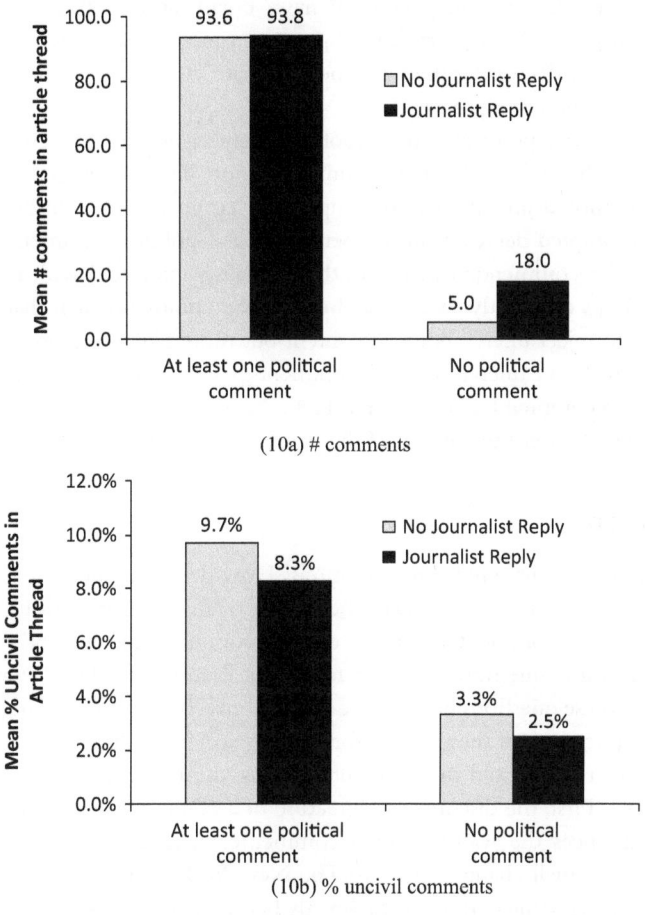

(10a) # comments

(10b) % uncivil comments

FIGURE 7.10 Mean # of Comments and Mean% of Uncivil Comments Posted in the Comment Thread of an Article Depending on the Presence or Absence of a Journalist Reply in that Thread

one political comment, however, were 1.4 percent less uncivil when there was at least one journalist reply in the comment thread.

Journalists at The New York Times treated incivility slightly differently when it appeared in comments with political language than when it appeared in comments without political language. A higher percentage of nonpolitical content with incivility was rejected by journalists than political content with incivility, a pattern that became slightly stronger after the redesign. Further, journalist replies to a comment thread did not substantially change the number of comments posted to a political thread but did relate to a lower percentage of uncivil comments in a political comment thread. Journalists did not seem comfortable outright rejecting political content with incivility, which aligns with previous research concerning political news norms and conflict (e.g., Semetko & Valkenburg, 2000). Yet journalists' engagement in comments sections may have played a role in decreasing the likelihood that site visitors posted uncivil content in political commenting spaces.

In many ways, political and nonpolitical content led to different patterns of behavior in The New York Times comment section. The redesign of the comment section promoted an increase in nonpolitical compared to political comment, but also prompted decreases in the percentages of political comments that were flagged and recommended each month. Journalists interacted with uncivil *political* comments differently than uncivil *nonpolitical* comments such that they were less likely to reject uncivil political content but more likely to reply to comment threads with fewer uncivil political comments. Contrastingly, when commenters received a recommendation or NYT Pick, they were likely to post more future comment no matter the content of the original comment.

Conclusion

This chapter has answered three questions: How does the discourse architecture of a comment section affect engagement with that comment section? How does interaction with commenters influence future commenting behavior? And are the answers to these questions different for political and nonpolitical content? The answers to these questions have been detailed above, leaving one last inquiry: what are the implications of these results for scholars and journalists?

To scholars interested in comment sections, the results provide a number of key insights. First, the discourse architecture of a comment section (e.g., Freelon, 2015) influences the way in which commenters engage with the space. Even the relatively small changes made to The New York Times comment section— including moving the comments to directly below an article and making the abuse flag less visible—influences the amount of content and interactive behaviors used by site visitors and journalists.

Second, interactivity needs more theorizing. Stromer-Galley (2004) made an important stride in discussing the difference between interactivity-as-product and interactivity-as-process. Yet the characteristics of comment sections straddle the boundary between these two types of interactivity. As the analyses in this chapter indicated, interaction with a digital tool in the comment section might prompt a person to write more comments in the future. Scholars should consider thinking of interactivity within the larger process of comment sections to complicate the approach to engagement with news sites.

Finally, the moments in which political and nonpolitical comments behaved differently are important to consider. Journalist replies made political comment threads more civil but did little to prompt more discussion in a comment thread. More generally, both users and journalists seemed to be more accepting of incivility when it occurred with political content than when it occurred with nonpolitical content. The potential discrepancy should be taken into account in future research—incivility may be more prevalent in political posts, but perhaps also more acceptable to news users and journalists in those political posts than in nonpolitical posts.

Practically, journalists and news organizations can learn from the results. First, they need to carefully consider the technological structure in their comment sections. Even small elements like whether an abuse flag is or is not visible to site visitors may affect commenting behavior. Testing new comment section designs prior to publishing them is necessary, especially if a change could decrease engagement with a site.

Additionally, the current study is the second recent project demonstrating that journalist involvement in the comment section can decrease incivility in a political comment thread (see also Stroud, Scacco, Muddiman, & Curry, 2015). If decreasing incivility is a goal of a news organization, encouraging the journalists to post a comment or two after their stories can help make strides toward reaching that goal.

This point leads to a final take-away for journalists and news organizations: consider the values most appropriate for the comment section on your news page. Deliberative norms would favor balanced discussion and civil discourse whereas more traditional news norms would favor allowing incivility for the sake of conflict and free speech, particularly in political comments. The New York Times leaned toward the second option, rejecting nonpolitical uncivil content at a higher rate than uncivil political content. There might be a trade off between these two approaches, however, so journalists should be clear about the goals of their own comment sections.

A few limitations are of note given the dataset and are useful for anyone considering big data analysis to consider. Most prominently, coding for incivility is difficult even when using human coding. Computer-aided content analysis, which is necessary with a dataset the size of the one discussed in the current chapter, adds another layer of difficulty. If people cannot agree on what is uncivil, teaching a computer to identify it is a difficult task. The dictionary approach, while helpful in identifying words that relate to a number of types of incivility, can only identify comments that reference some uncivil word. The approach cannot tell researchers whether a commenter is *engaging* in incivility or simply discussing an example of incivility that has made its way into the traditional news content. Small-scale human content analysis would be helpful in filling in this detail.

Next, even though a strength of the dataset is that it is longitudinal, the conclusions drawn from the data are not causal. Take the redesign conclusions, for instance. Although the redesign essentially amounted to a field experiment, there was no control group and no subset of users who did not receive the redesigned comments. As such, there could have been something else happening in 2011 and 2012 (for instance, the presidential election) that could have influenced commenting behaviors in ways the current study could not capture. Similarly, commenting behavior simply could be increasing overtime across all websites, meaning that time rather than the redesign could have driven increases in posted comments.

Finally, as large as the dataset is, it is still missing some important information that would allow researchers to better understand the commenting context. For example, the current project examined political content of the *comments* but could not examine political content in the *articles*. People could post a political comment on a nonpolitical news story and could post a nonpolitical comment on a political news story. Smaller-scale data analysis can fill in some of the information that big data analysis, at least with the current dataset, cannot answer.

Despite the limitations, what can people interested in comment sections learn from this analysis? I would argue that the take-away is this: technical aspects of a comment section matter but so does human interaction. Even in a giant dataset, the personal and small should not be lost. One recommendation could prompt an additional comment that may not have otherwise been posted. One reply from a journalist can decrease the amount of incivility present in a political discussion. The New York Times comments demonstrate that politics—even when presented in large datasets—is still personal.

Acknowledgments

The author would like to thank the Democracy Fund and the Hewlett Foundation for providing funding for this project. She also would like to thank Bassey Etim, Justin Bank, Lainie Cosgrove, and Paul Yorke from The New York Times for their assistance in obtaining the data and interpreting the results, as well as Josh Rachner and Stephen Roller for helping to prepare the data for analysis. Finally, she would like to thank the entire Center for Media Engagement team, and particularly Natalie Jomini Stroud, for assisting in the completion of this project.

Appendix: Content Analysis Procedure

The dictionaries were created using the following steps. First, I used an algorithm to pull the 5,000 most-used stemmed terms from all of the comment text in the dataset. I then pulled out all of the stemmed terms that seemed, on their face, to potentially be related to politics or incivility. However, these terms were out of context, meaning that they might have been used in unexpected ways. For instance, the word "farce" could be used to disrespect an opponent or to describe a movie. Thus for each word in each dictionary, I randomly selected 25 comments that included the stemmed term and had two Center for Media Engagement members code whether that comment referenced the stemmed term in a political or uncivil way, depending on the dictionary. Anytime 80 percent or more of the randomly selected comments contained that stemmed term in a way that the coder considered uncivil or political, the term was coded as a "1," meaning that it should be included in the incivility or political dictionary.

If fewer than 80 percent of the comments referenced the stemmed term in an uncivil or political way, the term was coded as a "0," meaning that it should not be included in the incivility or political dictionary. We then ran an intercoder reliability test on the coders' decisions to include or not include the terms in the dictionaries. Reliability was strong for both dictionaries. The incivility dictionary included 63 stemmed terms and the political dictionary included 137 stemmed words.

Notes

1 There were other changes, as well, including allowing certain commenters with a track record of approved comments to post without needing moderator approval. For more details, see Sonderman (2011).
2 Notably, this uptick is not likely due solely to an increase in the number of articles opened for comments after the redesign. Statistical models predicting the number of comments posted per article indicated that the number of comments per article increased after the redesign as well.
3 Because there were approximately 49 months of comments in the dataset posted prior to the redesign compared to only about 20 months of comments in the dataset posted after the redesign, the analyses below include averages of each of the engagement measures of interest across the number of months before and after the redesign.
4 Given the high percentage of comments that have at least one recommendation, there were a substantial number of comments that were both a person's first comment ever approved for publication in The New York Times comment section *and* a person's first recommendation. To ensure that this overlap was not the only driver of the results, I re-ran the analysis taking out the comments that were both someone's first comment and that person's first received recommendation. The result was the same: number of comments posted in the 30 prior to the recommendation was lower than the number of comments posted afterward.
5 Abuse flags were not studied here because nearly every comment with an abuse flag also included a recommendation, making it very difficult to tease out the specific effects of abuse flags. When only comments that included recommendations but no abuse flags were studied, the results held.
6 When the effects of the commenter who posted the comment and the article on which a comment is posted are held fixed, uncivil content of a comment significantly increases the likelihood that a comment is selected as a NYT Pick. However, the fixed effect regression coefficient for incivility is very small – less than .001 – suggesting uncivil content plays a rather small role in influencing journalists' decision to select NYT Picks.
7 To ensure that journalist replies were not artificially inflating the number of comments posted to a comment thread, the length of the comment threads did not include the number of journalist replies in that thread.

References

Anderson, A. A., Brossard, D., Scheufele, D. A., Xenos, M. A., & Ladwig, P. (2014). The "nasty effect": Online incivility and risk perceptions of emerging technologies. *Journal of Computer-Mediated Communication, 19*, 373–387.

Bartels, L. M. (2000). Partisanship and voting behavior, 1952–1996. *American Journal of Political Science, 44*, 35–50.

Chen, G. M., & Pain, P. (2016). Journalists and online comments. *Center for Media Engagement.* Retrieved from https://mediaengagement.org/research/journalists-and-online-comments/

Coe, K., Kenski, K., & Rains, S. A. (2014). Patterns and determinants of incivility in newspaper website comments. *Journal of Communication, 64*, 658–679.

Etim, B. (n.d.). The New York Times: How does the NYT determine which articles have comments? *Quora.* Retrieved from www.quora.com/The-New-York-Times-How-does-the-NYT-determine-which-articles-have-comments

Eveland, W. P. (2003). A "mix of attributes" approach to the study of media effects and new communication technologies. *Journal of Communication, 53*, 395–410.

Fishkin, J. S., & Luskin, R. C. (2005). Experimenting with a democratic ideal: Deliberative polling and public opinion. *Acta Politica.*

Freelon, D. (2015). Discourse architecture, ideology, and democratic norms in online political discussion. *New Media & Society, 17*, 772–791.

Gans, H. J. (2004/1979). *Deciding what's news: A study of CBS Evening News, NBC Nightly News, Newsweek, and Time.* Evanston, IL: Northwestern University Press.

Hoyt, C. (2007, November 4). Civil discourse, meet the internet. *The New York Times.* Retrieved from www.nytimes.com/2007/11/04/opinion/04pubed.html

Iyengar, S., Sood, G., & Lelkes, Y. (2012). Affect, not ideology: A social identity perspective on polarization. *Public Opinion Quarterly, 76*, 405–431.

Knobloch-Westerwick, S., Sharma, N., Alter, S., & Hansen, D. L. (2010). Impact of popularity indications on readers' selective exposure to online news. *Journal of Broadcasting & Electronic Media, 49*, 37–41.

Maisel, L. S. (2012). The negative consequences of uncivil political discourse. *Political Science & Politics, 42*, 405–411.

Messing, S., & Westwood, S. J. (2012). Selective exposure in the age of social media: Endorsements trump partisan source affiliation when selecting news online. *Communication Research, 41*, 1042–1063.

Mutz, D. C. (2015). *In-your-face politics: The consequences of uncivil media.* Princeton, NJ: Princeton University Press.

Papacharissi, Z. (2004). Democracy online: Civility, politeness, and the democratic potential of online political discussion groups. *New Media & Society, 6*, 259–283.

Santana, A. D. (2014). Virtuous or vitriolic: The effect of anonymity on civility in online newspaper reader comment boards. *Journalism Practice, 8*, 18–33.

Sonderman, J. (2011, November 30). New York Times overhauls comment system, grants privileges to trusted readers. *Poynter.* Retrieved from www.poynter.org/news/new-york-times-overhauls-comment-system-grants-privileges-trusted-readers

Semetko, H. A., & Valkenburg, P. M. (2000). Framing European politics : A content analysis of press and television news. *Journal of Communication, 50*, 93–109.

Stromer-Galley, J. (2004). Interactivity-as-product and interactivity-as-process. *The Information Society, 20*, 391–394.

Stromer-Galley, J. (2007). Measuring deliberation's content: A coding scheme. *Journal of Public Deliberation, 3*, Article 12.

Stroud, N. J., Muddiman, A., & Scacco, J. M. (2017). Like, recommend, or respect? Altering political behavior in news comment sections. *New Media & Society, 19*, 1727–1743.

Stroud, N. J., Muddiman, A., & Scacco, J. M. (2015). Engaging audiences via online news sites. In H. Gil de Zúñiga (Ed.), *New technologies and civic engagement* (pp. 178–194). New York, NY: Routledge.

Stroud, N. J., Scacco, J. M., Muddiman, A., & Curry, A. L. (2015). Changing deliberative norms on news organizations' Facebook sites. *Journal of Computer-Mediated Communication, 20,* 188–203.

Sullivan, M. (2013, August 2). Perfectly reasonable question no. 5: On comment "Picks." *The New York Times.* Retrieved from http://publiceditor.blogs.nytimes.com/2013/08/02/perfectly-reasonable-question-no-5-on-comment-picks/

Weeks, B. E., & Holbert, R. L. (2013). Predicting dissemination of news content in social media: A focus on reception, friending, and partisanship. *Journalism & Mass Communication Quarterly, 90,* 212–232.

Ziegele, M., Breiner, T., & Quiring, O. (2014). What creates interactivity in online news discussions? An exploratory analysis of discussion factors in user comments on news items. *Journal of Communication, 64,* 1111–1138.

8

IS YIK YAK A PLATFORM FOR POLITICAL COMMUNICATION?

Exploring College Students' Communication on an Emergent Social Media Platform

Chris Vargo and Toby Hopp

Social media platforms such as Facebook and Twitter have become an object of exploration for researchers interested in political discussion. This scholarly emphasis on social media has been driven, in large part, by the rapid adoption of social networking technologies, particularly among young adults. Available research suggests that young adults use social media for a wide array of political behaviors related to both information seeking and self-expression. Understanding the relationship between young adults' media use and political behaviors is especially important because research suggests that the habits underlying lifelong political engagement develop during one's college years (Chaffee, Ward, & Tipton, 1981; Diddi & LaRose, 2006).

The present study used computational social science techniques to explore the democratic potential of Yik Yak, an emergent social media platform that is especially popular among college students. Yik Yak is a location-based messaging service that allows users to anonymously post content (Northcut, 2015). Acquiring a better understanding of the degree to which Yik Yak is used for political purposes is important as it continues to increase in popularity.

In this study, we explored three specific research questions. First, we set out to better understand the degree to which college students generate politically oriented content on Yik Yak. We also assessed the degree to which responsiveness varies during nationwide political events. We then investigated the degree to which campus-wide contextual factors related to university profile, university learning environment, and social context could be used to describe political behavior on Yik Yak. To answer these research questions, we collected a month's worth of Yik Yak content from 63 major universities located in the United States (over 1.1 million individual messages). These data were collected in January of 2015, which allowed us to assess the degree to which a national political event

(President Obama's State of the Union address) would influence political discussion on Yik Yak. Using the collected data, we employed computer-assisted content analysis techniques to explore the degree to which political expression is present on Yik Yak. Finally, the work investigated the relationship between contextual factors (i.e., college-level data points) and political expression on Yik Yak.

Yik Yak

Yik Yak is a spatially bounded, anonymous messaging application that is primarily used by college students (Huet, 2014; Smith, 2015). The mobile phone-based application allows users to anonymously post messages, or "Yaks." Although users can post pictures, the majority of content posted on Yik Yak is text-based and limited to 200 characters. Depending upon site traffic, users must be within a radius of 1.5 to 10 miles of a central location (i.e., a college campus). Currently, Yik Yak is the most frequently downloaded anonymous social app in Apple's App Store, which reflects its enormous popularity among college students (Mahler, 2015). Users can "upvote" messages as a positive response and "downvote" messages as a negative response (Northcut, 2015). Messages receiving an aggregate of five downvotes disappear from view. Otherwise, user messages stay visible from several hours to several weeks, depending upon the volume of posted content.

College students can use Yik Yak to discuss upcoming finals, ask a question about campus life, or make a joke about a rival school (Mahler, 2015). Notably, serious concerns have emerged over the application's proclivity to harbor defamatory, uncivil, homophobic, and misogynistic discussion. Yik Yak has also been used to anonymously post threatening content. According to Mahler (2015), Yik Yak has been used to issue violent threats on more than a dozen college campuses. In one case, a Yik Yak user suggested that fellow users partake in a gang rape at the school's women's center. Concern over the nature of student conversation has led to organizations such as the Human Rights Campaign and the National Organization for Women to ask the Department of Education to address harassment and other verbally abusive behaviors on Yik Yak (Hess, 2015; Conner, 2015). In light of such behaviors, scholars, commentators, and community activists have primarily focused on the negative social effects associated with Yik Yak. However, as college students continue to adopt and use Yik Yak, it is important to appraise the degree to which the application can facilitate potentially positive social outcomes. One such outcome, contribution to the political public sphere, is the focus of the current study.

Political Expression and Social Media

As it specifically relates to political behaviors, prior research has linked factors such as community social status, community size, and neighborhood structure to both on and offline political involvement (e.g., Boardman & Robert, 2000;

Glascock, 2014; Kwak, Williams, Wang, & Lee, 2005). Vargo and Hopp (2015), for instance, used a big data approach to understand the relationship between community factors and political incivility on Twitter. The results suggested aggregated levels of education exerted a negative effect on political incivility—in other words, residents in better educated communities were more likely to discuss politics using civil language than those less educated communities.

Although scholars have yet to assess the degree to which Yik Yak is used for political communication, prior research has explored both why and how citizens use internet-based media platforms for political purposes. Research in this area tends to conceptualize political participation in terms of both content acquisition and content creation (e.g., Gil de Zúñiga, Molyneux, & Zheng, 2014; Shah, Cho, Eveland, & Kwak, 2005). As it relates to political participation, people use social media for a variety of activities, including sharing opinions about current events, commenting about public officials, and collectively organizing in response to proposed policies and initiatives (Gil de Zúñiga, Molyneux, & Zheng, 2014). In this study, we focus specifically on political expression, which in the current context can be defined as the posting of political commentary by individual site users.

Given the widespread adoption of social media, investigation of the discursive democratic potential of these platforms has been conducted. On one hand, scholars note that the accessible nature of the internet has the potential widen the public sphere. This would allow for the expression of additional perspectives that have traditionally been absent from institutional news sources (Yamamoto, Kushin, & Dalisay, 2015; Correa & Jeong, 2011). Moreover, online political conversation may be less resource intensive than offline political conversation (Valenzuela, Kim, Gil de Zúñiga, 2012), resulting in wider participation. Conversation is important because research suggests that people who talk about politics are more likely to engage in political activities (Shah, Cho, Eveland, & Kwak, 2005; Valenzuela, Kim, Gil de Zúñiga, 2012). On the other hand, researchers have observed instances where the democratic potential of social media is left unrealized (Papacharissi, 2004). Not all popular online platforms will contain political discussion and be responsive to political events.

One of the primary goals of this study was to examine the degree to which Yik Yak, an emergent social media platform, facilitates college students' political expressions. Therein, we were interested in exploring both the frequency of political discussion on Yik Yak.

RQ1: What percentage of Yik Yak discussion is devoted to political expression?

Moreover, scholars have noticed that the volume of political talk on social media is responsive to major offline social and political events. In one prior study, Vargo, Shaw and Basilaia (2015) tracked two ongoing situations. The first, the mortgage and housing crisis, featured relatively infrequent newsworthy developments and thus news coverage was primarily "speculative and debate-driven" (p. 225).

The second scenario, the BP oil spill, featured many newsworthy sub-events (i.e., repeated failed attempts to cap the spill), thus resulting in news coverage that was fueled by the consistent and continued emergence of cues. Generally speaking, the results suggested that the volume of Twitter-based discussion was, indeed, linked to offline occurrences. Therein, the data further suggested that scenarios featuring many real-word cues may be accompanied by volatile levels of social media conversation. Specifically, situations governed by the rapid and continued emergence of newsworthy information were likely to feature stark increases in Twitter conversation volume while scenarios with fewer news cues were characterized by a slow entropy in online conversation volume. Noting this difference, we were interested in exploring the degree to which general political talk volume on Yik Yak was associated with major political events, and how those periods might differ from periods that did not feature major offline news cues.

> RQ2: Is the amount of political discussion on Yik Yak associated with major offline political events (i.e., the State of the Union Address)? If so, to what degree?

Potential Contextual Correlates of Political Conversation on Yik Yak

In addition to exploring the relative frequency and responsiveness of political expression on Yik Yak, this study also explored the degree to which contextual factors associated with on-campus life were associated with aggregated patterns of political expression. Central to this line of inquiry is Dahlgren's (2000) *civic culture*, which suggests that surrounding social and cultural factors effectively constitute the pre-conditions for democratic participation. In other words, community profile factors fundamentally influence political behavior, including those behaviors related to citizen engagement in the online public sphere. This study focused on three contextual factors associated with campus life: university demographic profile, campus learning environment, and on-campus social factors. These dimensions are reviewed in the following section.

University Demographics

On the individual level, research indicates that social media usage may differ by demographic categories. For instance, African-American teenagers are more likely than white teenagers to use to Twitter (Madden, et al, 2013) and women have been found to be heavier users than men (Hargittai & Litt, 2011). Research has also shown that age cohorts use social media platforms differently and with varying frequencies (Duggan et al, 2015). Research suggests that these individual-level differences in social media usage may also be apparent at the community level. For example, a recent study by Murthy, Gross, and Pensavalle (2015) used big data to explore the relationship between Twitter usage intensity and community demographics. Here, the authors found a relationship between community demographics and tweet interval, concluding that African-American users living in densely populated urban areas may be the most active on Twitter.

Despite the foregoing, relatively little is known about the relationship between community-level characteristics and *political involvement* on social media. Thus, in the current study, we set out to explore whether university-level demographic factors related to political engagement on Yik Yak. Considering the unique characteristics of college campuses across the United States, the following factors were considered: school size, gender breakdown, average age, race share (African-American, Asian, Hispanic, and white), attendance cost, and public or private status. These factors are consistent with prior social media research on demographics, which has, as reviewed above, focused on age, gender, race, and socioeconomic status.

University Learning Environment

Research has suggested that college attendance has an appreciable impact on political values and involvement (e.g., Hillygus, 2005; McClintock & Turner, 1962). Less is known about the degree to which individual university learning environments affect either political participation generally or political expression specifically. Addressing this question may be important. Prior studies have concluded that the learning environments that surround college students influence student-centered outcomes, including studying habits (Lizzio, Wilson, & Simons, 2002), performance (Kuh, 1993), involvement (Karp & Yoels, 1976), and social integration (Braxton & McClendon, 2001). Thus, one of the goals of this study was to assess a given college's learning environment and its association with online political conversation.

University learning environments can be understood in both institutional/contextual (i.e., classroom size) and perceptive (i.e., student satisfaction) terms. For instance, Lizzio, Wilson, and Simons (2002) used a self-report measure to better understand college students' perceptions of their surrounding learning environment. From an institutional angle, scholars have used measures such as student retention (Braxton & McClendon, 2001), classroom size (Pulvers & Diekhoff, 1999), and graduation rate (Lau, 2003) as indicators of productive learning environments. Considered as a whole, research in this area suggests that college students who have access to ample faculty and administrative and material resources tend to perform better and demonstrate higher levels of engagement with their studies and campus life. Therefore, in the current study, factors such as freshman retention rate, average class size, and graduation rate were used to explore the relationship between college students' learning environment and the frequency of political communication on Yik Yak.

University Social Environment

This study's approach to revealing the relationship between campus social environment and online political communication is heavily influenced by the theory of social capital. Social capital refers to individual citizens' ability to access "resources embedded in their social networks" (Ellison, Vitak, Gray, & Lampe, 2014, p. 856). Social capital is linked to factors such as shared norms, shared language, social trust, and the sense of mutual obligation (Huysman & Wulf, 2004; Ellison, Steinfeld, & Lampe, 2007). It is both created and maintained via social interaction (Ellison, Vitak, Gray, & Lampe, 2014). The ability to form and maintain shared norms and trust is thought to be a pre-requisite for a civil and politically engaged society. According to Newton (2001), social capital helps "sustain civil society and community relations in a way that generates trust and cooperation between citizens and a high level of civic engagement and participation" (p. 201).

Previous research has explored social capital at both the individual and aggregate levels. On the individual level, social capital has been conceptualized as interpersonal trust (e.g., Lee & Lee, 2010; Shah, 1998), life contentment (e.g., Shah, Kwak, & Holbert, 2001), participation in civic behaviors (e.g., Blanchard & Horan, 1998; Onyx & Bullen, 2000) and involvement with political organizations (e.g., Wellman, Haase, Witte, & Hampton, 2001). On the contextual level, scholars have measured social capital using a variety of indexes, including aggregated composites of individual-level variables (Hendryx, Ahern, Lovrich, & McCurdy, 2002), voter turnout (e.g., Chamlin & Cochran, 1995; Rosenfeld, Messner, & Baumer, 2001), racial/ethnic heterogeneity (e.g., Costa & Kahn, 2003; Rupasingha, Goetz, & Freshwater, 2006) and number of civic/social/political groups within a community (e.g., Pretty & Ward, 2001).

To some degree, the relationship between social capital and political participation on social media remains an open question. On one hand, researchers have found links between the accumulation of social capital and use of social media (e.g., Ellison, Steinfeld, & Lampe, 2007; Valenzuela, Park, & Kee, 2009). However, less is known about the degree to which social capital formation, either *online* or *offline*, is associated with social media-based political expression. Therefore, one of the key questions driving the current study is related to the degree to which campus-wide social capital indicators are associated with political discussion on Yik Yak. Building upon previous research, we were specifically interested in exploring three contextually situated factors linked to campus-wide social capital formation.

The first factor of interest is *racial/ethnic heterogeneity*. Prior research has generally conceptualized high levels of racial/ethnic heterogeneity as exerting an inhibitory effect on collective organization and action (e.g., Alesina & Ferrara, 2002; Vargo & Hopp, 2015). The theory driving this perspective is that "similarity breeds connections" (McPherson, Smith-Lovin, & Cook, 2001, p. 415) and; as such, *high* levels of racial/ethnic heterogeneity are thought to be indicative of comparatively *low* levels of social capital potential. However, on university campuses racial heterogeneity has been associated with a number of positive outcomes related to on-campus democratic engagement (e.g., Guren, Nagda, & Lopez, 2004).

The second factor of interest is *organizational participation*. Previous research has conceptualized social capital in terms of organizational participation (e.g., Putnam, 2000; Wellman, Haase, Witte, & Hampton, 2001). Theoretically, associational involvement in the form of participation in religious, civic, voluntary, and interest oriented groups help encourage the development of shared norms and mutual trust (Portes, 1998).

Finally, we explored the degree to which participation in Greek life was a part of each university's social fabric. Participation in Greek organizations tends to "discourage interaction across difference" (Laird, 2005, p. 373). Specifically, involvement in Greek life has been conceptualized as an indicator of college students' involvement in "activities that do not challenge students to engage diverse peoples and ideas" (p. 373). On one hand, campuses featuring high levels of Greek involvement may feature heightened levels of social capital. Greek life forms strong, bonded networks between similar individuals. On the other hand, it may be the case that Greek involvement results in an insular social environment where the political and social striations necessary for democratic communication are suppressed.

Given the above literature, our third research question was interested in exploring if (and to what degree) contextual, campus-level characteristics (university demographics, university learning environment indicators, and university social environment factors) are associated with political communication on Yik Yak:

> RQ3: Do university demographics, university learning environment factors, and university social environment factors correlate with the frequency of political discussion on Yik Yak?

Method

Retrieving the Data from Yik Yak

Yik Yak is a freely available social media platform like Twitter. However unlike Twitter, it does not provide documentation for its Application Programming Interface (API). As such it is difficult to make standardized requests for data. This restriction is likely because of its policy to not to allow third-party apps and services to connect to it (Yik Yak, 2015). APIs are primarily used for these reasons. Computer science scholars have recognized this limitation and developed a solution to fetch Yik Yak data using python packages. The tool "Yik Yak Terminal" was used. It is an open source and freely available python program on GitHub

(YikYakTerminal, 2015). It enables users to enter a custom location and retrieve messages. The authors here altered the code to automate data collection. The program ran every 24 hours and stored data locally in a tabular format. Yaks that were at least 4 hours old were collected each day. To classify each message's geographic location, each version of the script specified the "geofence" that corresponded to the university of interest. In all, 64 versions of the script were generated, one for each full time member in the Atlantic Coastal, Big Ten, Big 12, Pacific-12 and Southeastern conferences. The decision to focus on the above-described schools was made because (1) all of the selected universities are similar in terms of institutional structure; (2) all schools compete in high profile college athletics, which is a significant part of the student experience and thus likely to comprise a substantial part of on-campus discussion; and (3) examination of approximately 60 contextual units is consistent with the number of clusters used by other researchers in similar big data analyses (e.g., Murthy, Gross, Pensavalle, 2015).

In the current study, data from 63 universities was analyzed. Data from the University of North Carolina were dropped because the geocoder incorrectly resolved the University of North Carolina at Chapel Hill to the Greensboro campus. This was because the term "the University of North Carolina" resolved to the latter on Google Maps. In all, 1,139,724 messages were acquired. Given that Yik Yak was in different stages of diffusion at each university, the number of messages per school ranged from 492 (Texas A&M) to 34,888 (University of Michigan). The average number of collected Yaks per university was 18,090.86 (SD = 9,058.16).

Coding for Political Talk

The researchers tried several approaches to extract political talk. First, the authors performed many iterations of Latent Dirichlet Allocation (LDA) modeling to extract the topics inside of the Yik Yak data. The authors finally settled on Dynamic Modeling via Non-negative Matrix Factorization (Green & Cross, 2015). The authors adopted this LDA method because of its scalability to large datasets and its temporal nature. Standard topic modeling approaches assume the order of documents does not matter, making them unsuitable for time-stamped corpora. In contrast, *dynamic topic modeling* approaches track how language changes and topics evolve over time. Here we applied a two-level approach for dynamic topic modeling via Non-negative Matrix Factorization (NMF), which links together topics identified in snapshots of text sources appearing over time (Greene & Cross, 2016).

The authors extracted the top 100 topics, the top 15 of which can be seen in Table 8.1. As seen, while these topical models provided some insight into the types of content posted on Yik Yak, no clear political topics emerged.

To better hone in on political talk, the researchers adopted a lexicon approach. The researchers leveraged existing wordlists from a previous study, which detected

TABLE 8.1 Top 15 LDA Topics

Topic Number	Topic Contents
1	*like look looks feels smells sounds act feeling doesn smell women days bitch person actually*
2	*just saw wanna realized said wish walked mean took did told tell doesn woke watched*
3	*don understand care anymore wanna tell worry talk wear need text mind work trust drink*
4	*people white actually black stop talk understand meet world lot use talking wonder tinder yaks*
5	*girl cute hot scout sorority ask date beautiful looking white saw cookies talk wants said*
6	*day valentine valentines snow single leg great having today beautiful classes mlk gonna long ll*
7	*fuck shut buddy yeah state did bu bitch uva wanna holy drunk gonna bitches floor*
8	*class professor minutes tomorrow late 30 walk early semester teacher morning cancelled sitting*
9	*time long spend start nap remember half waste having work hard actually phone free spent*
10	*guy cute hot saw nice black talking date looking friend tell wants said wearing ask*
11	*know didn doesn ll anybody real did person dont bad doing gonna ya won talking*
12	*girls sorority white hot talk tinder cute wear looking boys attractive black beautiful pretty*
13	*today need help stop didn open saw classes wearing work gonna weather buddy man did*
14	*feel bad makes better person way lonely making sad guilty sick doing weird sorry boyfriend*
15	*going tomorrow home gym semester weekend start instead im hell break alarm today outside*

political talk on Twitter from the 2012 election (Vargo & Guo, 2015). This list included 16 key political issues.[1] The lexicons originated from words that were traditionally associated with key political issues. In addition to the use of pre-existing wordlists, additional wordlists representing (1) words/phrases used to signify discussion of the State of the Union address (e.g., "State of the Union," "SOTU"); (2) key themes from the State of the Union address (e.g., "NATO," "McConnell"); and (3) words/phrases related to current events (e.g., "ISIS," "Charlie Hebdo") were created.[2]

Like intercoder agreement with traditional content analysis, "algorithms and dictionaries must often be repeatedly revised and tweaked to improve their performance" (Zamith & Lewis, 2015, p. 4). This process is only complete when a satisfactory level of construct validity is established. In this case, two coders should agree with each other to establish "gold standard" data. Then, the computer should agree with the gold standard data at an acceptable level. The researchers conducted three rounds of validity checks. Wordlists were altered at each iteration to improve performance. Words that caused false positives were removed and more specific uses of the word were incorporated, or the word was removed. In cases where neither solution yielded more valid results, an exclusion list for that word was created. Words were also added to dictionary lists when researchers noticed their absence. At each stage, two human coders read a random sample of messages and coded them as either political or nonpolitical in nature. Then, they compared their result with the computer-coded result. If the results did not match, the human coders reported an error. At all three stages the two human coders' intercoder agreement was acceptable ($\alpha > .85$). The two human coders agreed on whether talk was political or not with an acceptable degree of intercoder reliability.

For comparing the computer-coded data to the human-annotated data, percent agreement was used as an external validity check. A reliability check was not needed, because computers are presumed to be reliable (Riffe, Fico & Lacy, 2014). For the first iteration, the researchers examined a large subsample to explore the dataset and rigorously augment words. Subsequent sample frames were smaller, but matched the sample size standards set by previous research (Riffe, Fico & Lacy, 2014). The pairwise agreement for each round was as follows: Round 1 = 35.5% (n = 1,000); Round 2 = 73.4% (n = 282); Round 3 = 94.3% (n = 282).

University Data

U.S. News & World Report (USNWR) annually ranks U.S. post-secondary institutions. As a part of those rankings, USNWR analysts collect data points on 1,400 colleges and universities. The rankings have been compiled and published annually since 1985 and are the most widely quoted of their kind in the United States (Leiby, 2014). Data are collected via an annual survey sent to each school. There are several individual measures derived from this data.

University Demographics

To measure *university size*, USNWR data describing the estimated number of undergraduates enrolled at each university were used (M = 24,042.62, SD = 9,650.95). Here, we used undergraduate enrollment rather than total enrollment because Yik Yak is primarily used by undergraduate students (e.g., Huet, 2014; Northcut, 2015). For *attendance cost*, cost of attendance was used as the closest proxy for each university's relative socio-economic status. The cost of attendance was calculated as the total fulltime tuition cost for a single year of attendance. For public schools, we used the in-state rate (M = $16, 863.27, SD = $13, 785.78). In terms of *public/private status*, 17.46% (n = 11) of the universities were private institutions. To measure the *gender distribution* at each university, we used the percentage of undergraduate male students (M = 50.21%,

SD = 4.46). The average *age* of the undergraduate population at each school was 20.84 years (SD = 0.93 years). The *racial/ethnic distribution* at each university was measured as the percentage share of each university that was Asian/Asian-American (M = 8.25%, SD = 7.66%), Black/African-American (M = 5.87%, SD = 3.39%), Hispanic/Latino (M = 8.77%, SD = 5.96%), and White/Caucasian (M = 64.80%, SD = 13.64%).

University Learning Environment

Two measures were used evaluate *average classroom size*. The first measure was the percentage of classes at each university with less than 20 students (M = 42.45%, SD = 11.66%). The second measure was the percentage of classes at each university with greater than 50 students (M= 15.95%, SD = 5.26%). *Graduation rate* was measured as the percentage of students who graduate in six years or less (M = 75.73%, SD = 11.43%). *Freshman retention rate* was calculated as the percentage of first year students who return for a second year (M= 89.32%, SD = 5.77%).

University Social Environment

As it pertains to *campus heterogeneity,* the USNWR data provide the following racial/ethnic/identification categories: Black/African-American, American Indian/Native American, Asian/Asian-American, Hispanic/Latino, White/Caucasian, Pacific Islander, 2 or more races, International, and unknown. To generate an estimate of racial/ethnic heterogeneity on each campus, we employed the approach previously used by Costa and Kahn (2003). Use of this technique returned a value between 0 and 1, wherein higher values were indicative of greater levels of on-campus heterogeneity (M= 0.53; SD = 0.13).[3] Next, we measured the number of *university-affiliated organizations* using the USNWR's pooled estimate of number of campus-wide organizations (M = 613.83, SD = 290.24). Finally, we pooled the number of fraternities and sororities to create a single index measuring *campus-wide Greek involvement* (M = 38.34, SD = 21.21).

Results

The first research question addressed the degree to which Yik Yak featured political talk. Over the entire month of January, we observed 9,340 political comments. As such, political comments comprised less than 1% of all comments posted on Yik Yak (9,340 political messages/1,139,724 total messages = 0.82%). Averaged across all universities, the mean percentage of political talk was 0.84% (SD = 0.45%). Examination of the individual university totals suggested that Duke University's Yik Yak featured the lowest overall percentage of political discussion (0.29%) while the University of Kansas' Yik Yak featured the highest overall percentage of political discussion (3.41%).[4] percentage of political discussion at each university is shown in Figure 8.1.

The second research question was concerned with the degree to which discussion on Yik Yak is responsive to or reflective of national political events. January 20th, the day of the State of the Union address, saw the highest overall percentage of political discussion on Yik Yak (2.63%; M = 2.59%, SD = 2.24%). As seen in Figure 8.2, Yik Yak-based political talk was substantially elevated during the four-day period beginning on January 19. 16.10% percent (n = 1,504) of all observed political comments were posted on January 20th and 36.26% of all observed political comments (n = 3,387) were posted during the four-day period from January 19 to January 22.

On January 20th, the day of the State of the Union address, individual percentages for each university indicated that political talk had substantive variance, ranging from 0.00% (Texas A&M, University of Arizona, University of Texas) to 14.80% (University of Kansas). Five university accounts featured single-day averages in excess of 5.0% (University of Kansas = 14.80%, Northwestern University = 9.51%, University of Virginia = 7.18%, Boston College = 5.84%, Purdue University = 5.48%, Baylor University = 5.11%). The university with the greatest single-day percentage of political talk was the University of Kansas (21.05%; January 22).

Next, we explored the degree to which political discussion on January 20th differed from "normal" levels of onsite political discussion. Paired samples t-tests suggested that the mean percentage of political talk on January 20th was significantly higher than the percentage of political talk observed on January 19th, $t(62)$ = 5.94, p < .01, January 21st, $t(62)$ = 5.59, p < .01, and January 22nd, $t(62)$ = 5.88, p < .01. Given that January 19, 21, and 22 featured the three next highest percentages of political conversation (relative to January 20), these findings allow us to conclude that the percentage of political conversation on January 20th was statistically greater than on any other day in the period of observation.

Finally, the degree to which higher levels of political talk during "normal" periods was associated with political talk during the four-day period surrounding the State of the Union address (January 19 – January 22). To do so, two data points were calculated for each university. The first series of data points represented the percentage of all talk that was political for the periods between January 1 – January 18 and January 23 – January 31. The second series of data points represented the percentage of all talk that was political for the period between January 19 and January 22. Using these values, we estimated a bivariate correlation describing the relationship between "normal" levels of political communication and levels of political communication surrounding the State of the Union address. The results suggested that universities that featured higher levels of political communication during "normal" periods of the month also featured heightened levels of political communication during the four-day period bracketing the State of the Union address, r = .28, p < .05.

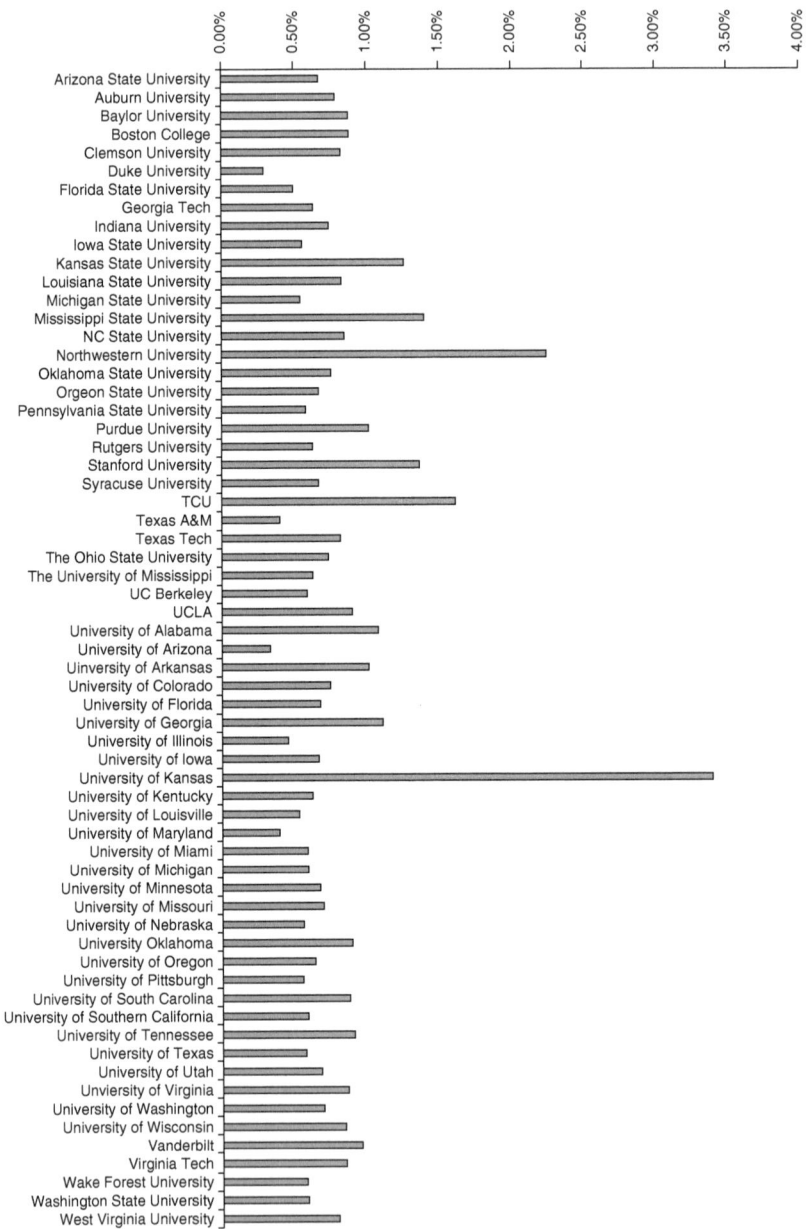

FIGURE 8.1 Percentage of Political Talk on Yik Yak for Each University in the Sample

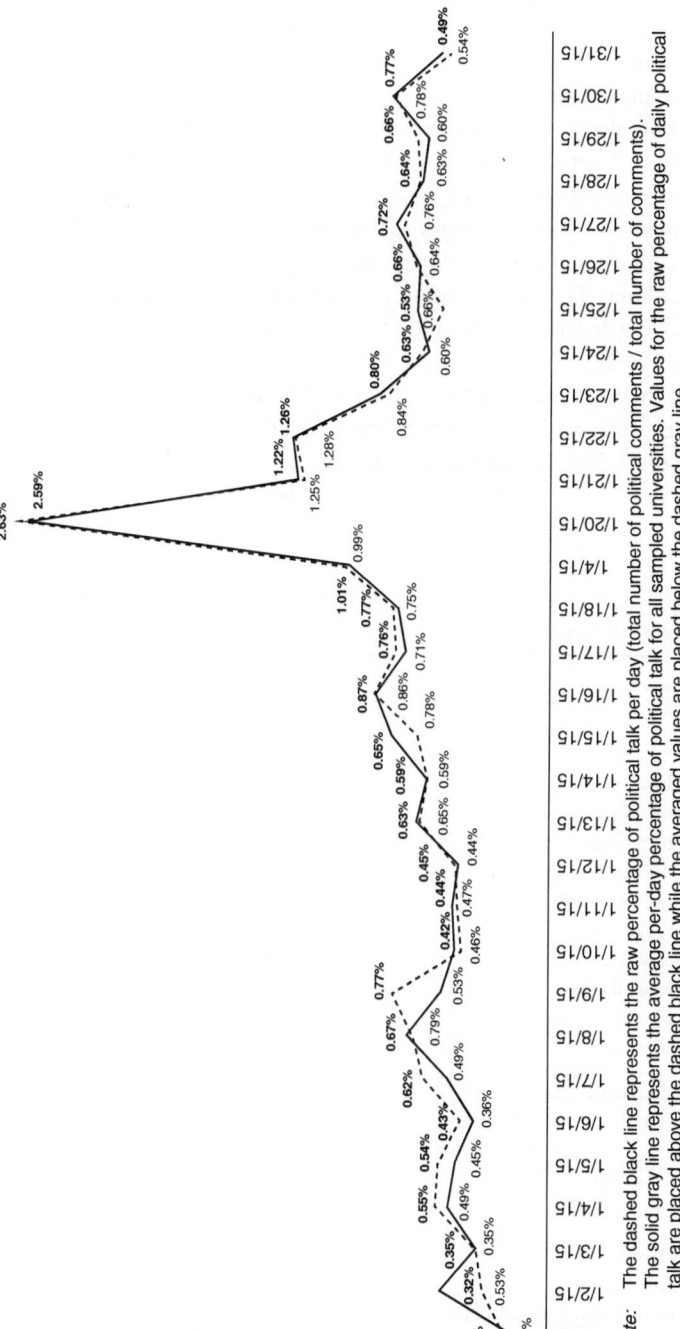

Note: The dashed black line represents the raw percentage of political talk per day (total number of political comments / total number of comments). The solid gray line represents the average per-day percentage of political talk for all sampled universities. Values for the raw percentage of daily political talk are placed above the dashed black line while the averaged values are placed below the dashed gray line.

FIGURE 8.2 Per-day Summary of Yik Yak Political Talk

The third research question was interested in exploring the degree to which university characteristics were associated with the prevalence of political discussion on Yik Yak. To explore this question, we examined the bivariate correlations between the percentage of political discussion on each campus and university-level indicators describing university demographics, learning environment, and social capital potential. Given that a bulk of the observed political communication occurred between January 19 and January 22 and that the nature of that talk was reflexive of a special event, correlations were estimated for both the full month percentage and the percentage for the period surrounding the State of the Union address. For the university demographic factors, we observed significant, negative correlations between university size and the amount of political talk for both the full month ($r = -.30, p < .05$) and the 4-day period surrounding the State of the Union address ($r = -.28, p < .05$). For the learning environment factors, there was a negative and significant correlation between the percentage of classes with > 50 students and the amount of political discussion for both the full month ($r = -.31, p < .01$) and the period between January 19 and January

TABLE 8.2 Bivariate Correlations between Percentage of Political Talk on Yik Yak and University Characteristics

	Political Talk January 1–31	Political Talk January 19–22
Demographics		
University Size	-.30**	-.28**
Attendance Cost	.13	.15
Private Status	.16	.16
Gender (Percent Male)	-.10	-.12
Average Age	-.07	-.06
Percentage Asian	-.09	-.09
Percentage Black	.05	.00
Percentage Hispanic	-.11	-.08
Percentage White	.12	.10
Learning Environment		
Percent of Classes < 20 Students	.22*	.17
Percent of Classes > 50 Students	-.31***	-.32***
Graduation Rate	-.09	-.10
Freshman Retention	-.13	-.14
Social Environment		
Campus Heterogeneity	-.13	-.09
Number of University-Affiliated Clubs	-.17	-.17
Number of Greek Organizations	-.32**	-.32**

Note: $* p < .10, ** p < .05, *** p < .01$

22 ($r = -.32$, $p < .01$). Finally, as it relates to university social environment, our results suggest that campuses that feature a high number of Greek organizations were less likely to feature political discussion. Specifically, we observed negative correlations between number of on-campus Greek organizations and the frequency of political discussion for both the month-long and four-day period from January 19 to January 22 ($r = -.32$, $p < .05$ for both periods). See Table 8.2 for a full summary of the observed correlations.[5]

Discussion

Political Talk Overall

Political discussion is increasingly located online. The rapid diffusion and adoption of social media has the ability to re-shape how, where, and when people talk about important political and social issues. However, as scholars have previously pointed out, the democratic potential of online platforms are not universally realized (e.g., Papacharissi, 2004). The current study explored the degree to which young adults use Yik Yak for political expression. To the best of our knowledge, this study is a number of firsts as it pertains to Yik Yak. It is the first to address political communication, the first to leverage computational social science methods with big data, and the first in communication sciences to explore the uses of Yik Yak.

Political engagement on Yik Yak appears to be low. Less than 1% of all observed comments were political in nature. However, evidence suggests that the volume of Yik Yak-based political commentary is responsive to highly visible major political events. The data indicated that 36.26% of all observed political comments were posted in the four days surrounding President Obama's 2015 State of the Union address. This is similar to what previous researchers have found for Twitter (e.g., Vargo, Shaw, & Basilaia, 2015).

Finally, the data suggested that political conversation on Yik Yak was lower at universities with large undergraduate enrollments, a large percentage of classes with greater than 50 students, and a large number of fraternities. Implications are discussed below.

LDA topic modeling (see Table 8.1) indicated that Yik Yak is dedicated to interpersonal relationships, sexual topics, and school-related topics. Political talk is completely absent from the most popular types of conversations. Yik Yak's potential for political discussion is primarily unrealized. However, Yik Yak is responsive to major political events. A large proportion of the observed comments were posted on or around the day of the State of the Union address. The results suggested a positive, linear relationship between amount of "normal" monthly political talk and amount of talk that occurred during the four-day period surrounding the address. This suggests some schools are more attentive to politics than others, and this effect is boosted by major events. These findings provide scholars and practitioners a baseline upon which to build more sophisticated predictive models of college students' political engagement on Yik Yak. Schools' relative political "baseline" seems to be a clue as to how it will respond during events.

The Technological Affordances of Yik Yak

Anonymity

Yik Yak is a unique in that it provides ability for users to be anonymous to other users. This technological affordance undoubtedly changes the nature of the discussion on the medium (see Table 8.1), which could lower barriers to political discussion. For instance, individuals could voice divergent opinions without fear of personal consequence. Unlike Facebook and Twitter, political messages that are controversial would not spill over into the identities of real people. Moreover, it is well-known that trolls, or individuals who deliberately post offensive or provocative online posting with the aim of upsetting someone, prefer anonymity (Phillips, 2015). Trolls are known to post divergent political opinions (Hmielowski, Hutchens, & Cicchirillo, 2014). For these reasons, it is interesting that Yik Yak has not afforded more political talk, whether it civil or uncivil in nature.

Instead, Table 8.1 shows that anonymity in a college setting appears to encourage more discussion about sex, drinking alcohol, and consuming illicit substances (e.g., marijuana and other drugs). Anonymity still plays a key role in these messages, as these behaviors can be illegal for college students. The reasons why these behaviors are discussed and political discussion is relatively absent is ripe for further study. At present, no known studies have tackled the uses and gratifications of Yik Yak.

Geolocations

Beyond privacy, Yik Yak also affords geofenced content. In one sense this is a novel feature of the platform. Users of Yik Yak can only see and post messages that correspond to their geographical area. Here, this design choice makes it easy for users to see the happenings of only their local area. This locus also seems to encourage discussion of events that pertain to those specific areas (e.g., here a specific college campus). Table 8.1 again reveals that the daily happenings of college students are prevalent in the data. Keywords that relate to campus life (e.g., classes and professors) appear often. Location-based messaging may itself also discourage certain types of messages. For instance, Twitter is a medium that does not filter data via geographical areas. Instead, all users can see the entire population of Twitter content. Twitter is also immensely popular during national events (e.g., a presidential debate) and usage of the platform spikes during these times (Hu et al., 2012). Here, we studied the State of the Union, a national event that does typically generate significant traffic on Twitter (Wang et al., 2012). It could be that the intentional design choice for Yik Yak to filter messages locally is itself quelling discussions that are more global in nature, instead giving preference to events that are more local in nature. Further research should examine politics at local levels to see if Yik Yak and other geofenced social media are more responsive in these situations.

Contextual Factors

The data tentatively suggested that contextual factors might have an influence on the frequency with which political discussion appears on Yik Yak. This is consistent with previous research that suggests similar interplays between online and offline behaviors (e.g., Dahlgren, 2000). Campuses with a high number of classes that had more than 50 students were less likely to feature high levels of political talk on Yik Yak. This finding could be due to a conditioning effect. Students in larger classrooms are given fewer opportunities for classroom discussion. Thus, they may be less likely to use their free time to discuss such issues. Similarly, our observation that the number of Greek organizations was negatively affiliated with political discussion could indicate that Greek associations institute social structures that are non-conducive to political talk.[6]

It is also important to note that we observed a large number of null relationships between the contextual factors of interest and the frequency of political posts on Yik Yak. One explanation for these findings could be the relative homogeneity of the modern university environment. Another explanation could be moderating factors that exert conditional influences on Yik Yak-based political behavior. As an emergent platform, Yik Yak could also be unevenly diffused across universities. This could mask potentially meaningful relationships. Clearly, in this area, future research is needed.

This study has a number of limitations. We did not address the quality of political communication on Yik Yak. A comprehensive understanding of any media's democratic potential must encompass both *quantity* and *quality* (Hopp & Vargo, 2015). As such, future research could investigate the degree to which political discussion on Yik Yak is free of namecalling, insults, and other indicators of low quality political discussion. Additionally, given the application's localized nature, it may be the case that Yik Yak is more frequently used to discuss local, rather than national, political, social, and cultural issues. Future research could comparatively explore the degree to which Yik Yak is used for discussion of local political issues. Third, the structure of the USNWR data framed the operationalization of some of the campus-level variables used in this study. In some cases, this may have resulted in measures with less-than-ideal properties or restricted us from exploring potentially meaningful relationships. Future research should seek to employ more robust contextual measures as a means of substantiating and building upon the current results.

Twitter and Facebook have played a prominent role in the discussion of the last two elections, especially among young adults. Campaigns have reacted to this new reality by building sophisticated social media campaign strategies aimed at building and sustaining candidate-friendly narratives. Given the rapid adoption of Yik Yak among young voters, it seems entirely conceivable that platforms such as Yik Yak may play a role in future elections. As such, we hope that scholars build upon this initial work in order to build a fuller understanding of Yik Yak's democratic potential.

Notes

1 The 16 ongoing issues frequently discussed in political context are: (1) taxes; (2) jobs/unemployment; (3) federal budget deficit; (4) general economy; (5) foreign affairs; (6) immigration; (7) healthcare; (8) public order; (9) LGBT/same-sex marriage; (10) abortion; (11) environment/climate; (12) energy; (13) education; (14) role of government; (15) middle class issues; and (16) welfare/entitlements.
2 Complete lexicons and Python code used to classify the data are freely available from the author.
3 The formula used to generate the heterogeneity measure was

$$1 - \sum_k s_{ki}^2$$

where s_{ki} is the share of race/ethnic/identification category k for university i.
4 Additional analyses suggested that the number of total university-wide messages was not related to the percentage of political messages, $r = -.02, p > .05$.
5 The USNWR data included some missing values. Specifically, 1 observation was missing for the gender breakdown measure, 2 observations were missing for the measure describing university-affiliated clubs/organizations, and 7 observations were missing for the measure describing number of on-campus Greek organizations. To determine the degree to which these missing values biased our results, we used the R package "mice" to impute missing values. Using these values, we estimated all relevant correlations. These correlations were then compared to the correlations acquired using listwise deletion. In all cases, the relational magnitude and significance levels were essentially identical, suggesting that missing values did not bias our reported results.
6 Given the exploratory nature of the current study, the relatively small number of campus units, the presence of missing data, and the strong correlations between many of the contextual indicators, we chose not to use regression analyses to model the current data. However, when the three significant factors identified in Table 8.2 (undergraduate enrollment, class sizes > 50, and number of Greek organizations) were simultaneously entered into a regression equation, class size emerged as the strongest overall predictor, followed by number of Greek organizations and undergraduate enrollment.

References

Alesina, A., & Ferrara, E. L. (2000). Participation in heterogeneous communities. *Quarterly Journal of Economics, 115*, 847–904.

Blanchard, A., & Horan, T. (1998). Virtual communities and social capital. *Social Science Computer Review, 16*, 293–307.

Boardman, J. D., & Robert, S. A. (2000). Neighborhood socioeconomic status and perceptions of self-efficacy. *Sociological Perspectives, 43*(1), 117–136.

Braxton, J. M., & McClendon, S. A. (2001). The fostering of social integration and retention through institutional practice. *Journal of College Student Retention*, *3*, 57–71.

Chaffee, S. H., Ward, S. L., & Tipton, L. (1981). Mass communication and political socialization. In M. Janowitz & P. Hirsch (Eds.), *Reader in public opinion and mass communication* (pp. 74–88). New York, NY: Free Press.

Chamlin, M. B., & Cochran, J. K. (1995). Assessing Messner and Rosenfeld's institutional anomie theory: A partial test. *Criminology*, *33*, 411–429.

Conner, C. (2015). Activist groups ask the Department of Education to address Yik Yak harassment. *Student Press Law Center.* From www.splc.org/blog/splc/2015/10/activist-groups-ask-the-department-of-education-to-address-yik-yak-harassment

Correa, T., & Jeong, S. H. (2011). Race and online content creation: Why minorities are actively participating in the web. *Information, Communication, & Society*, *14*, 638–659.

Costa, D. L., & Kahn, M. E. (2003). Civic engagement and community heterogeneity: An economist's perspective. *Perspectives on Politics*, *1*, 103–111.

Dahlgren, P. (2000). The internet and the democratization of civic culture. *Political Communication*, *17*, 335–340.

Diddi, A., & LaRose, R. (2006). Getting hooked on the news: Uses and gratifications and the formation of news habits among college students in an internet environment. *Journal of Broadcasting & Electronic Media*, *50*, 193–210.

Duggan, M., Ellsion, N. B., Lampe, C., Lenhart, A., & Madden, M. (2015). Social media update 2014. *Pew Research Center.* From: www.pewinternet.org/files/2015/01/PI_SocialMediaUpdate20144.pdf

Ellison, N. B., Steinfeld, C., & Lampe, C. (2007). The benefits of Facebook "Friends": Social capital and college students' use of online asocial network sites. *Journal of Computer-Mediated Communication*, *12*, 1143–1168.

Gil de Zúñiga, H., Molyneux, L., & Zheng, P. (2014). Social media, political expression, and political participation: Panel analysis of lagged and concurrent relationships. *Journal of Communication*, *64*, 612–634.

Glascock, J. (2014). Contribution of demographics, sociological factors, and media usage to verbal aggressiveness. *Journal of Media Psychology*.

Greene, D., & Cross, J. P. (2016). Exploring the political agenda of the European parliament using a dynamic topic modeling approach. *arXiv preprint arXiv:1607.03055*.

Guo, L., & Vargo, C. (2015). The power of message networks: A big-data analysis of the network agenda setting model and issue ownership. *Mass Communication and Society*, *18*, 557–576.

Hargittai, E., & Litt, E. (2011). The tweet smell of celebrity success: Explaining variation in Twitter adoption among a diverse group of young adults. *New Media & Society*, *13*, 824Media

Hendryx, M. S., Ahern, M. M., Lovrich, N. P., & McCurdy, A. H. (2002). Access to health care and community social capital. *Health Services Research*, *37*, 85–101.

Hess, A. (2015). Don't ban Yik Yak. *Slate.* From www.slate.com/articles/technology/users/2015/10/yik_yak_is_good_for_university_students.html

Hillygus, D. S. (2005). The missing link: Exploring the relationship between higher education and political engagement. *Political Behavior*, *27*, 25–47.

Hmielowski, J. D., Hutchens, M. J., & Cicchirillo, V. J. (2014). Living in an age of online incivility: Examining the conditional indirect effects of online discussion on political flaming. *Information, Communication & Society*, *17*, 1196–1211.

Hu, Y., John, A., Seligmann, D. D., & Wang, F. (2012, May). What were the tweets about? Topical associations between public events and Twitter feeds. In *ICWSM*.

Huet, E. (2014). Yik Yak wants to be a news hub but it needs to grow up first. *Forbes*. Retrieved from www.forbes.com/sites/ellenhuet/2014/10/20/yik-yak-wants-to-be-a-news-hub-but-it-needs-to-grow-up-first/

Huysman, M., & Wulf, V. (2004). *Social capital and information technology*. Cambridge, MA: MIT Press.

Karp, D. A., & Yoels, W. C. (1976). The college classroom: Some observations on the meanings of student participation. *Sociology & Social Research, 60*, 421–439.

Kwak, N., Williams, A. E., Wang, X., & Lee, H. (2005). Talking politics and engaging politics: An examination of the interactive relationship between structural features of political talk and discussion engagement. *Communication Research, 32*, 87–111.

Kuh, G. D. (1993). In their own words: What students learn outside the classroom. *American Educational Research Journal, 30*, 277–304.

Laird, T. N. (2005). College students' experiences with diversity and their effects on academic self-confidence, social agency, and disposition toward critical thinking. *Research in Higher Education, 46*, 365–387.

Lau, L. K. (2003). Institutional factors affecting student retention. *Education, 124*, 126–136.

Lee, J. & Lee, H. (2010). The computer-mediated communication network: Exploring the linkage between online community and social capital. *New Media & Society, 12*, 71–727.

Leiby, R. (2014, September 9). The guru behind the U.S. News college rankings. *The Washington Post*. Retrieved November 9, 2015, from www.washingtonpost.com/lifestyle/style/the-us-news-college-rankings-guru/2014/09/09/318e3370-3856-11e4-8601-97ba88884ffd_story.html

Lizzio, A., Wilson, K., Simons, R. (2002). University students' perceptions of learning environment and academic outcomes: Implications for theory and practice. *Studies in Higher Education, 27*, 27–52.

Madden, M., Lenhart, A., Cortesi, S., Gasser, U., Duggan, M., & Smith, A. (2013). Teens, social media, and privacy. *Pew Internet and American Life Project*.

McClintock, C. G., & Turner, H. A. (1962). The impact of college upon political knowledge, participation, and values. *Human Relations, 15*, 163–176.

McPherson, M., & Smith-Lovin, L. (1987). Homophily in voluntary organizations: Status distance and the composition of face-to-face groups. *American Sociological Review, 52*, 370–389.

Murthy, D., Gross, A., & Pensavalle, A. (2015). Urban social media demographics: An exploration of Twitter use in major American cities. *Journal of Computer Mediated Communication*. Online before print. doi: 10.1111/jcc4.12144

Newton, K. (2003). Trust, social capital, civil society, and democracy. *International Political Science Review, 22*, 201–214.

Onyx, J., & Bullen, P. (2000). Measuring social capital in five communities. *The Journal of Applied Behavioral Science, 36*, 23–42.

Papacharissi, Z. (2004). Democracy online: Civility, politeness, and the democratic potential of online political discussion groups. *New Media & Society, 6*, 259–283.

Phillips, Whitney (2015). *This is why we can't have nice things. Mapping the relationship between online trolling and mainstream culture*. Cambridge, MA: The MIT Press.

Portes, A. (1998). Social capital: Its origins and applications in modern sociology. *Annual Review of Sociology, 24*, 1–24.

Pretty, J., & Ward, H. (2001). Social capital and the environment. *World Development, 29*(2), 209–227.

Pulvers, K., & Diekhoff, G. M. (1999). The relationship between academic dishonesty and college classroom environment. *Research in Higher Education, 40*, 487–498.

Putnam, R. (2000). *Bowling alone; The collapse and revival of the American community*. New York, NY: Simon & Schuster.

Riffe, D., Lacy, S. & Fico, F. (2014). *Analyzing media messages: Using quantitative content analysis in research*. New York, NY: Routledge/Taylor & Francis Group.

Rosenfeld, R., Messner, S. F., & Baumer, E. P. (2001). Social capital and homicide. *Social Forces, 80*, 283–309.

Rupasingha, A., Goetz, S. J., & Freshwater, D. (2006). The production of social capital in US counties. *The Journal of Socio-Economics, 35*, 83–101.

Shah, D.V. (1998). Civic engagement, interpersonal trust, and television use: An individual level assessment of social capital. *Political Psychology, 19*, 469–496.

Shah, D. V., Cho, J., Eveland, W. P., & Kwak, N. (2005). Information and expression in a digital age: Modeling internet effects on civic participation. *Communication Research, 32*, 531–565.

Shah, D.V., Kwak, N., & Holbert, L. (2001). "Connecting" and "disconnecting" with civic life: Patterns of internet use and the production of social capital. *Political Communication, 18*, 141–162.

Wellman, B., Haase, A. Q., Witte, J., & Hampton, K. (2001). Does the internet increase, decrease, or supplement social capital? Social networks, participation, and community commitment. *American Behavioral Scientist, 45*, 436–455.

Valenzuela, S., Kim, Y., & Gil de Zúñiga, H. (2012). Social networks that matter: Exploring the role of political discussion for online political participation. *International Journal of Public Opinion Research, 24*, 163–184.

Valenzuela, S., Park, N., & Kee, K. F. (2009). Is there social capital in a social network site?: Facebook use and college students' life satisfaction, trust, and participation. *Computer-Mediated Communication, 14*, 875–901.

Vargo, C. J., & Hopp, T. (2015). Socioeconomic status, social capital, and partisan polarity as predictors of political incivility on Twitter: A congressional district-level analysis. *Social Science Computer Review*. doi: 10.1177/0894439315602858

Vargo, C., Basilaia, E. & Shaw, D. (2015). Event vs. Issue: Twitter reflections of major news, a case study. *Studies in Media and Communication, 9*, 215–239.

Wang, H., Can, D., Kazemzadeh, A., Bar, F., & Narayanan, S. (2012, July). A system for real-time Twitter sentiment analysis of 2012 US presidential election cycle. In *Proceedings of the ACL 2012 System Demonstrations* (pp. 115–120). Association for Computational Linguistics.

Yamamoto, M., Kushin, M. J., & Dalisay, F. (2015). Social media and mobiles as political mobilization forces for young adults: Examining the moderating role of online political expression in political participation. *New Media & Society, 17*, 880–898.

YikYakTerminal on GitHub. (2015, November 4). Retrieved from https://github.com/djtech42/YikYakTerminal

Yik Yak Terms of Service. (2015, November 4). Retrieved from www.yikyakapp.com/terms/

9

DATA-DRIVEN CAMPAIGNING

Jessica Baldwin-Philippi

Although the 2008 Obama campaign has been described as groundbreaking for its use of social media in academic and journalistic literature alike, its true break-through in campaigning was in the area of analytics and data strategy. This area has not exactly been overlooked, as the strategic choices involving data-driven campaigning have been detailed in popular press books (Issenberg, 2012) and how-to manuals (Delany, 2011, 2013) and have become central components of training young activists at major workshops like RootsCamp and conferences like Netroots Nation and RightOnline. The analytics teams that supported a variety of the Obama campaigns' work in both 2008 and 2012 have been mythologized by reporters as a cave full of geeks, hipsters, and hacks, insulated from the trad-itional campaign world of horserace coverage and process stories, and from which winning strategies emerged in computerized fluidity (Madrigal, 2013). While these practices mark important changes to the work of political communica-tion and campaign strategy more broadly, the tendency of both journalists and academics to focus on the winners and innovators in order to discern how polit-ical communications strategies change and what tactics are most successful does not tell the whole story.

This chapter aims to describe the state of data-driven campaigning as it has been taken up by campaigns that have fewer resources—in skills, labor, money, and sometimes all three. Following an overview of what data strategy has looked like over time and the concerns that have accompanied its rise, this chapter gives an account of the evolution and status of data campaigning across Field Operations—the team behind voter registration and often volunteer outreach, making contact with likely supporters via phone and in-person canvassing, and getting out the vote (GOTV) on Election Day—and Communications—those who craft email, traditional and digital advertising, and most often have a hand in producing social media content. Overall, it argues that data-driven campaigning is a more limited practice than many popular accounts of contemporary campaign strategy acknowledge, and that beyond presidential campaigns and the most competitive of senate runs, staffers limit data-driven strategy to field operations and advertising.

As part of a volume about the role of data and analytics in political communication research, this project takes the somewhat counter-intuitive approach of using qualitative methods to investigate the topic. In doing so, I take an epistemological approach to data, investigating how campaigns think about data, the conditions under which data produces meaningful knowledge, and the types of knowledge it produces, rather than looking at data itself as the object of study. Moreover, I focus on the everyday ways that data is (and is not) used, discussed, requested, or ignored by campaigns. This chapter is not merely about the contemporary practices of campaigns, but how and why those practices have emerged. In doing so, I find two somewhat divergent stories. On one hand, presidential and advanced senate-level campaigns are staffed by vocal advocates of data-driven practices and the most analytically advanced activists. On the other hand, more local campaigns—congressional, gubernatorial, and even some of the less competitive senate campaigns—are not engaging in these practices in all facets of campaigning. This chapter goes beyond documenting these differences, and highlights where and why such divergence has emerged. Far from a simple story of merely needing data skills, this chapter uncovers other variables that prevent the uptake of data-driven analytics in certain types of campaigns and particular aspects of campaign strategy. In doing so, it also speaks to lessons that the field of political communication can glean from attention to this gap between the data haves and have-nots.

The Development of Data-Driven Campaigning

The roots of data-driven campaigning go much deeper than digital campaigning. Beginning with the rise of public opinion polls in the late 1940s and early 1950s (Berelson, Lazarsfeld, & McPhee, 1954; Lazarsfeld, Berelson, & Gaudet, 1948), data has been used to inform political campaigns of what issues are important to voters, which stances are most popular, and which arguments are persuasive. Over time, this data also provided insight into how different populations viewed issues and could be persuaded and/or mobilized to vote on Election Day. In the 1980s, campaigns began using data from Census Block Groups to combine economic data with racial demographics, education levels, and religious beliefs to construct archetypes of Americans, which were then understood to have political valences. For instance, "Furs & Stationwagons" living in "expensive new neighborhoods in the greenbelt suburbs of nation's major metropolitan areas," their empty-nester equivalents, "Pools and Patios," or the recently-divorced "New Beginnings" set (Klein, 1989). During the 1996 election, the Clinton campaign further refined such tactics by collecting highly segmented opinion polls and lifestyle data to construct archetypes of voters with varying levels of persuadability and issue focuses. "Soccer Moms" were suburban women who the Clinton campaign saw as likely persuadable swing voters, while a reconstructed version of "Pools and Patios" voters were more likely to vote Republican.

Contemporary visions of data-driven campaigning combine these tactics of population defining and targeting with improved database technology that can provide more data to parse, more precisely slice and re-combine populations, and even test how messages perform across groups. As early as 1992, the California Democratic party began organizing voting records, matching that with other available information, and adding its own data about voter contacts (phone calls and canvassing). In the 2004 election, the Bush campaign engaged in extensive efforts to identify potential and likely voters, and built complex models to test and improve turnout (Kreiss, 2016). Over a decade later, these digital platforms have made the collection and organization of information relevant to political decision-making and mobilization of all types easier. While most mobilization efforts are still aimed at turning out voters on Election Day, other, higher-dedication actions such as getting individuals to donate or come into a campaign office to volunteer—and moving them up the so-called "ladder of engagement" to increasingly important and time-consuming actions—are also part of mobilization efforts and are increasingly data driven. Cookies record which parts of campaign websites we click on and when, email systems can organize individuals into separate groups and document which individuals opened which emails and if links inside of the email were clicked, and social media platforms construct our identities out of the information we willingly provide in profiles, the articles we click on, and the preferences of individuals we connect with, and then target political advertisements accordingly. Even more advanced campaigns go beyond relying on targeting to perceived political values, and empirically test particular messages, images, and calls to action with small samples of users before sending the perfectly tailored versions of each message to all available parties (Baldwin-Philippi, 2016). Embedded in this drive toward increasingly precise targeting is what Beth Coleman (2016) has called the "hegemony of big data," or the belief that more data and more specific data will allow campaigns to truly know their audience, and therefore know how to persuade or mobilize them. Although Eitan Hersh's (2015) book *Hacking the Electorate* has demonstrated that the data that is most valuable to campaigns is that which is publicly available and much more overtly tied to past political behaviors and broad demographic information—voter registration, census data, vote history, rather than consumer or lifestyle data—microtargeting and subsequent message testing makes up a significant portion of the discussion of campaign practice.

Even prior to the precision offered by data and analytics that contemporary digital campaigning has enabled, concerns about the democratic impacts of targeting messages to specific populations have existed. First and foremost of these concerns is the fear that with the rise of microtargeting, we will miss out on information that we may disagree with, thereby leading to further polarization and a diminished level of informed citizenry (Pariser, 2011; Sunstein, 2007). The production of a so-called filter bubble in which people find themselves immersed in content they are likely to agree with is not simply a function of gravitating toward information you agree with or avoiding information you do not, though digital information consumption practices certainly reflect this tendency to selectively expose oneself to agreeable content (Garrett, Carnahan, & Lynch, 2011; Stroud, 2011). It is also a function of the technological platforms campaigns and citizens alike rely on. Facebook allows individuals to mute other users and group accounts, as well as particular publications. Facebook, YouTube, Twitter, Instagram, and so on, also provide candidates with highly targeted options for ad buys, including categories that are based not only on political leanings, but of hobbies and interests as well. As campaigns not only target people who are likely to be persuaded or mobilized, they also avoid or segment those who are unlikely to support the candidate, thereby impoverishing certain populations of information. Both of these practices harm the potential citizens have to become informed, and therefore hinder the potential for democratic deliberation and debate. Data-driven practices like microtargeting are not just about ensuring the public is informed so that deliberative democracy can flourish, but also about ensuring opportunities for participatory democracy are present. Just as certain populations can be segmented and end up with less information, the same practices of segmentation leads campaigns to avoid mobilizing certain individuals and groups. Moreover, as Philip Howard (2006) has argued, these tools also reward the loudest voices, rather than the most informed, thereby enabling the rise of "thin" citizens, who "can respond quickly to political urges and need not spend significant amounts of time contemplating political matters" (p. 185). That said, practitioners often argue that voters are more likely to respond to and become mobilized by content they are interested in—especially in an age of information overload—thereby giving microtargeting a valuable role in constructing a more participatory democracy (Issenberg, 2012).

As described, data-driven campaigning strategies are available to campaigns, but central questions remain: Where is data-driven campaigning occurring, and where is it faltering? The following analysis describes how Field and Communications operations within campaigns have made use of data-driven strategy, and where such practices remain lacking. Rather that treat lack of adoption as a failure, this chapter highlights the reasons behind some campaigns' lack of data-driven strategy, and in certain aspects of campaign communications in particular. This chapter then discusses the implications of these findings on the field of political communication, asking what this means for scholars who study campaigns, and scholars who study emergent and changing strategies. Rather than using big data or analytics to conduct my inquiry, I inquire about what these things mean for campaigns.

To answer these questions, this research does not look to big data itself, but to a qualitative investigation of the practices, strategies, and tactics of campaign practitioners and their reflections on these practices, as well as content from training materials and campaign manuals. As a result, it draws on data spanning from 2010–2014, including in-depth interviews of over 40 campaign consultants following the 2010 and 2012 campaigns, brief (~ 20–30 minute) interviews with an additional fifteen staffers and consultants in 2014—nine of whom were staffers in single campaigns in 2014 (three in senate races, six in congressional, across six different states) and six of whom were consultants working on multiple campaigns across a variety of states, often including lower state-level candidates as well. It also uses content presented at professional consulting conferences and written manuals by leaders in the field over the course of those four years. Additionally, as it draws on shifts in analytics-based strategy and the rise of the culture of testing over time, it draws on prior fieldwork as a participant observer inside an Illinois race for federal office in 2010 (Baldwin-Philippi, 2015).

Field Operations: Data-Driven Voter Contact

Historically speaking, Field Operations have the greatest experience with data-driven politicking. While public opinion polls may contribute to how campaigns construct persuasive messages, the use of publicly available, privately purchased, and privately collected data is where the most meaningful and widespread use of data exists. Using combinations of the above data types, campaigns have long used such information in their "ground game"—to predict which individuals and households campaigns need to directly contact in order to ensure they turn out on voting day. While stories of declining ground efforts and the rise of mass media campaigning define the 1980s and 1990s, the late 1990s marked the beginning of increased interest in expanding turnout efforts. Campaigns began devoting significant amounts of money and labor to GOTV efforts in the early 2000s, which were themselves increasingly based on rigorously-tested experiments concerning what worked when trying to get people to the polls (Nielsen, 2012). Early academic experiments conducted during the 1998 midterm elections tested how effective various forms of voter contact were, pitting direct mail, phone calls, and in-person canvassing against each other, and were released just before the 2000 election, to much attention from the consulting class (Gerber & Green, 2000). Daniel Kreiss (2016) goes into great detail discussing the histories of database technologies and use of data on the right and left, explaining how, like the California State Democratic Party began to do in 1992, the Republican National Committee (RNC) had a relatively robust system of sharing voter records and other data that was then used to canvas and target individuals for GOTV efforts. As his book, *Prototype Politics: Technology-Intensive Campaigning and the Data of Democracy*, details, this system, called VoterVault, was developed in a federalized manner in 1995, and by the 2002 midterms was turned into a major database where state parties could connect directly with an interface that would allow them to work with (and add to) data from their local voter files. This system widely outpaced that of the Democratic National Committee (DNC) during that time period, and marked a major development in data at the national level. With this buy-in from parties, databases began to be widely shared, accessed, and added to in a decentralized manner. Following subsequent failures of the RNC to keep the data and technology up to date and the DNC's increased efforts in the area, the DNC caught up to and surpassed the RNC.

In 2004, the AFL-CIO conducted experiments on which unions and which kind of members were more likely to be persuaded by political appeals and ads from leading Republicans (Issenberg, 2010). As the resulting empirically proven tactics were taken up by campaigns on both side of the aisle, and data-driven GOTV tactics and targeting took off in earnest, the political left decided it would be in their interest for more of these findings to be proprietary. In 2007, the Analyst Institute was established to do just that, and brought academic rigor to the experimental field-testing of voter-contact methods. Over the next seven years, the Analyst Institute continued to test methods of voter contact (text messages are helpful (Malhotra, Michelson, Rogers, & Valenzuela, 2011)), and actual scripts to increase turnout (social pressure works (Gerber & Green, n.d.)). Organizationally speaking, while Obama's digital and analytics staffers contributed to many projects—using social media data to target emails and other communications, fundraising, and so on—their crowning achievements in both 2008 and 2012 were turnout models and data-driven organizing. Although it was infamous for its failure, the 2012 Romney campaign's ORCA project—a data-driven Field project designed to show the campaign precisely who had turned out in real time on Election Day—became a cautionary tale against failing to properly invest in technological infrastructure.

Importantly, the use of such data for field operations has not been limited to presidential races—in fact, its power has laid in its usefulness for state-level and local races. While many campaign innovations, such as learning best practices for social media or email writing, take time to trickle down from the presidential level to that of congressional or gubernatorial races (Baldwin-Philippi, 2015), using data to personalize voter contacts was occurring in congressional level elections by 2008 in a way that was more than haphazard, long before they adopted social media (Nielsen, 2012). Additionally, on a more ad-hoc basis, campaigns have long kept lists of "1s," who they know to be likely to attend an event or lend a last-minute hand if needed, as well as "2s" and "3s" who are reliable bets for some volunteer or donor activities. While campaigns at the congressional level and all but the most well-supported senate races lack the type of data that would allow them to make the predictive analysis regarding what type of persuasive messages were likely to work (which the Obama 2012 campaign did do), major party candidates have had access to voter data that is decently well-organized and pretty complete since 2008. Importantly, public records, more than specific lifestyle data, are what have significant impact on strategy at all levels of campaigning—including the presidential (Hersh, 2015). At the congressional level, as early as 2008, campaigns were not only using vote history data to decide who to directly contact by phone, in-person canvassing, and/or mail, but were adding to the database of information about those voters by recording how likely they were to vote for the candidate or entire party ticket, and whether or not they would be willing to volunteer or donate. In 2010, much of the data added to the system was first recorded by volunteers in analog, and was subsequently entered manually. With the proliferation of smartphones and further decentralization of this data, volunteers can add to the file at their fingertips, and the practice is now nearly universal. Daniel Kreiss's (2012, 2016) work explains the differences in database infrastructure and the divergence in the effectiveness of data-driven strategy across the right and left in great detail, but what is notable is that data is used across the board, even if the left has been more adept in its uses over the past decade.

Communications Operations: Email, Social Advertising, and Social Media Content

In a modern congressional campaign, the communications team sends out multiple messages directly to potential voters and supporters every day. From national ad campaigns to responses to Facebook comments, mass emails to tweets, campaigns communicate constantly. Increasingly, we have heard about campaigns' ability to target such messages. The Obama 2012 campaign used new, increasingly personal data from the television ratings industry to develop data-driven practices that allowed the campaign to target television ads by personal political information rather than the traditional television industry terms—likelihood of voting, level of information they'd received, and political leanings, rather than the demographics of viewers of certain shows or genres (Davidsen, 2015) As companies like Facebook and Twitter depend on ad revenue, they have made possible targeting very particular groups of people based on interests that are both self-reported and determined by content sought on the platform, friend networks and interests, and traditional demographic information like location and age. Most campaigns use customer management systems (CRMs) that can organize email lists and facilitate targeting and testing of messages. These practices all fall under the banner of what many consultants have, since 2010, called a "culture of analytics" or a "culture of testing" that advocates for rigorously testing messages across many platforms in order to ensure they are not only well-crafted, but well targeted, and also provide campaigns with more information about what works moving forward (Baldwin-Philippi, 2016).

Mixed Inbox: Targeting without Testing

With little effort or infrastructure, campaigns can purchase subscriptions to off-the-shelf Customer Relationship Management (CRM) systems that allow them to organize recipients and target messages based off of information they ask citizens to provide, such as political interests, types of events they might be interested in, and basic demographic information. CRM systems can also collect data on whether an email was opened, if it was shared in other social media spaces, and/or what links were clicked. Such systems return the data concerning which messages were opened and otherwise responded to in varying degrees of detail, often allowing campaigns to easily see which emails were opened, or which populations did the most opening. Although campaigns can learn a lot from eyeballing the popularity of data like open and click-through rates, consultants and staffers with more advanced analytics experience have begun to advocate for what has been called a culture of testing, which involves scientifically testing messages, rather than merely eyeballing trends. Major proponents of the culture of testing also use consulting conferences to advocate for more advanced testing involving randomized controlled studies to train activists and consultants to be efficient in how and when they communicate. Although the language of cultivating a culture of testing is seemingly more widespread than the actual use of such tactics (Baldwin-Philippi, 2016), advocates argue that their use allows campaigns to improve their outreach by small, but meaningful numbers, which is what will result in more persuasion, dollars raised, and ultimately more electoral victories (Michelson & Nickerson, 2011; Schwartz, 2009). Many of these tactics are based on the field experiments pioneered by Field teams to mobilize voters to turn out on Election Day, and have since been applied to mobilization efforts surrounding getting supporters to donate, volunteer, or take online action such as petition signing.

While presidential campaigns have made use of these practices since 2008, congressional and even senate level races' use of rigorous scientific testing is limited, despite their professed enthusiasm for analytics. Generally, communications directors for Senate and Congressional campaigns were well versed in targeting email lists according to issue interests and geography. Campaigns will send invitations to events to those they know are local, based on self-reported zip codes while sending fundraising requests outside of their district, and campaigns will send out updates about an environmental policy or event with environmental groups to those they who have checked a box stating they were interested in that particular issue. Well-funded congressional campaigns were practicing this regularly as early as 2010, even though they also sent out mass emails to their entire lists as well for things like fundraising, calls to action, and occasional campaign updates such as new ads and endorsements (Fieldnotes Aug 25, 2010). The practice of sending some emails to an entire list persisted at the congressional level, where they were largely used to update supporters on events like fundraising dinners with major elected officials, and "newsletter-type" emails with multiple updates (Personal communication Dec 15, 2014). Interestingly, even at the presidential level, a common critique of the 2016 Trump campaign was that the communications office was not even targeting its email list at this basic level, and engaging in practices that made it likely that messages would go to spam (Kaye, 2016; Samuelsohn & Vogel, 2016).

Calls to go beyond this simple list splicing and move toward testing messages are relatively widely discussed in professional trade publications like *Campaigns & Elections* and major conferences such as *Netroots Nation, Conservative Political*

Action Conference (CPAC), and the now-defunct *Right Online,* as well as by leading consultants. Outside of the presidential level, those who do attend to controlled sample testing are, overwhelmingly, either consultants or staffers for the most competitive of senate races. With a recent organizational study showing that roughly 20 veterans of the Obama campaign who focused on digital and analytics went to down-ballot races in 2014 and 2016 (Kreiss & Jasinski, 2016), it makes sense that these spaces are where the most innovative tactics would take place, leaving the rest of campaigns to less rigorous methods of message testing.

In most campaigns, these practices are simply not a predominant aspect of local races. In 2010, only the most advanced campaigns at the senate level were testing those messages in order to determine what type of subject header, content, and images were best at gaining attention or mobilizing constituencies (Baldwin-Philippi, 2016). By 2014, those at the congressional level and less competitive senate races had made little headway in this area. At the congressional and senate level in 2014, few consultants and staffers engaged in randomized, controlled sample testing in 2014, though some did regularly compare two or three versions of a message and send the one that worked best to the whole list. This practice, known as A/B testing, does not separate test subjects into controlled samples or isolate particular variables of the message. Campaign consultants in particular, rather than staffers on single campaigns, reported A/B testing, and most used it for both website and email content—five out of six I spoke with used this tactic for any type of message, from website content to social media ads, although only three reported using it for email. Although staffers were far less likely to use A/B testing, it was still a viable tactic, with three of the nine staffers interviewed engaging with such comparative analysis. Two of these worked at the senate level, and each of them reported that they mostly A/B tested their website content, rather than emails. Despite using this tactic, staffers (especially at the congressional level) were unlikely to describe conducting such tests in a routine or ongoing way.

Advanced-level Advertising

Advertising tells a slightly different story, as campaigns' facility with targeting ads far surpasses any other communications efforts, at all levels of election. While social media were not always ad-supported, the presence of advertising in the digital campaigning landscape is unavoidable. Facebook has been home to a robust ad system since 2008, and Twitter has since April of 2010.[1] Because social media platforms subsist on advertising revenue, they have long lured businesses with the very fact that they have enormous amounts of data about their users' interests and behaviors and can target them accordingly. Over time, platforms like Facebook and Twitter have made ads look more and more like the content produced by other users, changing their placement in the user interface and using small, less noticeable disclaimers about promoted content. Broadly, campaigns have more experience with advertising within Facebook than Twitter, due to Facebook's audience size and the perception that Twitter is best for talking to journalists (Hamby, 2013; Kreiss, 2012) and driving the campaign's narrative.

As early as 2010, even congressional campaigns were much more familiar with targeting ads in Facebook and looking at the ad analytics Facebook provides in order to assess whether an online ad was succeeding, and making the appropriate changes from these findings. For instance, campaign staffers who did not A/B test any email or web content were familiar with targeting Facebook ads by location, age, education, gender, and other demographic features. In fact, they used the advertising platform easily as early as the 2010 midterm election (Fieldnotes, August 25, 2010). Moreover, Facebook allowed microtargeting based on keywords that users had entered as interests of theirs, and specific places users work. Opportunities for microtargeting have only gotten more specific as Facebook moved past using only user-provided information, and began to assemble their own "shadow" profiles of users based on what we click on, what we like, and who our friends are. As one congressional staffer explained, "Facebook has always made it so easy, with drop down menus of demographics and interests and everything. Now there are even more options [than in prior years]—you can boost posts, not just ads even" (Personal communication, December 18, 2014). As early as 2010, another widely used method of targeting that Facebook provided was to segment populations of those who were fans of a page, those who are not, and those who have "friends" who are fans of a page, enabling campaigns to target new potential supporters while also adding social pressure by showing them which of their friends have already liked their campaign. Similarly, as early as 2008, campaigns began to match their voter files to ad networks, Yahoo!, and Google, so they could better-target ads on search engines, and on scores of websites that subscribe to various ad networks. The ability to microtarget has only gotten more precise over time. By 2015, campaigns could even target individual "political influencers" across the political spectrum through Facebook's ad interface, and the Trump 2016 campaign's digital team claimed that highly targeted Facebook ads were key to their success (Green & Issenberg, 2016).

In all of these cases, the corporations selling the ad buys have made it cheap and, even more importantly, easy for campaigns and have shared best practices and advice for how best to use their platforms for targeted advertising. One staffer from the congressional level explained that corporations not only made their ad interfaces intuitive, but have doubled down on offering support to encourage campaigns to advertise within their platform: "There have always been newsletters or listservs I read for best practices of all kinds of messaging, but Facebook ads were always pretty easy. And now Facebook even emails advice and best practices if you sign up for their list" (Personal communication, Dec 3, 2014). Campaigns could also use the data they receive from their own fans to design strategies that expand beyond advertising. In 2012, the amount of data that Facebook provided to campaigns about anyone who had liked their page allowed the Obama campaign to target emails encouraging people to vote by telling them which of their friends had pledged to do so (Judd, 2011).

While the 2008 Obama campaign used Facebook to both broadcast and target their messages via public posts and advertisements respectively, the platforms and strategies for doing so have changed dramatically over the past eight years. In 2010, the line between public and targeted content was clearly drawn—posts were public (unless sent directly and privately to individuals), and advertisements were available to be targeted based on users' location, age, gender, and interests. Though many campaigns engaged in both tactics, they were sometimes surprised and often frustrated at the difference in affordances, and their inability to use the targeting tools they used for advertising to target regular public posts or messages (Fieldnotes, Aug. 31, 2010; Sept. 1, 2010).

Social Media Analytics: Using What's There

While figuring out if ads worked, and how competing versions tested against each other was relatively easy for campaigns, understanding what worked for content of social media posts has been more difficult for campaigns. Of course, testing particular social media messages ahead of time is not feasible—the posts are public and dispersed on a mass scale. Instead, campaigns use social media post-fact to determine if messages worked, although defining what success means in this space has been difficult. Social media platforms like Facebook and Twitter are also continuously developing analytics and dashboards to help their users—especially those related to consumer marketing, who also buy ads—make sense of these numbers. They are also developing improved ways to help campaigns expand the reach of messages and even target them, including both paid and free options.

If campaigns like looking at click-through rates of emails, they love looking at the social media metrics provided in the platforms' dashboards—for instance, Facebook Insights' clear illustration of which posts got the most hits, as represented as overall bar graphs, and by impressions per day. One extolled their virtues of being immediately available and easy to decipher, exclaiming "Of course! They're right there! You can just take a quick look and see what type of messages perform well" (Personal communication, December 18-b, 2014) when asked if she looked at them. Another laughed when asked the question, noting "I was a little compulsive with them. You want people to see your messages, and to be able to see that feels good—as opposed to like calling, where who knows what the guy who hangs up on you will do or if he'll vote." (Personal communication, December 13, 2014). Even though likes and retweets can tell staffers little about what Election Day turnout will be like, metrics provided some window into how potential voters would respond, and that was gratifying, even when anxiety-provoking. This staffer explained this feeling of anxiety as well, saying he "had to say 'Ok, you can't look until tomorrow morning'" so he could both unwind when home, or work on other things that required more focus.

When looking at these analytics, it's important to acknowledge that even as campaign staffers and consultants say "they show what works," the very definition of success if complicated and not measured particularly well by the available analytics.

At their core, these analytics focus on popularity, highlighting the amount of impressions content makes, how many times it is liked or favorited, and how often it is shared about other metrics. Visually, the native analytics of Facebook overwhelmingly emphasize these very measures. In each of these, the number of likes, the reach (total impressions), and "engagement" (a combination of likes, comments, shares, and how many times links are clicked) are provided. These engagement analytics begin to provide insight that is deeper than popularity of topics or issues, but also require more advanced strategies in combination with other forms of analytics to understand if other action such as donating, or signing up for a newsletter are taken. Facebook highlights notifications specifically for likes and shares and bar graphs that visually represent the amount of people reached. Although popularity and reach of messages are important to campaigns—not least of all to seem well supported—these messages are unlikely to persuade undecideds, or those leaning the other way. Instead, social media messaging—and digital messaging more generally—has largely been viewed as a mechanism to deepen commitment and mobilize those committed supporters (Baldwin-Philippi, 2015; Bimber, 2003; Vaccari, 2008). And social media platforms are particularly bad at measuring that. The analytics provided by platforms like Facebook and Twitter do measure instances of mobilization or commitment-building, such as engagement, or if audiences click on links provided, but the systems themselves cannot track analytics of more action-oriented behavior, such as which users donate once a link is clicked, or how long they stay on that page. While Twitter provides data on a user's audience through a "followers" section of their analytics and a very skilled campaign could perform social network analysis of its users, that information harder to access than analytics displaying an account and individual tweet's impressions, retweets, favorites, or an account's mentions. While campaigns know that popularity is not necessarily the most important metric, it is one they often fall back on.

Just as the material constraints of privately owned platforms impacted campaigns' ability to control and sensor public commentary, they also constrain campaigns' ability to work with analytics. The data that platforms like Facebook and Twitter automatically provide to users—especially the data that they choose to visually represent and make the most easily interpretable—will be the data that campaigns turn to, and that therefore drives content creation. Popular social media analytics packages such as SproutSocial, CrowdTangle, Attentive.ly, and so on, provide more complex metrics of "engagement" than those baked into social media platforms themselves, like Facebook Insights. In these third-party tools, algorithms rank combinations of measures such as likes, shares, attention, users' networks, and so on, and sometimes compare them with other similar pages. These uses of analytics are certainly an important beginning step into testing messages and engaging analytics more rigorously, but their limited use results in attention to the type of content that encourages campaigns to focus on messages that are popular, rather than mobilizing.

What campaigns are doing with social media analytics is rather mundane, and not particularly helpful to creating more nuanced messages, but it is also in the platforms' interest to develop tools that enable campaigns and consumer marketers to make better use of the vast quantities of data social media platforms collect. In one major change, by the time the 2012 campaigns occurred, Facebook had blurred the line between public posts and ads, giving campaigns the ability to "promote" (now "boost") individual posts to audiences that could be targeted based on user location, age, gender, and interests. Social platforms like Facebook and Twitter have continued to blur the line between advertising and content by allowing campaigns to pay to "promote" their posts to larger audiences and target the populations who make up that audience. While these posts are still publicly visible, and therefore subject to checks by journalists, supporters, and the opposing campaign alike, campaigns can now extend the reach of messages they choose, and do so to populations that are microtargeted. Still, some campaign staffers are skeptical of such options. One reported, "It's just like $3, so of course I did it sometimes, but I never really felt great about it. Like, what do those extra people reached mean? I'm glad when it says more, but is that worth paying for regularly? Is this just Facebook making us think it works?" Interestingly, this tactic brought forth skepticism that was previously not discussed among consultants and staffers.

Why Are Local Campaigns Falling Behind in Communications?

In many cases, new campaign strategies trickle down from the well-funded presidential campaigns that are staffed by well-known and successful staffers to more local races, staffed by more local politicos with less experience and less exposure to cutting-edge best practices. Of course, there are outliers, but this trickle-down narrative wherein innovation happens at the presidential level and adoption occurs first by well-funded, competitive campaigns, then by local campaigns has held true for how campaigns made sense of how to navigate the type of content to post in social media, how to craft websites, and so on (Baldwin-Philippi, 2015; Foot & Schneider, 2006; Nielsen, 2012; Serazio, 2015; Stromer-Galley, 2014). Most of the arguments for why local campaigns are falling behind in the move toward microtargeted and analytics driven emails and social media messaging assume that staffers and consultants at this level lack the skills or professional experience to believe in data-driven strategy.

At a certain level, this is true, but it does not tell the whole story. Daniel Kreiss's study of where presidential campaign staffers work off-election years shows that they do go to major senate races, but are very unlikely to work at the congressional level, using their skills and knowledge to improve the tactics in their races and leaving others to catch up over time. Races at the congressional level, therefore, do lack the individuals associated with data-driven campaigning, but they do not necessarily lack the skills to do so, or the more general cultural norms needed to want to invest in doing so. When speaking with staffers of and consultants for senate and congressional level races, nearly all of them report whole-heartedly supporting moves toward data-driven campaigning. Moreover, not all local races are lacking skilled practitioners, as hundreds of local activists, advocacy workers, and campaign staffers have been trained by data-oriented grassroots organizations like the New Organizing Institute and Wellstone. What this means is that at the level of senate and even congressional campaigns, staffers often have these skills, but are unable to make use of them for other reasons. In particular, more local campaigns stress the amount of labor data-driven practices take, the limited payoff, and the availability of other information that gets "close enough" to data-driven practices.

Campaigns, especially local ones, are staffed by very few people, and the time of those who decide and implement strategy is stretched very thin. At the level of congressional campaigns, the best-funded campaigns generally have fewer than fifteen staffers, with many campaigns working with fewer. For senate races, the higher end of these employ around 25 paid staffers. While volunteer labor and party resources provide reinforcements, those individuals are not usually tasked with strategic positions or the power to craft much content. With the time of digital and communications directors stretched so thin, they are unlikely to have the time to devote to data-driven practices. One staffer who had been trained in and previously engaged in email targeting and testing for an advocacy group reported, "we just didn't have the bandwidth—or the time really—to write a bunch of different emails [to test against one another] (Dec 15, 2014b)." Despite knowing that he could increase the number of people who read an email or click on its link, he was not willing to use his valuable time to write multiple versions of an email to test whether different images, narrative frames, or tone would change the results. Similarly, as another communications staffer for a congressional level race explained, "I don't have to take time to set something up before posting a message [...] I can look at the numbers [of who liked or shared social messages] when I have the time" (Personal communication, December 3, 2014).

Moreover, the ultimate payoff of taking the time to do so is not immediately beneficial to campaigns at local, and even statewide levels. The success of data-driven campaigning in many ways relies upon large sample sizes. When the most successful of messages increases your desired outcome by 3 percentage points, and most of the time testing only increases desired behaviors at a rate below 1%, the payoff is markedly less for local races. When the Obama campaign nets a 1% increase in donations on a list of about 20 million, that number is massive; when a local race has a list numbering in the single thousands, 1% makes much less difference. The tradeoff between time and reward is fundamentally different for local races, and decisions to forego data-driven email and social media tactics can be rational, considered responses to the high cost and lesser reward they offer smaller campaigns. The constraint of Election Day looming as the ultimate arbiter of success and failure becomes especially visible when considering how much more advanced the uses of analytics-based messaging activist organizations—even relatively small organizations—engage in (Karpf, 2016). When an investment in labor can pay off later on in future campaigns, months down the road, such practices become much more widespread.

Campaigns have also found workarounds for adopting what they assumed were best practices. One very popular method of assessing social media content, as discussed earlier, is using available analytics that measure popularity and reach, rather than more nuanced metrics that measure which messages are successfully being circulated, shared, or liked. As discussed earlier, campaigns of all sizes had staffers who paid attention to the analytics that social media platforms provide users. A staffer who said she didn't have the time to test messages noted that she could come to social media metrics after content had been posted, see if it became well-shared, well-liked, or even just seen by many people, and "still use that [finding] the next time we need to post a message" (Personal Communication, Jan 12, 2015). These metrics are how, as the 2010 midterm elections began to progress, campaigns realized that posting long, text-heavy, issue-focused content in social media did not get much attention in the space. As one digital consultant handling many races explained, this learning process happened over the course of the campaign, and by the end of 2010, they realized that "anytime we dabbled with actual policy, it was a disaster" (Personal Communication, March 4, 2011). While close attention to metrics or testing email messages might have revealed that sooner, campaigns caught on nonetheless.

Sometimes foregoing data all-together, campaigns often looked to each other for best practices, and copied the style, tone, and content of campaigns that are better resourced, assuming knew what they were doing. In 2010, congressional communications and digital directors constantly referenced Cory Booker's use of Twitter as something they wanted to emulate in order to reach out to constituents. "Look at [our opposing campaign's] pictures. You need to use images that are better framed and use filters, like [our opponent]" (Fieldnotes, Oct 18, 2010). Another staffer who worked on a senate race in 2014 explained how they had adopted certain email writing practices, saying "You know how Obama's emails [subject lines] are all short—like, "Hey…"? We know that works better. So we started doing short subject lines too" (Personal Communication, Jan 16, 2015). Other work investigating the use of social media strategy in the 2016 presidential primaries showed that even at this level, staffers from lesser-known candidates would look to the perceived leaders in the field (McGregor, Kreiss, & Lawrence, 2016). For instance, if a campaign of either party saw the Clinton campaign creating a new style of image or content, they would be imitated, because the perception was that their campaign knew best practices. In these cases, campaigns can decide to forego testing messages (whether it is outside their skill level or at too high a cost), while thinking of their strategy as benefitting from the move toward data-driven messaging.

Of course some opportunities to use new strategies and analytics are missed due to campaigns' inabilities or lack of vision about the importance of such methods. Even as campaign staffers and consultants extol the virtues of data-driven practices, the culture of campaigns can privilege tried and true methods and gut instincts that have worked in the past, rather than pay attention to what new methods are seemingly working in the present. But these cultural clashes between traditional and new campaign strategies are not limited to the local level. In both 2008 and 2012, the Obama campaign's data and analytics department clashed with more traditional media and communications departments. Staffers from competitive senate races report repeated arguments between Communications and Digital operations. The Romney campaign famously required 22 people to sign off on anything the campaign tweeted, to the great frustration of the Digital team (Kreiss, 2014).

Implications for Studying Data-Driven Campaigning

As the study of data-driven campaigning reaches beyond accounts of what the most successful and well-funded of presidential campaigns are doing, we not only learn how strategies differ across levels of campaigning, but how and why they spread—or do not. At a fairly surface level, data like that presented here tells us that the whole terrain of political campaign strategy does not look like that of presidential campaigning. While presidential races tell us much about cutting-edge tactics, it is the midterm elections where these practices get picked up or left behind, and they play a vital role in continuing, evolving, and sometimes changing or ignoring strategies from presidential campaigns. These campaigns are home to many who continue to work in local politics and advocacy organizations, and we miss a significant amount of what political strategy looks at by looking only to presidential campaigns.

Moreover, the assumption is that innovative, productive tactics and strategies that are developed at the presidential level will trickle down as skills or tools disperse. Given that testing messages and using analytics does rely on a particular set of skills, it is sensible that we might attribute more local campaigns' failure to adopt a product of missing skills or because those in charge of campaigns are rooted in prior norms. Consequently, that tactics that work at the presidential level will, over time, work their way into down-ballot races. This research points to flaws in that thinking. The trickle-down model depends on the only variable precluding adoption being knowledge of the strategy or skills/tools needed to enact it.

This work points to alternative reasons, such as differing constraints on labor and resources, that makes congressional and all but the most competitive senate races unlikely to make such choices. We discuss email as a mode of communication that is free of cost, and that does not tell the whole story. While email is, obviously, cheaper than advertising, it does take significant labor to produce good, effective emails, and costs the communications director and digital director valuable time—a resource they cannot fundraise to get more of. Gubernatorial, congressional, and senate races (to say nothing of mayoral or state senate) are unlikely to raise enough money to simply hire more staffers to make up for this labor, as presidential campaigns could do. Moreover, while the cost is higher to down-ballot campaigns, the payoff is likely to be much lower. Due to the number of people these campaigns are trying to communicate with, marginal increases in effective outreach on the scale of 1% are unlikely to make a big dent in their numbers. These choices are not a failure to adopt, but a logically considered strategy not to do so.

That field teams have adopted these practices shows that the problem is not that campaigns avoid or overlook data, but that its adoption relies on being useful under constrained resources. With volunteers able to canvas, there is willing and able volunteer labor that can immediately put the data-driven targeting choices to work without much additional cost to the campaign. Moreover, as face-to-face voter contacts remain one of the most effective tactics for getting people to the voting booth, the payoff is much greater.

These findings not only call into question assumption about strategy adoption, but also about broader democratic implications of such strategies. Political communication has long been concerned about the potential for microtargeting in campaign communication—from individualized ads playing before YouTube videos, emails highlighting policies we are sure to approve of, to improved targeting of "traditional" media such as television ads. The concern that these messages can place people in a filter bubble, isolating them from important political content that would otherwise shape their views, then leads to concerns about the loss of true public deliberation and debate, increased polarization, and the development of limited versions of citizenship, wherein individuals are seen as little more than manipulable combinations of various data markers. While we should be critical of the data-driven choices and algorithms that impact our lives constantly now, we must also acknowledge that there are many areas of political messaging for which microtargeting is not of great strategic benefit, and that as a result, many of the messages we receive still follow a mass media.

Finally, just as Leticia Bode's chapter in this volume discusses how the use of big datasets can be beneficial to qualitative researchers, so too can qualitative work about how and why big data is used give insight into the role of big data in the field of political communication. By treating big data as the object of analysis, rather than a methodological choice, this chapter reveals that campaigns' use of data and analytics, while increasing, is not as widespread as popular press accounts may imply, and it may not be of great strategic benefit to many campaigns. Simply because it is there, and people can use it does not mean they will. Moreover, while big datasets are enticing to study because they can reveal political behaviors and trends in content on a large scale, those inquiries do not get to core questions about why campaigns create that content or citizens engage with it in a particular way. Simply because big data is there for the picking—campaigns' Twitter feeds and Facebook posts can be scraped and catalogued—does not mean it should be the focal point of what we ought to study. Combining the use of big data with qualitative methods investigating the actions, purposes, dispositions, and values behind such data and its strategic uses provides a holistic approach to the field of political communication as we move forward in a field that needs to keep up with rapid changes in communication technology.

Note

1 Facebook had specific deals with companies to do site-wide advertising prior to this.

References

Baldwin-Philippi, J. (2015). *Using technology, building democracy: Digital campaigning and the construction of citizenship.* New York, NY: Oxford University Press.

Baldwin-Philippi, J. (2016). The cult(ure) of analytics in 2014. In J. A. Hendricks & D. Schill (Eds.), *Communication and midterm elections: Media, message, and mobilization.* New York, NY: Palgrave Macmillan.

Berelson, B., Lazarsfeld, P., & McPhee, W. (1954). *Voting: A study of opinion formation in a presidential campaign.* Chicago, IL: University of Chicago Press.

Bimber, B. (2003). *Information and American democracy: Technology in the evolution of political power.* New York, NY: Cambridge University Press.

Coleman, B. (2016). Let's get lost: Poetic city meets data city. In Gordon, Eric & P. Mihailidis (Eds.), *Civic media: technology, design, practice.* Cambridge, MA: MIT Press.

Davidsen, C. (2015, June). *You are not your data: What we actually do with your data.* Presented at the Personal Democracy Forum, New York, NY. Retrieved from https://personaldemocracy.com/media/you-are-not-target-what-we-actually-do-your-data

Delany, C. (2011). *Online politics 101: The tools and tactics of digital political advocacy.* Colin Delany (self published).

Delany, C. (2013). *How to use the internet to win in 2014: A comprehensive guide to online politics for campaigns & advocates.* Epolitics.com.

Foot, K., & Schneider, S. (2006). *Web campaigning.* Cambridge, MA: MIT Press.

Garrett, R. K., Carnahan, D., & Lynch, E. K. (2011). A turn toward avoidance? Selective exposure to online political information, 2004–2008. *Political Behavior, 35*(1), 113–134.

Gerber, A. S., & Green, D. P. (2000). The effect of a nonpartisan get-out-the-vote drive: An experimental study of leafletting. *The Journal of Politics, 62*(3), 846–857.

Gerber, A. S., & Green, D. P. (n.d.). Field experiments on voter mobilization: An overview of a burgeoning literature. In *Handbook of field experiments.* Cambridge, MA: Abdul Latif Jameel Poverty Action Lab (J-PAL). Retrieved from www.povertyactionlab.org/handbook-field-experiments

Green, J., & Issenberg, S. (2016, October 27). Inside the Trump bunker, with days to go. *Bloomberg BusinessWeek.* Retrieved from www.bloomberg.com/news/articles/2016-10-27/inside-the-trump-bunker-with-12-days-to-go

Hamby, P. (2013). *Did Twitter kill the boys on the bus? Searching for a better way to cover a campaign.* Cambridge, MA: Shorenstein Center on Media, Politics, and Public Policy.

Hersh, E. (2015). *Hacking the electorate: How campaigns perceive voters.* New York, NY: Cambridge University Press.

Howard, P. (2006). *New media and the managed citizen.* New York, NY: Cambridge University Press.

Issenberg, S. (2010, October 31). Nudge the vote: How behavioral science is remaking politics. *The New York Times*. New York, NY. Retrieved from www.nytimes.com/2010/10/31/magazine/31politics-t.html

Issenberg, S. (2012). *The victory lab: The secret science of winning campaigns*. New York, NY: Crown Books.

Judd, N. (2011, October 22). Why campaigns are happy your vote isn't as private as many think it is. *TechPresident*. Retrieved from http://techpresident.com/news/23032/do-you-care-if-obama-knows-you-voted-what-about-if-he-told-your-friends

Kaye, K. (2016, June 23). Trump's first fundraising email had a 60% spam rate. Retrieved November 1, 2016, from http://adage.com/article/campaign-trail/trump-s-fundraising-email-a-60-spam-rate/304673/

Klein, D. (1989, April 16). You are where you live : Neighborhoods by the numbers: How ZIP codes can pigeonhole people like widgets in a digit factory. *Los Angeles Times*. Retrieved from http://articles.latimes.com/1989-04-16/news/vw-2346_1_zip-code-clusters-smithsonian-magazine

Kreiss, D. (2012). Acting in the public sphere: The 2008 Obama campaign's strategic use of new media to shape narratives of the presidential race. *Media, Movements, and Political Change: Research in Social Movements, Conflicts and Change, 33*, 195–223.

Kreiss, D. (2014). Seizing the moment: The presidential campaigns' use of Twitter during the 2012 electoral cycle. *New Media & Society, 18*(8), 1473–1490.

Kreiss, D. (2016). *Prototype politics: Technology-intensive campaigning and the data of democracy*. New York, NY: Oxford University Press.

Kreiss, D., & Jasinski, C. (2016). The tech industry meets presidential politics: Explaining the Democratic Party's technological advantage in electoral campaigning, 2004–2012. *Political Communication, 33*(4), 544–562.

Lazarsfeld, P., Berelson, B., & Gaudet, H. (1948). *The people's choice: How the voter makes up his mind*. New York, NY: Columbia University Press.

Madrigal, A. (2013). When the nerds go marching in. *The Atlantic* (November 16).

Malhotra, N., Michelson, M. R., Rogers, T., & Valenzuela, A. A. (2011). Text messages as mobilization tools: The conditional effect of habitual voting and election salience. *American Politics Research, 39*(4), 664–681.

McGregor, S., Kreiss, Daniel, & Lawrence, R. (2016). Instastyle: Campaign communication in the selfie era. Presented at the American Political Science Association, Philadelphia, PA.

Michelson, M. R., & Nickerson, D. (2011). Voter mobilization. In J. Druckman, D. P. Green, J. H. Kuklinski, & A. Lupia (Eds.), *Cambridge handbook of experimental political science* (pp. 228–242). New York, NY: Cambridge University Press.

Nielsen, R. K. (2012). *Ground wars: Personalized communication in political campaigns*. Princeton, NJ: Princeton University Press.

Pariser, E. (2011). *Filter bubble: How the new personalized web is changing what we read and how we think*. New York, NY: Penguin Books.

Samuelsohn, D., & Vogel, K. P. (2016, June 28). Trump's secret data reversal. *Politico*. Retrieved from http://politi.co/28YAt3B

Schwartz, R. (2009). *Cutting edge evidence-based best practices*. Presented at the Netroots Nation, Pittsburgh, PA. Retrieved from www.youtube.com/watch?v=HE7mgWHnI0g

Serazio, M. (2015). Qualitative political communication| Managing the digital news cyclone: Power, participation, and political production strategies. *International Journal of Communication, 9*(0), 19.

Stromer-Galley, J. (2014). *Presidential campaigning in the internet age.* New York, NY: Oxford University Press.

Stroud, N. J. (2011). *Niche news: The politics of news choice.* New York, NY: Oxford University Press.

Sunstein, C. (2007). *Republic 2.0.* Princeton, NJ: Princeton University Press.

Vaccari, C. (2008). From the air to the ground: The internet in the 2004 US presidential campaign. *New Media & Society, 10*(4), 647–665.

10

"LITTLE MARCO," "LYIN' TED," "CROOKED HILLARY," AND THE "BIASED" MEDIA

How Trump Used Twitter to Attack and Organize

Ayellet Pelled, Josephine Lukito, Fred Boehm, JungHwan Yang, and Dhavan Shah

Donald Trump received an unprecedented amount of news coverage during his presidential campaign (Confessore & Yourish, 2016), on occasions drawing as much as five times more volume than all of the other candidates combined (Patterson, 2016a). Trump, the controversial contender, a reality-television celebrity and media persona, mainly known for his business empire, has been an object of public interest for decades. Long before *The Apprentice* even aired, Trump had been dabbling in the entertainment arena, promoting his hotels, casinos, and golf courses, alongside his products, programs, and events (Yanofsky, 2015). His presidential candidacy reflects the quintessential intersection between media, politics, and entertainment (Ouellette, 2016; Williams & Delli Carpini, 2011).

In the early pre-primary stages of the campaign, Trump's celebrity status and prominence garnered a significant amount of media attention. He enjoyed relatively favorable coverage, with the press avoiding harsh criticism (Patterson, 2016b). Perhaps the tendency to cover Trump "forgivingly" during this period was tied to the perception held by many journalists that he was not a serious candidate. Furthermore, the press had a vested interest in covering Trump's many public remarks, as his name created a magnet for click-bait and online viewership (Azari, 2016; Karpf, 2016). In fact, he was frequently mentioned in news items even when he was not the focus of the story, or when covering other candidates.

The volume of news coverage Trump received cannot be explained by his audience-attracting propensity alone. Rather, Trump did much to cultivate coverage. Not only did the media seek Trump out, he also actively pursued the media, amplifying his visibility and presence on the media agenda. He lent himself to the press by frequently engaging in interviews, hosting press conferences, and holding public events, such as rallies, and townhalls, attempting to enhance his brand and visibility through earned media exposure (Eddy, 2016; Borchers, 2016). More important, he was able to generate media coverage through his use of Twitter and the amplification of his message by his followers (Wells et al., 2016, also Chadwick & Stromer-Galley, 2016). This differs greatly from candidates such as Clinton, who held fewer media events, avoided interviews, and lacked the social media following and enthusiasm that Trump enjoyed (Jacobson, 2016). Trump's experience garnering news attention meant he understood publicity and visibility (Marwick, 2013).

A major focus of Trump's messages on Twitter was, and continues to be, the targeting of "enemies." The press responded to these missives, abiding by the news norm to focus on conflict, especially when occurring among elites and in the midst of a horserace campaign. Our focus in this paper are Trump's four main targets during the campaign, which emerged from Latent Dirichlet Allocation topic modeling of his full corpus of tweets issues during the campaign: Marco Rubio, Ted Cruz, Hillary Clinton, and the "biased" media.

Trump and Social Media

Trump's use of social media, specifically Twitter, set him apart from other candidates who have been slow to adopt or fully integrate this channel into their campaign communications. For comparison, Hillary Clinton, the presidential nominee of the Democratic Party, only joined Twitter in the summer of 2013. When she announced her candidacy, on April 2015, her follower count was slightly over 3 million; larger than Trump's count at that time, which was around 2.7 million. After announcing his candidacy, in June 2015, Trump's follower count began to expand rapidly, and by October 2015 he had surpassed Clinton. Near the end of 2016, Clinton and Trump had 10.5 and 13 million followers, respectively, with his tweets garnering much more attention and retweet activity (Keegan, 2016; Lee & Quealy, 2017). His ability to leverage attention into coverage reflects a novel, hybrid campaigning strategy, which allowed him to bypass expensive advertising buys and a large campaign infrastructure, earning rather than paying for media exposure (Confessore & Yourish, 2016).

Of course, political actors have previously utilized social media and hybrid media campaigning for their coordination and mobilization efforts. Howard Dean campaign operatives were early adopters, as they learned the possibilities of these new interactive platforms as the campaign unfolded (Kreiss, 2012). Obama's campaign staff built on the infrastructure developed by Dean's campaign, in a more organized and hierarchical manner, infiltrating content into blogs, accumulating media presence, SMSing supporters, and raising funds via the web, in addition to mobilizing voters and volunteers (Chadwick, 2013).

Even though Trump's campaign is not the first to employ social media in a hybrid media campaigning, his strategies are somewhat distinct from those who preceded him. In both Dean's and Obama's campaigns, messages on social media were often directed to supporters with a recognition that these messages would get picked up by the mainstream media. Messaging was handled with some discipline, careful not to use inflammatory or ridiculing language, so that the campaign was presented in a positive light when exposed to a greater audience. Trump's use of social media was both more personal and vicious, less conventional and politically correct. That is, previous hybrid media campaigns were well orchestrated and planned efforts, organized by staffers in a central position overlooking the online arena, unlike Trump's campaign.

Trump's unique manner of directly addressing his followers, bypassing the restrictions and requirements of mainstream media intermediaries, and seemingly earning media coverage for these interactions, proved a powerful tool. His use of Twitter enabled him to respond, almost immediately, to any issue that arose on the media agenda. Understanding the structure and content of Trump's tweets and the retweets of his messages provides insight into the focus of Trump's attention and his linguistic style during the election (Anderson, 2015; Chadwick, 2013; Tumasjan, Sprenger, Sandner, & Welpe, 2010; Swigger, 2013).

His Twitter activity and the response of his followers also influenced news coverage, with the volume of retweets being the strongest predictor of subsequent media coverage (Wells, et al., 2016). Within this cycle of media channels feeding off each other, the press amplified Trump's message and, in this manner, aided his surprising dominance in the campaign. Traditional media outlets continue to play a significant role in spreading Trump's "brand" (Oates & Moe, 2016), amplifying his messaging in an ongoing cycle. As noted above, Trump's abundant media coverage aided him in the race for the presidency, and his Twitter practices were a major catalyzer of his news coverage (Wells, et al., 2016). If his use of Twitter generated media visibility, it is both interesting and important to examine the content of those messages, and how they are amplified.

What was Trump Saying?

From before his announcement, it was clear that Trump had no intention of presenting himself as a polished political candidate. On the contrary, he sought to distance himself from the "corrupt institution" which he claimed he could correct. Rather, by emphasizing his image as the straight-talking businessman who "tells it like it is" (Campbell, 2016), he offered a "fresh" voice in the political sphere—a non-politician who spoke candidly and in unvarnished terms about the social ills affecting America. By branding himself as an alternative to traditional politicians, as a leader who would "drain the swamp" if elected, his message appealed to disaffected voters, who felt resentful of those who they believed had benefitted from past policies, disappointed in their economic and social prospects, and neglected by previous administrations of both political parties (Cramer, 2016, Lakoff, 2016).

Trump's specific use of Twitter seems to center on targeting and attacking his enemies, many of who were also viewed by his followers with a sense of resentment, disappointment, and neglect. As others have commented, a reliable method to identify Trump's current "opponent" is simply to check who he is insulting (Quealy, 2017). Targeting others emphasized his efforts to distinguish himself from the other candidates who represent the "corrupt institution" that he aims to fix. This rhetoric of conflict was also a means for mobilizing supporters, as Trump frequently used terminology of "us against them."

Notably, the tendency to use certain pronouns in speech can indicate the level of solidarity one feel toward the audience for the message (Pennebaker, 2011). For instance, by employing the terms 'us' and 'we,' a speaker projects high level of solidarity, compared to the terms 'I' and 'me.' Third-person pronouns prime schemas of distant others; therefore, the use of the third-person pronoun in its plural form, 'them,' bundles those distant others into abstract homogenous groups (Pennebaker, Mehl & Niederhoffer, 2003). Trump uses this rhetorical technique to enhance group cohesion by repeatedly contrasting us (in-group) to them (out-group). 'Them,' as we find, can refer to other Republican candidates, Democratic opponents, the Media, or any entity that Trump deems worthy of his hostile attention.

Even a casual observer of Trump's Twitter use can observe his efforts to target his opponents, ridicule them, and label them with diminutives that circulated among his followers. Marco Rubio, the youthful Senator from the State of Florida, one of the biggest electoral prizes in the primary season and general election, was dubbed "Little Marco." Ted Cruz, the Texas Senator who is widely viewed within Congress as self-serving and uncooperative, was saddled with the moniker of "Lyin' Ted." And Trump's eventual opponent, Hillary Clinton, who was under investigation for her use of a private email server, was tagged "Crooked Hillary." These labels stuck, resonating with the media and the public.

Trump's attacks and criticisms of the media were also a feature of news attention, as the media self-reflexively cover themselves (Lee, 2005; Watts, Domke, Shah & Fan, 1999). When Trump accused the media of being untrustworthy and slanted against him, and raised claims of liberal bias, this often became news, as media dutifully reported the claim. We examine the prevalence and content of Trumps tweets, and the retweets of those posts, as they relate to these four targets: Marco Rubio, Ted Cruz, Hillary Clinton, and the news media. In doing so we aim to shed a light on the psychological and rhetorical characteristics of the language used by Trump and his followers to discuss, frame, and attack these campaign targets. We attempt to address the following research questions:

RQ1: Does the targeting of these opponents emerge as topics from Trump's tweets?

RQ2: What are the psychological and tonal features of these target topics?

RQ3: Does this targeting emerge as topics from retweets of Trump's posts?

RQ4: What are the psychological and tonal features of these retweet target topics?

Methods

To address these questions, we examined Trump's tweets and the retweets of his posts employing three different methods of computational text analysis. First, we employed Latent Dirichlet Allocation (LDA), a type of topic modeling, to understand the themes that emerge from these collections of tweets. We follow this with deeper analysis using two linguistic analysis systems to understand the features of these messages: the Linguistic Inquiry and Word Count (LIWC2015) system, to gauge the psychological meaning of word choice along multiple dimensions, and Diction 7.0, to assess the tonal qualities of word choice in terms of certainty, activity, optimism, realism, and commonality and their sub-dimensions.

Data Collection

For the present study we constructed two datasets. The first is comprised of all of the tweets sent from Donald Trump's Twitter account (@RealDonaldTrump), from January 1, 2015, to November 9, 2016, the day following the U.S. presidential elections. The second set is a random sample of retweets of Trump's messages, which accounts for 1% of all global retweets of Trump that were posted during the corresponding period. We aggregated this sample through the Twitter streaming Application Program Interface (API), and identified retweets by searching messages with 'RT @RealDonaldTrump' in their text.

Our datasets consist of 9,978 Trump tweets and 313,047 retweets of Trump's posts. In addition to the content of each message, the dataset also includes descriptive information such as date and time of original tweets and retweets, number of followers, and number following, and profile descriptions. The set also contains information regarding the device from which the tweet was sent, enabling differentiation among users of Trump's account, as he reportedly uses an Android device whereas his campaign staffs use iOS devices (Robinson, 2016).

Latent Dirichlet Allocation

Latent Dirichlet Allocation (LDA) is a generative probabilistic model for collections of documents. Like other topic modeling approaches, it offers an efficient way to analyze a large text corpus. LDA employs a "bag of words" approach, treating each document as a vector of word counts. It allows for the clustering of words into topics and documents into "mixtures of topics." Specifically, it employs a Bayesian inference model that associates each document with a probability distribution on topics, where topics are probability distributions on words. It is generative in the sense that it prescribes a model by which documents are created. Since its development (Blei, Ng & Jordan, 2003), researchers have applied LDA in a diverse collection of disciplines, including genomics (Dawson & Kendziorski, 2012), information retrieval (Krestel, Fankhauser & Nejdl, 2009), data mining (Han, Pei & Kamber, 2011), biomedical informatics (Hripcsak & Albers, 2013), and others.

We fitted LDA models to discover topics in each of our two corpora: (1) the texts of all tweets from the account @realDonaldTrump and (2) the texts of a 1% subset of retweets of posts from the account @realDonaldTrump, which also included any additional text appended to the original text by the retweeter. For both model fittings, we arbitrarily assigned the number of topics to 30. With the posterior parameter estimates, we had two goals: to (1) interpret and summarize each inferred topic by using its inferred posterior distribution over the vocabulary and (2) to classify each tweet by its distribution over topics.

Initially we queried our Hive database of tweets to collect both the tweets from @realDonaldTrump and the 1% sample of retweets of @realDonaldTrump posts. The pull extracted the text, date, and time for each tweet. For the retweets of Trump's posts, we chose to extract the full text of the tweet, which typically included the text of the original tweet (i.e., from @realDonaldTrump) and text appended by the user who retweeted the tweet from @realDonaldTrump. We analyzed tweets within a tidy data framework (Wickham, 2014). We filtered text of each tweet by removing words that belong to a list of short words (Silge & Robinson, 2016), and also removed the following terms: "http", "rt", "@realdonaldtrump", "#trump2016", "#makeamericagreatagain", "trump", "donald", "donaldtrump", "#maga". We justified their removal by the fact that they provided little information about the underlying themes of the two collections of tweets due to their commonality across much of the content.

We fitted LDA models, with 30 topics each, in the R statistical environment (R-Core Team, 2016). We estimated posterior parameter values via variational inference, as implemented in the topicmodels-R package (Hornik & Grün, 2011). We summarized each topic by examining its distribution over the vocabulary. Specifically, we examined for each topic those 30 words with the greatest posterior probabilities and attempted to create a concise summary of each topic (Chang, Boyd-Graber, Gerrish, Wang & Blei, 2009). We also sought to use the posterior distributions over topics to classify each tweet. Specifically, for each tweet, we considered posterior distribution over topics, and assigned a topic if the tweet's posterior distribution over topics placed at least probability 0.2 on a topic. We allowed for tweets to be assigned to more than one topic.

LIWC2015 & Diction 7.0

For the linguistic analyses we used two well-established computational text analysis programs, LIWC2015 and Diction 7.0. The Linguistic Inquiry and Word Count (LIWC2015) system allowed us to assign psychologically meaningful dimensions to each message by proportion of use of words used representing that dimension. LIWC dimensions include linguistic features and psychological categories, and include many sub-dimensions (Tausczik & Pennebaker, 2010; Pennebaker & Francis, 1996). For example, LIWC contains dictionaries for positive and negative emotions, as well as specific emotions such as anger and anxiety.

Diction offered a complementary analyses by determining the tone of verbal messages along five major dimensions—i.e., certainty, activity, optimism, realism, and commonality—and multiple sub-dimensions. Tone categories reflect word choice, or the ways a speaker chooses to discuss a subject. For example, Diction includes a dictionary for concreteness, or whether the speaker uses language referring to tangible, specific events. One unique feature of Diction is the ability to compare one's corpus with a database of 50,000 previously analyzed texts, allowing comparison to established norms of language use.

We processed each dataset separately, that of Trump's original tweets, and that of the retweets of his messages by his followers. By calculating the total number of a recurring message, we were able to distinguish between the "popular" and "unpopular" tweets—those that amplified by Twitter users, compared to those that received less resonance among users.

In a second step, we compared the psychological dimensions and tonal features by topic. We grouped the messages according to the topic they were assigned in the LDA procedure, and calculated the average of each dimension as computed by LIWC or Diction. To standardize the averages we created an index value, by calculating the average of a dimension by topic over the average of the entire data set. Index ratios that were greater than .3 from the total average (i.e. > 1.3) were noted as loading high for a category, while values lower than .3 from the total average (< 0.7) were noted as loading low on that dimension.

Results

Our Latent Dirichlet Allocation of the full corpus of Trump's tweets (N =9,978) and the 1% sample of the retweets of these posts (N = 313,047) produced a diverse array topics: attacking the establishment, event and interview announcements, praising positive coverage, polling and electoral success, expressions of gratitude to prominent supporters, self promotion of Trump businesses and brands, and, of course, Make America Great Again (#MAGA). Four of the most prominent topics across both LDA topic models were attacks on his key opponents during the campaign: Marco Rubio, Ted Cruz, Hillary Clinton, and the "biased" media. LIWC and Diction analyses identified distinct ways in which Trump and his followers tweeted about these different topics, revealing their word choice characteristics.

Trump's Tweets

Trump's tweets could be largely categorized into two major groups. The first are negative, criticism messages that raise conflict, specifically targeted at an opponent, focusing his efforts on one main "nemesis" at a time. He first aimed at Rubio, one of the most promising GOP candidates and a force in the pivotal State of Florida. During this time, there were many candidates in the Republican primaries, supplying multiple targets for Trump, yet he focused on Rubio. However, as the candidate pool diminished, particularly after Rubio dropped out of the race in March 2016, Trump reoriented his attacks to Ted Cruz—once an ally, now an emerging competitor. After the primary cycle, Trump shifted once against to focusing exclusively on Clinton, his last direct obstacle to the presidency. The exception to this temporal targeting is Trump's criticism of media, which persisted throughout the election. These four opponents represent the four themes found within the first group, alongside general and recurrent targeting of the political establishment, especially the conservative establishment as embodied in figures such as Mitt Romney and Megan Kelly.

The second category, which was comparatively retweeted less often, consisted of supportive and positive messages, often thanking supporters or motivating followers to engage with the campaign. These tweets encouraged followers to watch his interviews or media appearances, attend his townhalls or rallies, with multiple tweets sent from Trump's account prior to major events. The major topics centered on announcements of events or appearances, strong poll standing or electoral success in primary elections, gratitude directed at supporters, promotion of Trump brands, and the promise to Make America Great Again.

Despite our LDA model's ability to very concretely distinguish these two groups, it is important to note that his individual tweets often operated within this same binary. In other words, his opponents were not only portrayed negatively, but Trump would insert himself into the tweet as a contrast to these targets. If his opponents were weak, Trump was strong. This binary also existed in reverse. Trump identified himself as honest, forthright and uncorrupted, in direct contrast "Lyin' Ted" or "Crooked Hillary." Our analysis below focuses on the four major targets of his critical messages: Marco Rubio, Ted Cruz, Hillary Clinton, and the news. Figure 10.1 plots the frequency of Trump's tweets on these four topics.

"Little Marco"

In the early months of the election cycle, Trump's campaign competed with as many as 16 Republican primary candidates. In this bloated field, Senator Marco Rubio persisted as one of the frontrunners both in terms of polls and financial support (FoxNews.com, 2015). This inevitably made him a major target for Trump's criticisms. The top panel in Figure 10.1 presents the trend of tweets for the topic defined as targeting Senator Rubio, along a timeline of the two years preceding the elections. This topic emerges through the early primaries, peaking after debates when Rubio made substantive remarks. In terms of Trump's tweets, and the retweets related to Rubio (not shown), another peak occurs in early 2016, prior to March 15, 2016, the day Rubio dropped out of the primaries. Another

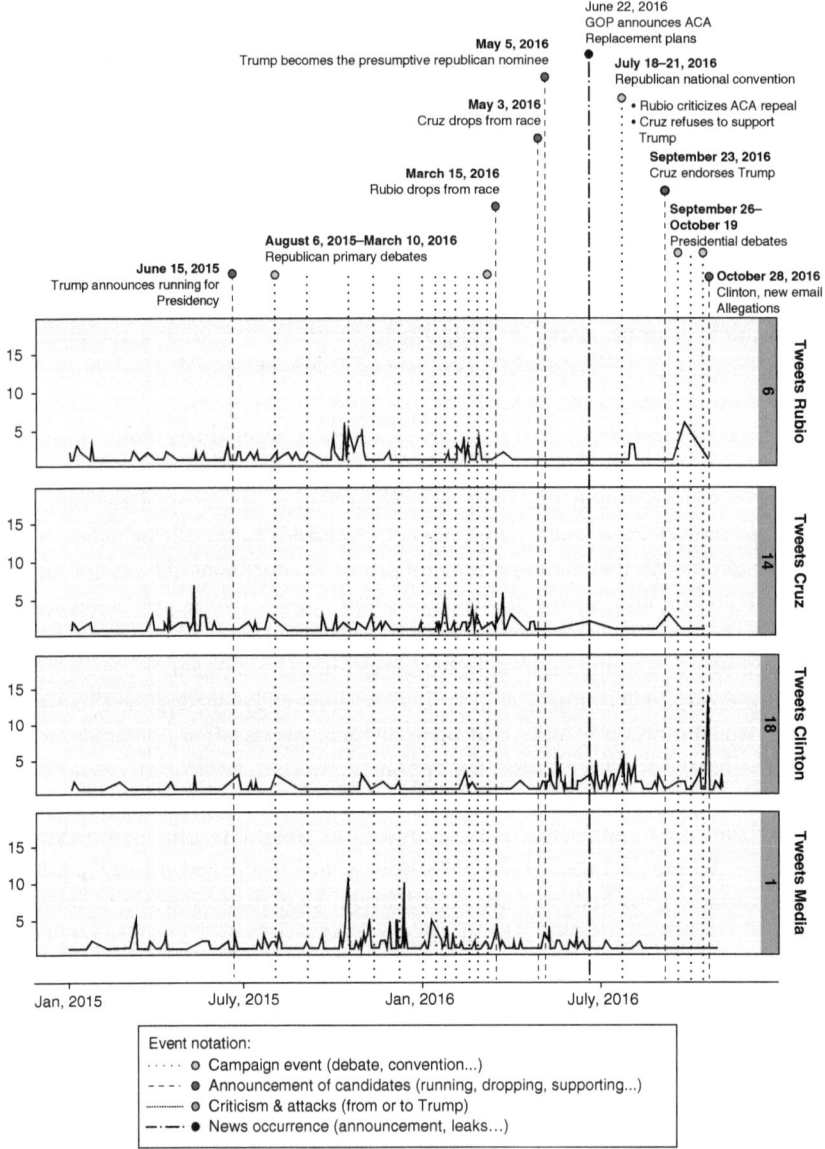

June 22, 2016
GOP announces ACA
Replacement plans

July 18–21, 2016
Republican national convention

May 5, 2016
Trump becomes the presumptive republican nominee

• Rubio criticizes ACA repeal
• Cruz refuses to support
Trump

May 3, 2016
Cruz drops from race

September 23, 2016
Cruz endorses Trump

March 15, 2016
Rubio drops from race

September 26–
October 19
Presidential debates

August 6, 2015–March 10, 2016
Republican primary debates

June 15, 2015
Trump announces running for
Presidency

October 28, 2016
Clinton, new email
Allegations

Event notation:
⋯⋯ ○ Campaign event (debate, convention...)
- - - ● Announcement of candidates (running, dropping, supporting...)
⋯⋯⋯ ○ Criticism & attacks (from or to Trump)
—·—· ● News occurrence (announcement, leaks...)

FIGURE 10.1 Trump's Tweets

peak arises in September 2016, when Trump dismissed Rubio's criticism regarding the repeal of the Affordable Care Act.

The LIWC and Diction analyses revealed that tweets in this topic had greater uses of third-person singular pronouns (index = 1.41) and references to masculinity (index = 1.83). This is understandable given the emphasis on Republican candidates, most of whom were male. Trump's rhetoric about "Little Marco" also scored high in social exclusion (index = 1.55), likely because Trump's tweets portrayed Marco Rubio as dishonest and ineffective. Tweets in this topic also loaded high on emotional tone. For example, two of the popular tweets, loading strongly to the Rubio-focused topic in the weeks prior to the Florida primary: "*Little Marco Rubio, the lightweight no show Senator from Florida, is set to be the 'puppet' of the special interest Koch brothers. WATCH!*" (Trump, 2/28/2016). "Little Marco Rubio is just another Washington D.C. politician that is all talk and no action. #RobotRubio" (Trump, 2/28/2016). Although the Republican primaries were filled with many candidates, Trump targeted "Little Marco" specifically, portraying his opponent as a "lightweight" representative of a corrupt establishment—deeming him not only as untrustworthy, but also incapable and robotic. This targeting strategy would be used repeatedly against other opponents as the campaign unfolded, and at other entities that criticized him. After Rubio dropped from the race, on March 15, 2016, Trump diverted his Twitter attention to the other contender, Ted Cruz.

"Lyin' Ted"

Like Rubio, Cruz became a frontrunner early in the campaign, appealing most to Evangelicals and former members of the Tea Party movement. He successfully won a plurality of the votes in the Iowa Causes, beating Trump out by 4%. The second panel in Figure 10.1 presents the trend of tweets for the topic defined as targeting Ted Cruz. Although he was less successful in subsequent contests, Cruz maintained a strong hold throughout the Republican primary season. This topic appeared sporadically in the primary season and increased from January to April 2016. Although this trend is similar to Rubio's timeline, Trump continued to post about Cruz after this peak period, until Cruz dropped out of the election in May. Retweets related to Cruz, which also emerged as a topic in our LDA analysis of Trump's followers' posts, are plotted in Figure 10.2. Large volumes of retweets targeting Cruz appeared twice after the main primary period: first, during the waning days of the primary campaign, when both candidates were attacking each other, and during the Republican National Convention, when Cruz refused to endorse Trump (Schleifer, Borger & Bash, 2016).

Analysis of linguistic features through LIWC revealed that language in these topics scored highly on negative emotions (index = 4.28), anger (index = 2.78), and references to men (3.62). This should unsurprising, as Trump was highly critical of Ted Cruz, and often grouped him with other, less successful, Republican candidates. For example, one tweet that loaded highly to a topic almost exclusively about Ted Cruz said, "Lyin' Ted Cruz lost all five races on Tuesday-and he was just given the jinx—a Lindsey Graham endorsement. Also backed Jeb. Lindsey got 0!" (Trump, 3/18/2016). Diction revealed similar patterns, with tweets using blame (index = 1.61), hardship (index = 1.93), and denial (index = 2.08) language. Tweets

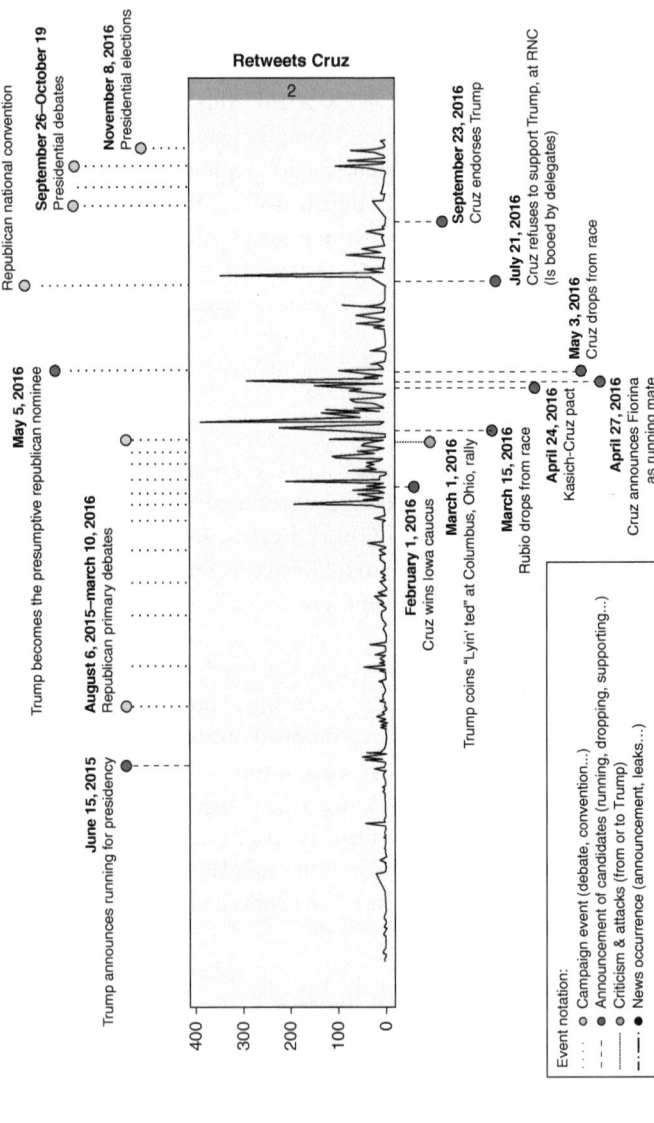

FIGURE 10.2 Retweets—Ted Cruz

in these topics were also somewhat more concrete (index = 1.41), suggesting Trump used tangible examples to criticize Cruz as dishonest. For example, one tweet noted, "Lyin' Ted Cruz just used a picture of Melania from a G.Q. shoot in his ad. Be careful, Lyin' Ted, or I will spill the beans on your wife!" (Trump, 3/23/2016). Here, Trump referenced a concrete event, implied deception by Cruz, and threatened his expose him.

"Crooked Hillary"

From the moment Trump became the presumptive Republican nominee in early May, with Cruz dropping out of the race after his loss in the Indiana primary, Trump then set his sights on his last opponent, Democrat candidate Senator Hillary Clinton. The third panel in Figure 10.1 presents the trend of tweets for the topic defined as targeting Hillary Clinton. Unsurprisingly, tweets about Clinton appeared frequently after Cruz drops out of the race, rising dramatically in June and July, especially during the Republican National Convention, where the Democratic ticket and platform were broadly targeted. In terms of the retweets targeting Clinton, which also emerged as a topic in our LDA modeling of his followers' posts, they spike in the period surrounding the resignation of the DNC chair, Debbie Wasserman Schultz and the Democratic National Convention. This trend is plotted in Figure 10.3. Another spike occurred in early November 2016, when the FBI decided to reopen its investigation into Clinton's use of a private email server. What is notable is Trump's strong shift away from Republican targets toward his Democratic opponent the moment he secured the nomination.

Linguistic analyses identified features that were both similar to and different from other themes. LIWC showed that tweets in this topic used second-person pronouns (index = 1.78), scored high on negative emotions (index = 1.30), as well as language related to power (index = 1.92). Additionally, our Diction analysis showed these topics scored high on blame (index = 1.79) and hardship (index = 1.31) language, and very low on cooperation (index = 0.31). The topic also included mentions of Clinton's former Democrat primary opponent, Senator Bernie Sanders though these targeted Clinton as well. Specifically, they highlighted the supposed biased manner in which the DNC treated Sanders during the primaries, mainly to highlight the corruption of Clinton and the DNC in rigging the system.

This rigged system theme was connected to Clinton in other ways, and used to support the "Crooked Hillary" theme: "Hillary Clinton should have been prosecuted and should be in jail. Instead she is running for president in what looks like a rigged election" (Trump, 10/15/2016). Clinton was also framed as deficient in other respects over the course of the campaign: "Crooked Hillary Clinton over-regulates, over-taxes and doesn't care about jobs. Most importantly, she suffers from plain old bad judgement!" (Trump, 5/24/2016). In other tweets, he focused on specific topics such as emails and used them to argue for her unfitness for office: "Crooked Hillary Clinton and her team "were extremely careless

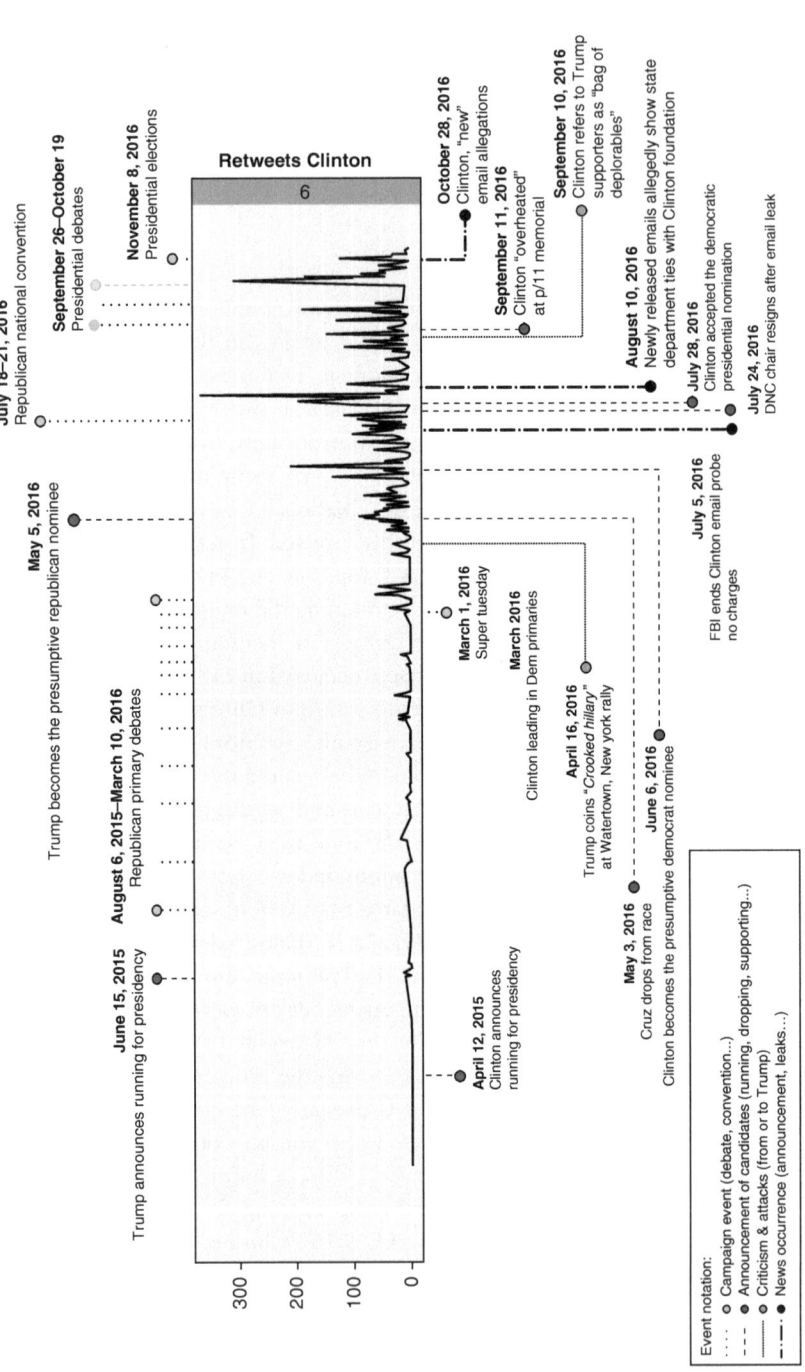

FIGURE 10.3 Retweets—Hillary Clinton

in their handling of very sensitive, highly classified information." Not fit!" (Trump, 7/6/2016). That is, Trump used Twitter to attack Clinton in a variety of ways, with some tweets focusing on her intended policy, others criticized her past behavior, and yet others emphasizing how she was operating within a rigged system. For Trump, "crooked" referred to incompetent, corrupt, and reckless.

The "Biased" Media

Unlike other opponents, this last theme focuses on news media as an institution, rather than a specific individual. Trump identified any news outlet that was critical of him as "mainstream" media, more of a tool of the establishment than a watchdog for the public. Some of this was subsumed under Trump's posts about Clinton, who he claimed was treated in an overtly favorable manner by major media outlets. Topics that focused on media criticism contained many references to specific outlets or news commentators; unsurprisingly, names of different television shows appeared as the words that loaded highest to these topics. The treatment of media as the opponent persisted through the primaries and general election, and continued to define Trump as he began his presidency, reflecting how often Trump criticized news media. LDA modeling of the retweets of Trump's posts reveal his followers echoed this theme. The trend of this topic is plotted in Figure 10.4. This shows that retweets about media criticism grew steadily over time, with more retweets in the general election season as opposed to the primaries, spiking in periods surrounding the initial closing the FBI investigation in Clinton's email server and after the first presidential debate.

Importantly, Trump distinguished supportive media outlets from critical "news media," which was a part of the establishment. For example, one tweet in a topic about "the political establishment" said, "Media desperate to distract from Clinton's anti-2A stance. I said pro-2A citizens must organize and get out vote to save our Constitution!" (Trump, 8/10/2016). By associating mainstream media with the corrupt establishment, Trump portrays critical news outlets as the enemy. Topics focusing on biased, mainstream media also shared similar linguistic features. As identified by LIWC, negative emotions were a key feature of tweets in this theme (index = 1.73), with different topics focusing on sadness, anger, and anxiety. Diction also identified greater use of hardship language (index = 1.40) in these topics, likely because Trump focused on disagreements between his campaign and certain outlets.

Some tweets focused on specific misinterpretations, such as Trump's use of a six-pointed star: "Dishonest media is trying their absolute best to depict a star in a tweet as the Star of David rather than a Sheriff's Star, or plain star!" (Trump, 7/4/2016). Other tweets more generally criticized reporting strategies or negative portrayals: "The failing @nytimes reporters don't even call us anymore, they just write whatever they want to write, making up sources along the way!" (Trump, 10/15/2016). Linguistic features identified by LIWC showed that these topics often used a combination of first-person singular pronouns (indexes = 1.35),

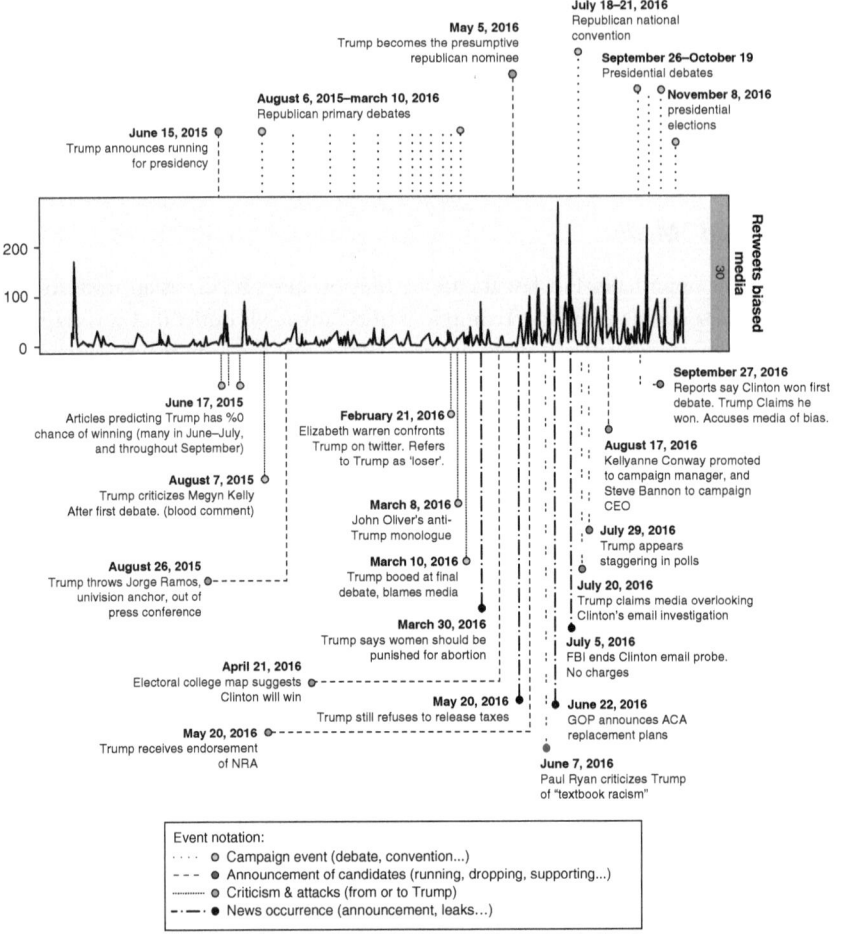

FIGURE 10.4 Retweets—"Biased" Media

and third-person plural pronouns (index = 1.44). This is because Trump often contrasts himself against the media. For example, Trump posted that "The main stream media wants to surrender constitutional rights – I believe #ISIS needs to surrender!" (Trump, 12/7/2015). In this way, Trump and his followers, through their retweeting of his posts, established a new enemy in the latter half of the campaign, and the hero who could save the public from it.

Discussion

Taken together, the focus on enemies and opponents across Trump's posts and his followers retweeting of those posts reflect a clear temporal pattern, a strong dose of negative emotions, and plenty of pointed criticism. Trump varied when and how he attacked each opponent. While Rubio was portrayed as weak and ineffective early in the primary process, Trump framed Cruz as untrustworthy and Clinton as corrupt. Perhaps earlier in the race, "dis-qualifying" opponents for being too weak or ineffectual was a fruitful strategy, such as with "Little Marco" and "Low energy Jeb." Later in the race, when the stronger candidates remained, Trump continued to refer his opponent's strength (or lack of it), for instance Clinton's "lack of stamina," or Cruz's not being "leadership material." However, dismissing them as weak may not have been sufficient. Whether intuitively or strategically, his efforts to frame their unfitness in terms of untrustworthiness ("Lyin Ted") and corruption ("Crooked Hillary") found traction among his followers, who were quick to retweet those posts.

Criticisms of news media, representing a more enduring threat, were longer lasting, with continued use of in-group/out-group language despite attacking an institution rather than a specific individual. Importantly, Trump used more concrete language to criticize new media opponents, suggesting more specific references to events and actions. Throughout this, Trump portrayed himself as the candidate who would "drain the swamp" of people who were like his opponents. Tweets served two purposes in this manner, first to highlight negative qualities of his opponents, second to emphasize the contrast between them and himself.

As mentioned above, this is not to say that Trump and his followers dwelled exclusively on attacking perceived enemies and expressing negative emotions. A major set of themes revealed through LDA topic modeling emphasized Trump's successes, his supporters, his allies, and his events. Given the attention surrounding Trump's Twitter account, a logical and shrewd strategy would encourage followers to track and support Trump's campaign. He regularly invited media and the public alike to follow him as he traveled from city to city, or from one television interview to another. For example, one tweet promoting Trump's appearance on *The Tonight Show* encouraged viewers to tune in: "I will be on The Tonight Show with Jimmy Fallon tonight at 11:30. Should be fun!" (Trump, 9/11/2016). These tweets often started similarly, with the words "I will be" or "Join us," followed by followed by either a media appearance (e.g., "on the Tonight Show") or a rally location.

In addition to calls for support, Trump also frequently thanked supporters for attending events or tweeting out to him. For example, one tweet said, "Thank you Concord, North Carolina! When WE win on November 8th, we are going to Washington, D.C. and we are going to #DrainTheSwamp!" (Trump, 11/3/2016). Aside from thanking supporters, Trump also specifically thanked supportive media, politicians who endorsed him, Twitter users who mention him in a positive light, and his family. For example, he often expressed gratitude to his wife, children, and in-laws: "Thank you for the incredible support- Melania, Barron, Ivanka, Jared, Tiffany, Don, Vanessa, Eric, and Lara!" (Trump, 4/26/2016).

LIWC and Diction results further reinforce the distinction between the attack messages detailed above and these supportive messages, as topics covering this theme loaded high on positive emotions (index = 1.90) and references to friends (index = 1.46). Perception processes, such as seeing (index = 1.54) and hearing (index = 1.64) were prominent as well, reflecting the media mentions. Diction also revealed that tweets tended to be more inspirational (index = 1.58), emphasized accomplishments (index = 1.85) and implied cooperation (index = 2.82). These more positive qualities suggest a marked difference in how Trump spoke about his supporters as opposed to his opponents.

Conclusions

Studies have indicated that Trump's retweets drove the volume of his news-media coverage (Wells et al., 2016). In the present study, we examine the content of Trump's tweets and the retweeting of these messages by Trump's followers, identifying major topics and their linguistic characteristics. Our findings highlight message characteristics and emotional tenor that might explain why certain Trump tweets were highly popular, while others were comparatively less shared.

We find Trump used Twitter to focus attacks on opponents (e.g. Rubio, Cruz, Clinton, and the "biased" media) and promote himself (e.g., his brands, his media appearances, his rallies). Yet it was his attacks that resonated most with his supporters, with all four of his focal targets—"Little Marco," "Lyin' Ted," "Crooked Hillary," and the "Biased" Media—emerging as topics in the LDA analysis of Trump's tweets and his followers' retweets of his messages. The relationship between retweets of Trump's posts and earned media coverage suggests that Trump's strategy of attacking paid coverage dividends (Wells et al., 2016).

This is particularly ironic given Trump's critique of a liberal media bias. Scholars have argued that individuals who work in media tend to be liberal, resulting in media content that is distorted to support liberal beliefs (Groseclose, 2011). Additionally, even without an actual bias, research finds that individuals tend to perceive a liberal media bias (Lee, 2005; Watts, Domke, Shah & Fan, 1999). However, Trump's interpretation of liberal media bias is more insidious and troubling, elevating media from a left-leaning source to a corrupt, direct enemy. In a society founded on principles of press freedom, such attacks on the press are potential corrosive, delegitimizing a major social institution.

The use of "them" versus "us," and "I" is a recurring theme in Trump's messages. It seems as though Trump defines the in-group by focusing on the out-group, contrasting them against what the in-group is not. From a social psychological perspective, this results in a stronger and more cohesive in-group. This reinforces the value of using LIWC as a tool for analyzing function words in Twitter discourse (Pennebaker, Boyd, Jordan, & Blackburn, 2015) and emphasizes the need for future studies to examine these often ignored features.

This corresponds with the trend of recent campaigns, a rise in negative campaigning—i.e., opponents attack each one another's personal characteristics and policy positions in their race for political office. Trump used this tactic via social media, allowing his followers to amplify his message through their own expression into their social networks. He also employed this platform to attack individuals other than his opposing candidates, targeting groups based on ethnicity, religion, political party affiliation, and, of course, gender.

It is worth noting that these insights were generated using a combination of three different computational text analysis techniques: Latent Dirichlet Allocation, LIWC2015, and Diction 7.0. The use of topic modeling to discover emergent themes, followed by employing LIWC and Diction to better understand the nature of the language used within these topics, provided an efficient yet powerful means to gain insights about Trump's successful use of Twitter. As other research has found, it was via his use of Twitter that he was able to earn so much free media coverage, and bypass the need for traditional ad buys (Wells et al., 2016).

The 2016 US presidential elections witnessed a new age of hybrid media campaigning (Chadwick, 2013), with social media traction serving as a central feature of Trump's campaign communications. The significant role of Twitter in the 2016 election cycle was at least partly a function of its unique affordances, and its place in the evolving media ecology. Twitter, its usage patterns, and its consequences, cannot be understood in a vacuum. Trump used Twitter to circumvent news media, and speak to his supporters directly, who could then amplify his perspectives into their social networks. Moreover, in the process of speaking directly to his supporters, he was also able to generate news coverage because of the controversial nature of so many of his posts and his followers' willingness to disseminate those posts to a wider audience.

In this study, we examined the linguistic features of Trumps tweets, and identified categories into which these messages group. The next step for these data involves examining whether certain topics or linguistic features explain how Trump drove news coverage. Previous work has simply examined the volume of Trump's tweets and retweets to understand their relationship to news coverage in major print and online news outlets. Future research should combine detailed linguistic analysis of Trump's tweets and retweets with the volume of news coverage to examine whether his attacks were the root of his media attention. In fact, we hope to conduct a series of multiple linear regression models predicting the volume of news coverage earned by Trump with the nature of his Twitter messaging.

Future research would also benefit from a comparison of multiple candidates. For example, an analysis of the tweets and retweets of Hillary Clinton, Ted Cruz, and Bernie Sanders could be particularly valuable. As described earlier, Trump is an avid Twitter user, far beyond any of his opponents. However, it may be that they utilized Twitter in much the same way as Trump, but with less amplification through follower networks, and less media attention because of their less controversial utterances. This, of course, remains an open question, and one that merits special attention given the role of the press in Trump's rise.

Another possible venue of study is the examination of Trump's retweeters' political ideology. This information can then be analyzed in tandem with semantic data in order to identify whether there is a difference between the tweets shared by each ideological group. It is likely that Trump supporters would tend to share positive messages such as "make America great again" and self-endorsements where Trump presents himself as a savior for the American people. In contrast, one might assume that his negative posts—in which he criticizes individuals, insults social groups, or makes controversial comments—get amplified not only by his supporters but also by those angered and disturbed by these messages. Future research should examine the question of retweeting posts by allied and opposing follower groups to better understand partisan information flows in this new media ecology. The use of machine learning to classify users based on their network of connections or pattern of posting is a necessary next step in this work, extending the LDA, LIWC, and Diction analysis we conducted here to gain deeper insights into message propagation.

References

Anderson, M. (2015, April 1). 6 facts about Americans and their Smartphones. *Pew Research Center Fact Tank: News in the Numbers*. Retrieved from www.pewresearch.org/fact-tank/2015/04/01/6-facts-about-americans-and-their-smartphones/

Azari, J. R. (2016). How the news media helped to nominate Trump. *Political Communication, 33*(4), 677–680.

Blei, D. M., Ng, A. Y., & Jordan M. I., (2003). Latent Dirichlet allocation. *Journal of Machine Learning Research, 3*, 993–1022.

Borchers, C. (2016, June 6). The Clinton campaign's totally bogus claim about its press availability. *The Washington Post*. Retrieved from www.washingtonpost.com/news/the-fix/wp/2016/06/06/the-clinton-campaigns-totally-bogus-claim-about-its-press-availability/?utm_term=.eab5578142fa

Chadwick, A., & Stromer-Galley, J. (2016). Digital media, power, and democracy in parties and election campaigns: Party decline or party renewal? *The International Journal of Press/Politics, 21*(3), 283–293.

Chadwick, A. (2013). *The hybrid media system: Politics and power*. New York, NY: Oxford University Press.

Chang, J., Boyd-Graber, J. L., Gerrish, S., Wang, C., & Blei, D. M. (2009). Reading tea leaves: How humans interpret topic models. *Nips, 31*,1–9.

Campbell, J. P. (2016). Trump Supporters: In their own words. Available at *SSRN 2750480*

Confessore, N., & Yourish, K. (2016, March 16). $2 Billion worth of free media for Donald Trump. *The New York Times*. Retrieved from www.nytimes.com/2016/03/16/upshot/measuring-donald-trumps-mammoth-advantage-in-free-media.html.

Cramer, K. J. (2016). *The politics of resentment: Rural consciousness in Wisconsin and the rise of Scott Walker*. Chicago, IL: University of Chicago Press.

Dawson, J. A., & Kendziorski, C. (2012). Survival-supervised latent Dirichlet allocation models for genomic analysis of time-to-event outcomes. *arXiv preprint arXiv:1202.5999*.

Eddy, B. (2016). *Trump bubbles: The dramatic rise and fall of high-conflict politicians*. BookBaby.

Fox News (2015, October 31). Rubio's momentum picks up support with increased donor support, endorsements. *Fox News Politics*. Retrieved from www.foxnews.com/politics/2015/10/31/rubio-momentum-picks-up-with-increased-donor-support-endorsements.html

Groseclose, T. (2011). *Left turn: How liberal media bias distorts the American mind*. London, UK: Macmillan.

Han, J., Pei, J., & Kamber, M. (2011). *Data mining: Concepts and techniques*. New York, NY: Elsevier.

Hornik, K., & Grün, B. (2011). Topicmodels: An R package for fitting topic models. *Journal of Statistical Software, 40*(13), 1–30.

Hripcsak, G., & Albers, D. J. (2013). Next-generation phenotyping of electronic health records. *Journal of the American Medical Informatics Association, 20*(1), 117–121.

Jacobson, W. (2016, January 29). Walter Jacobson explains why Donald Trump is beating everyone, including the media. *WGN Radio*. Retrieved from http://wgnradio.com/2016/01/29/walter-jacobson-explains-why-donald-trump-beating-everyone-including-the-media/

Karpf, D. (2016, June 19). The clickbait candidate. *The Chronicle of Higher Education*. Retrieved from www.chronicle.com/article/The-Clickbait-Candidate/236815?cid=rc_right

Keegan, J. (2016, July 19). Clinton vs. Trump: How they used Twitter. *Wall Street Journal*. Retrieved from http://graphics.wsj.com/clinton-trump-Twitter/

Kreiss, D. (2012). *Taking our country back: The crafting of networked politics from Howard Dean to Barack Obama*. Oxford, UK: Oxford University Press.

Krestel, R., Fankhauser, P., & Nejdl, W. (2009). Latent Dirichlet allocation for tag recommendation. In *Proceedings of the 3rd ACM Conference on Recommender Systems*, 61–68.

Lakoff, G. (2016, August 19) Understanding Trump's use of language. George Lakoff Blog. Retrieved from http://georgelakoff.com/2016/08/19/understanding-trumps-use-of-language/

Lee, T. T. (2005). The liberal media myth revisited: An examination of factors influencing perceptions of media bias. *Journal of Broadcasting & Electronic Media, 49*(1), 43–64.

Lee, J. C., & Quealy, K. (2017, January 28). The 325 people, places and things Donald Trump has insulted on Twitter: A complete list. *The New York Times*. Retrieved from www.nytimes.com/interactive/2016/01/28/upshot/donald-trump-twitter-insults.html

Oates, S., & Moe, W. W. (2016). Donald Trump and the "Oxygen of Publicity": Branding, social media, and mass media in the 2016 presidential primary elections. In *American Political Science Association (APSA) Annual Meeting*.

Ouellette, L. (2016). The Trump show. *Television and New Media, 17*(7), 647–650.

Patterson, T. E. (2016a, July 11). News coverage of the 2016 presidential primaries: Horse race reporting has consequences. *Shorenstein Center on Media, Politics and Public Policy*. Retrieved from http://shorensteincenter.org/news-coverage-2016-presidential-primaries/

Patterson, T. E. (2016b, June 13). Pre-primary news coverage of the 2016 presidential race: Trump's rise, Sanders' emergence, Clinton's struggle. *Shorenstein Center on Media, Politics and Public Policy*. Retrieved from https://shorensteincenter.org/pre-primary-news-coverage-2016-trump-clinton-sanders/

Pennebaker, J. W., Boyd, R. L., Jordan, K., & Blackburn, K. (2015). The development and psychometric properties of LIWC2015. *UT Faculty/Researcher Works*.

Pennebaker, J. W. (2011). *The secret life of pronouns*. London, UK: Bloomsbury Press.

Pennebaker, J. W., & Francis, M. E. (1996). Cognitive, emotional, and language processes in disclosure. *Cognition & Emotion, 10*(6), 601–626.

Pennebaker, J. W., Mehl, M. R., & Niederhoffer, K. G. (2003). Psychological aspects of natural language use: Our words, our selves. *Annual Review of Psychology, 54*(1), 547–577.

Quealy, K. (2017, December 6). How to know what Donald Trump really cares about? *The New York Times*. Retrieved from https://nyti.ms/2jRoJFk

R-Core Team. (2016). R: *A language and environment for statistical computing*. Vienna, Austria: R Foundation for Statistical Computing.

Robinson, D. (2016, August 09). Text analysis of Trump's tweets confirms he writes only the (angrier) android half. *Variance Explained*. Retrieved from http://varianceexplained. org/r/trump-tweets/

Silge, J., & Robinson, D., (2016). Tidytext: Text mining and analysis using tidy data principles in R. *The Journal of Open Source Software, 37*, 1–3.

Schleifer, T, Borger, G. & Bash, D. (2016, September 23) Ted Cruz endorses Donald Trump. *CNN*. Retrieved from www.cnn.com/2016/09/23/politics/ted-cruz-endorses-donald-trump/

Swigger, N. (2013). The online citizen: Is social media changing citizens' beliefs about democratic values? *Political Behavior, 35*(3), 589–603.

Tumasjan, A., Sprenger, T. O., Sandner, P. G., & Welpe, I. M. (2010). Predicting elections with Twitter: What 140 characters reveal about political sentiment. *ICWSM, 10*, 178–185.

Tausczik, Y. R., & Pennebaker, J. W. (2010). The psychological meaning of words: LIWC and computerized text analysis methods. *Journal of Language and Social Psychology, 29*(1), 24–54.

Watts, M. D., Domke, D., Shah, D. V., & Fan, D. P. (1999). Elite cues and media bias in presidential campaigns: Explaining public perceptions of a liberal press. *Communication Research, 26*(2), 144–175.

Wells, C., Shah, D. V., Pevehouse, J. C., Yang, J., Pelled, A., Boehm, F., Lukito, J., Ghosh, S. & Schmidt, J. (2016). How Trump drove coverage to the nomination: Hybrid media campaigning. *Political Communication, 33*(4), 669–676.

Wickham, H. (2014). Tidy data. *Journal of Statistical Software, 59*(10), 1–23.

Williams, B. A., & Carpini, M. X. D. (2011). *After broadcast news: Media regimes, democracy, and the new information environment*. Cambridge, UK: Cambridge University Press.

Yanofsky, D. (2015, July 22). A list of everything Donald Trump runs that has his name on it. *Quartz*. Retrieved from https://qz.com/461688/a-list-of-everything-donald-trump-runs-that-has-his-name-on-it/

INDEX